D1806835

Integrating Market, Credit and Operational Risk

Integrating Market, Credit and Operational Risk

A Complete Guide for Bankers and Risk Professionals

By Lampros Kalyvas & Ioannis Akkizidis
with Ioanna Zourka & Vivianne Bouchereau

Published by Risk Books, a Division of Incisive Financial Publishing Ltd

Haymarket House
28–29 Haymarket
London SW1Y 4RX
Tel: +44 (0)20 7484 9700
Fax: +44 (0)20 7484 9800
E-mail: books@incisivemedia.com
Sites: www.riskbooks.com
       www.incisivemedia.com

ISBN 1 904339 96 4

British Library Cataloguing in Publication Data
A catalogue record for this book is available from the British Library

Publisher: Laurie Donaldson
Assistant Editor: Hannah Berry
Designer: Rebecca Bramwell

Typeset by Mizpah Publishing Services Private Limited, Chennai, India

Printed and bound in Spain by Espacegrafic, Pamplona, Navarra

Contents

Dedications

This book is dedicated to:

My daughter Sophia (Lampros Kalyvas)
My father (Ioannis Akkizidis)
My parents (Vivianne Bouchereau)
My family (Ioanna Zourka)

Acknowledgements

The authors would like to specially thank all those who gave them support in different ways for the completion of this book. All authors would like to thank Panagiotis Panagopoulos for his constant effort to produce a part of the results used in this book. Special thanks go to Vasilios Masmanidis and Christos Ventiadis for their support and Nikos Akkizidis for his good ideas and discussions on the contents of this book. Lampros Kalyvas would like to thank Dr Athanasios Sfetsos for his helpful ideas and his continuous support of the research, carried out throughout the last years, which was the basis for the publication of this book and Professor Costas Siriopoulos for his psychological support. The authors would also like to thank each other for all the great effort and many sleepless nights that enabled them to put words on paper. They would also like to thank Risk Books, for giving them the opportunity to publish their work. And last, but not least a great thank you goes to all their individual families for the constant support, encouragement and patience.

Authors' Note

At the heart of all credit institutions, no matter in which sector they operate, there are in particular, three types of risks: *market*, *credit* and *operational*. Market risk measures the risk of adverse movements in market factors, such as asset prices, foreign exchange rates and interest rates. The risk of loss resulting from failure of obligors to respect their payments is called credit risk, while operational risk (from Basel II) can be defined as "the risk of direct or indirect loss resulting from inadequate or failed internal processes, people and systems or from external events".

Definitions of market and credit risk come, as expected, from the related businesses: investment, market trading and money lending. Definitions of operational risk are based on an identification of causes whose consequences are not always directly measurable. Credit institutions are facing the challenge of developing internal models in order to provide adequate solutions for quantifying, supervising and managing all these three major types of financial risk. Such institutions are developing the corresponding internal models in order to provide objective, tailor-made solutions for each of the risk types and align them with the Basel II Accord and the Sarbanes–Oxley Act. The challenge is not only to identify and measure these individual risks, but, since they are correlated, to integrate them in some way.

The topic of risk integration has only recently become an area of investigation. The goal of integrated risk management in financial institutions is to measure and manage risk and capital across a series of diverse business activities. This book regards integrated risk management as a technique whereby market, credit and operational risks of credit institutions are taken into account and, furthermore, an attempt is made to optimise them as part of sophisticated, novel approaches.

The book is divided into six chapters consisting of different sections. The first chapter introduces the idea of market risks and how they affect credit institutions. It discusses the identification of market risk factors, modelling market risks, specific risk models and, finally, backtesting and stress-testing market risk exposures.

The second chapter focuses on credit risk. In this chapter, the basics of credit risk are described and different ways of modelling credit risk are introduced. It also reviews credit risk assessment models, as well as the definition and estimation of credit risk. In addition, credit-rating systems and validation are examined.

The third chapter focuses on operational risk. It highlights operational risk capital requirements and discusses the identification of operational risk and loss profiling. Finally it introduces the concept of operational value-at-risk (VAR).

Chapter 4 examines extreme-value theory (EVT) in the application of risk management. Furthermore, it shows the application of clustering analysis in EVT.

Chapter 5 focuses on the characteristics, strengths and weaknesses of the Basel II accord within the framework of market, credit and operational risks.

The sixth chapter concentrates on integrated risk management frameworks, where the integration of market, credit and operational risk is discussed. It then goes on to highlight the integration of market, credit and operational losses. Furthermore, it talks about economic and regulatory capital with regard to integration, and finally it considers aspects on integrated VAR.

The concluding chapter reviews all the topics discussed in the book. An Appendix supports the theoretical background necessary to help readers to familiarise themselves with certain subjects of the book. Finally, a list of the acronyms and initialisms used in the book is listed to give fast access to the abbreviations employed.

References are given at the end of each chapter for those interested in reinforcing their know-how beyond the scope of the book.

About the Authors

Dr Lampros Kalyvas is a risk analyst and his main concerns involve risks undertaken by credit institutions. He is currently employed at the Bank of Greece and he is a visiting lecturer at the University of Ioannina, Greece. He received his PhD in risk management from the University of Macedonia, Greece, his MSc in international banking and financial studies from the University of Southampton, UK, and his BSc in applied informatics from the University of Macedonia, Greece.

Lampros has been employed at the Hellenic Central Securities Depository and has taught at various seminars organised by several institutions. He has also published several scientific papers and presented at several international conferences. His research interests lie in the quantification of market risk, the quantification of credit risk, interest rate modelling, regulatory treatment of credit institutions' portfolios, securitisation, credit derivatives and risk integration.

Dr Ioannis S. Akkizidis is a consultant in risk management working for IRIS integrated risk management ag, in Zurich, Switzerland. His main interests lie in designing and implementing solutions as well as consulting in the risk management field for credit institutions. He is the author of the book *Guide to Optimal Operational Risk & Basel II*.

Ioannis's first degree is in engineering, whereas his postgraduate master's degree is in control systems and applied mathematical analysis from the University of Portsmouth, UK. He holds a PhD in artificial intelligence and applied mathematics obtained from the University of Wales, UK. He has also published several scientific papers in international journals and presented at several international conferences and events. He has given many talks on the subject of risk optimisation and management. He has worked worldwide for many years in business and risk analysis and in implementing advanced solutions in risk analysis for large organisations and financial institutions.

Dr Vivianne R. M. Bouchereau is an analyst in the field of risk, quality and process management. She has undertaken projects in the field of business performance and operational risk analysis and optimisation as well as quality management. She is the co-author of *Guide to Optimal Operational Risk & Basel II*. Vivianne has given several seminars and talks on operational risk management and Basel II, and has an extensive academic background and working knowledge in this field.

She has several years' working experience in the quality engineering field and has also written numerous papers on the subject of total quality management, as well as presenting at numerous international seminars and conferences. She obtained her combined bachelor's and master's (MEng) in electronic and electrical engineering and her PhD in quality engineering in the UK.

Ms Ioanna Zourka works as an examiner in the Risk Analysis and Supervisory Techniques Division at the Department for the Supervision of Credit and Financial Institutions in the Bank of Greece. She received her MSc in statistics and operational research and a BSc in mathematics. Her main focus is on the examination of credit risk models developed by Greek banks and the observance of their adaptation processes in the new sophisticated environment, outlined by the new capital adequacy framework (Basel II).

Ioanna is also responsible for stress-testing exercises in order to examine the sensitivity of the Greek banking system to the changes of critical economic factors. In the past, she has worked in the risk management and underwriting sector as a credit analyst and developer of scoring systems used to determine the creditworthiness of obligors.

Contacts

The authors will be pleased to receive feedback and are open to any discussion on the subject and material presented in this book. Please contact them at the following e-mail addresses:

lkalyvas@bankofgreece.gr (Lampros Kalyvas)
ioannis.akkizidis@iris.ch (Ioannis Akkizidis)
v.bouchereau@riskoptimisation.com (Vivianne Bouchereau)
izourka@bankofgreece.gr (Ioanna Zourka)

Forewords

On one hand, the last few years have been the most demanding years regarding additional regulatory requirements for financial institutions. The Basel Committee on Banking Supervision and the Bank of International Settlement (BIS), define not only new standards for minimum capital requirements, but demand in its Pillar II principles a supervisory review process and in its Pillar III vast disclosure requirements. The International Accounting Standards Board (IASB) has unified the valuation of financial instruments, has defined principles for hedge accounting and furthermore requires disclosure regarding market and credit risk. The Sarbanes–Oxley (SOX) act requires that senior officers follow a code of ethics that makes them personally liable for incorrect disclosures to the public and The Committee of Sponsoring Organizations of the Treadway Commission (COSO) suggests an integrated framework for enterprise risk management, where the most critical challenges are determining how much risk an entity is ready to accept as it strives to create value.

On the other hand, the financial industry is facing globalisation, stronger competition and reduced margins. In order to cope with more and more complex regulatory demands and margin erosion at the same time, there is only one way forward; namely to start looking at risk management in an integrated and unified way. This is exactly the purpose of this book, which gives an excellent overview of current methods used regarding market, credit and operational risk. It provides a good mix of comprehensive explanations along with examples of the quantitative methods used.

If integrated risk management is applied on the level of management information systems, then it is able to provide a significant comparative advantage since it reduces dramatically the

workload and risk in terms of data interfacing, testing and recon-
ciliation between too many systems doing similar calculations.

Andreas Jäk
Vice President Business Development
IRIS integrated risk management ag

The efforts of regulatory and supervisory authorities to identify and analyse the risks that credit and financial institutions face, in order to reduce their impact at an institutional-wide, country-wide or international-wide level is not a recent advance. What is new is the expansion of market globalisation and the Basel II implementation challenge, which respectively demand, on the one hand, continual data analysis, concerning operations of credit institutions in different financial environments and their exposures to heterogeneous risks, and on the other hand, the enhancement of banks and supervisory staff capabilities to assess these risks.

This challenge requires the utilisation of knowledge and information that is not bound by the supervisory authorities' assessments of credit institutions' risks. What is needed is the independent and integrated evaluation of risks made by the credit institutions, which actually possess detailed information about the risks that they face at a micro and macro level.

Moreover, the long period of low interest rates and the search for excess returns makes the pricing and management of market, credit, liquidity, concentration and operational risk, along with the non-quantifiable risks (like reputation and compliance risk), a crucial factor. Some of the aforementioned risks can be categorised under market, credit and operational risk; for example, concentration risk can be categorised under market, credit or operational risk, while reputation and compliance risk under operational risk.

It is encouraging that risk professionals do not limit themselves in the theoretical analysis of risks, but they employ their operational and/or supervisory experience to contribute to the creative exchange of opinions in searching for innovative tools and models towards the identification of reliable methods for the quantification of risks. Of particular importance is the need to adapt the supervisory review process of Pillar II to the risk profile of each particular bank and the effectiveness of banks' Internal Capital Adequacy Assessment Process (ICAAP).

In pursuing the optimal quantification of risks, credit institutions should convince regulatory authorities that the aggregation of individual risks overestimate the overall risk they face, which means that not all sources of risk exhibit absolute positive linear correlation. This is a very difficult task since not all sources of risk follow the same return distribution and at the same time innovative methodologies, such as value-at-risk, are currently tested at a practical level. In this context, I welcome the attempt of this book to provide adequate theoretical background as an initiative for credit institutions to establish the application of innovative internal models on real data concerning the integration of market, credit and operational risk. At the same time, it undoubtedly contributes to the dialogue between supervisory authorities and banks, in particular with regard to the diversification benefits in capital requirements resulting from the application of integrated risk management models. An important outcome of the aforementioned dialogue is to appease the concerns of banks that supervisors may impose extreme capital requirements under Pillar II of the new Basel II framework.

Panagiotis Kyriakopoulos
Director, Bank of Greece
Member of CEBS and BSC

Introduction

The beginning is the most important part of the work
                                                    – Plato

In recent years, the banking and financial services industry has become more global, more integrated, more competitive and also more complex, with risk management emerging into the spotlight. The transformation of financial products into commodities and the reduction in margins are encouraging credit institutions to take more risks. Meanwhile, there is an increasing requirement for more transparency. These developments require credit institutions to have systems that make possible efficient measurement, reporting and management.

To assist the risk management decision process in large institutions, the overall risk faced by these institutions is broken down into different risk groups. These groups are defined through different causes and/or effects. In the banking industry, market risk is defined as the systemic risk intrinsic in the capital market – that is, it is the risk that is not diversifiable through trading in financial contracts. Credit risk is defined as loss exposures due to counterparties' default on contracts. Although the definitions of market risk and credit risk are relatively clear, the definition of operational risk has evolved rapidly over the past few years. At first, it was commonly defined as every type of unquantifiable risk faced by a bank. However, further analysis has considerably refined the definition. The current definition of operational risk proposed by Basel II is "the risk of loss resulting from inadequate or failed internal processes, people and systems or from external events".

In credit institutions it is recognised that market, credit and operational risks are integrated to a certain extent, due to the fact that many financial portfolios or even single financial products are exposed to more than one type of risk. The need for efficient integrated risk management has increased in importance with the appearance of global financial enterprises, increased cross-border trading and an increase in the use of complex financial products, services and systems. Apart from that, increasing rules and the advance of new risk management standards such as the new Basel II capital accord, have also been added to this list of issues. Some risks, such as market risk, are easier to quantify than others (eg, operational risk), but much less is known about the relationship between the risks. Credit risk and market risk are driven by the same fundamental market variables, with both market and credit risk being derived from the same market value distributions.

The great use of financial techniques that reduce credit and market risk may create increased operational risk. Market risk, for instance, can cause a change in another type of market risk, or in credit risk, or in operational risk. On the other hand, credit risk may be reflected in the market and may change the operational risk in an adverse direction. Some examples of where financial institutions have been affected by the different types of risk are highlighted in Table 1. In most of the cases they were affected by more than just one risk, which shows how correlated these risk types are.

A sound and sophisticated approach for integrating these types of risk, which are interrelated and whose distributional shapes differ significantly, is thus required. Market risk typically displays distributions that are nearly symmetric and are often approximated as normal. Credit and especially operational risk, on the other hand, produce more skewed distributions because of occasional, extreme losses. For credit risks, these may be due to large lending exposures and, in the case of operational risk, a large tragedy such as 11 September, 2001. Figure 1 shows the distribution shape of the three types of risk.

Although many financial institutions are capable of adequately quantifying, supervising and managing their financial risks individually, they have not yet developed sufficient techniques and

Table 1 List of famously reported losses

Year	Description of loss	Type of risk
1987	Stock market crash – blamed on "portfolio insurance" derived from option pricing theory under unrealistic assumptions	Market
1991	BCCI: reported losses of US$10 billion. Wide range of illegal activities that included fraudulent loans, fictitious deposits, and money laundering	Operational
1994	Metalgesellschaft: reported losses of DM1.8 billion on its operations and DM1.5 billion on hedging programme	Operation and market
	Proctor & Gamble: mistaken long-term views, improperly hedged by Bankers Trust; US$20 million and US$147 million losses respectively	Operation and market
	Orange County: trading in securities not legally approved; nondisclosure of massive potential losses; US$1.6 billion losses	Operational
1995	Barings: concealed huge (US$1.4 billion) losses on options and futures trading	Market and operational
	Orange County: forced gamble to make up under funding with exotic fixed income products (lost US$1.6 billion)	Market and operational
1996	Sumitomo Copper scandal: concealed huge (US$2.6 billion) losses on forwards and futures trading	Operational and market
	Daiwa Securities: concealed huge (US$1.4 billion) losses on bond trading; US operations terminated	Market and operational
1997	NatWest Capital Markets: £90 million losses concealed on mispricing swaps	Operational
1998	Long Term Capital Management: Bailed out by 14 financial institutions in a US$3.6 billion rescue package	Operational and credit
	Lost heavily on bond arbitrage when Russia defaulted on short-term bonds	

Table 1 (continued)

Year	Description of loss	Type of risk
11/09/2001	Cantor Fitzgerald, Bank of New York, Morgan Stanley, etc World Trade Center attack: The largest ever single operational risk loss with estimates of total losses to the insurance industry up to US$70 billion (prior event was Hurricane Andrew in 1992 with insured losses in the region of US$18 billion)	Operational
2001	Lehman Brothers, London: a dealer traded a £300 million lot instead of an intended £3 million. A hundred and twenty points fall on the FTSE100 index, temporarily removing about £40 billion of the UKs top companies	Operational
	Eurex derivatives exchange: a large erroneous trade of Dow Jones Euro Stoxx 50 future contracts. Eight hundred point fall on the DAX future index	Operational
	UBS Warburg: the number of shares and the share price were inadvertently transposed during a sale from its Japanese equity trading book; lost around US$50 million	Operational
	Allied Irish Banks reported a fraud that had gone on undetected since 1997 and had cost the bank US$691 million (£483.20 million)	Operational

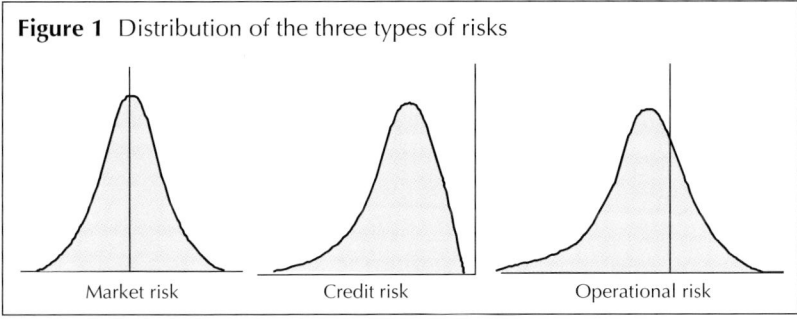

Figure 1 Distribution of the three types of risks

methodologies for approaching the integration among them. Therefore, an insightful aim for financial institutions is to evaluate and minimise the overall risk undertaken and initiated from the integration among the financial risks. For integration purposes, there is a need to discover the effect of business mix and inter-risk correlations to determine the total financial risk. Total financial risk first declines considerably (operational risk has lower volatility than the other two), but then flattens as the impact of fatter tails counteracts the effect of lower volatility. On the other hand, as the correlation of market and credit risk with operational risk increases, both volatility and fat tails increase. Integration of market and credit risks results in the combination of the profit-and-loss (P&L) distribution at different levels of organisational hierarchy, whereas extreme operational losses are at the far tail of the aggregated P&L distribution.

In order to conclude to an integrated risk distribution, there needs to be a common currency for risk. Market risk is typically based on the return distribution of the end-of-day positions in the trading book. Similarly, in credit risk, the output may be a loss or return distribution, typically in terms of percentage of exposure. In both cases there is a need to know the exposure at risk – for example, trading or lending assets – in order to compute money at risk. Operational risks measure financial losses when operations go wrong or are affected by external or internal events. Moreover, operational risk can be measured based on operational failures and undesirable performances. Through these failures both market and credit risk can be generated.

The overall risk distribution is somehow a weighted combination of the individual risks, where the weights, which add up to one, are determined by the risk-specific exposures. For market risk, it is trading assets plus liabilities (the trading book may contain both long and short positions); for credit risk it is lending assets; and for operational risk it is total assets. The "total book" is then the sum of these three. The weights assigned to the types of risk depend on the business activity the financial institution is engaged in. For example, most regional banks focus their business activities on lending and have little trading activity. As a result, they are likely to have relatively more credit risk and less market risk. In addition, they may have less exposure to traditional sources of operational risk such as processing related activities. On the other hand a "processing bank," that has a wide spread of trading activities and is performing in various markets, would likely have more operational risk than the average bank. Finally, a trading-intensive bank is likely to have relatively more market risk.

Action taken to manage risks should be integrated with existing planning and operational processes. As a part of decision making, risk management should be supported by other management techniques.

Our key objective here is to introduce the theoretical background that corresponds to different types of risk. The ultimate objective of the book is to integrate the methodologies for different types of financial risk (market, credit and operational). We provide an overview for evaluating and managing all three major types of financial risk and, furthermore, address the issue of how to identify and quantify different types of risk based on multifactorial and multidimensional measurements. Moreover, we will demonstrate current techniques and methodologies on modelling integrated risks and evaluate their overall effect on financial institutions.

Apart from the traditional market risk quantification techniques, the book focuses on some new variations in order to better integrate the market risk incorporated in different types of financial products. Moreover, the book examines the trade-offs between the conservatism of the prediction of each model and the multiplication factor proposed by the Basel Committee for this prediction, in order to select a benchmark model for credit institutions.

In turn, the credit risk quantification is calculated through various means, spanning from internally self-estimated credit risk measures to market-implied credit risk measures, in order to propose a benchmark model that will be used as an element in the "inter-risk" aggregation and integration. In addition to the traditional static estimations of credit risk parameters, the book provides the reader with their alternative empirical or fuzzy approximations. These approximations will be specifically useful for resolving retail and SME credit in cases where there is no definite time horizon for these loans.

Concerning operational risk, now one of the major topics in risk management, this book presents all the key aspects by providing guidelines on how to identify and qualitatively map risks in operations. It further discusses how to transfer their qualitative attributes to quantitative measurement indicators and how to estimate the operational value-at-risk (VAR) based on such measurements.

In addition, we present a unique way of evaluating integrated risks within complex operational processes using advanced approaches for monitoring the operational risks that are integrated to credit and market risks, and affect in parallel or complementarily the functionality of credit institutions.

Furthermore, the book provides the reader with a continuous clarification of the meanings of "aggregation" and "integration". It also identifies certain aspects of market, credit and operational risks that will serve as linkages among the aforementioned types of risk. In turn, these linkages will interconnect all three types of risk in a unique quantification, providing the risk manager with an "all-in-one" figure.

Ultimately, we are developing here a common integrated framework for the quantification of economic capital, identifying potential weaknesses of the newly publicised Basel II Accord, in defining the capital requirements for the integrated risk framework.

Several innovative approaches that combine aspects of advanced financial modelling, mathematical algorithmic modelling and business intelligence techniques are outlined in here. Practical examples of the approaches are introduced to support the guidelines offered, and we present useful illustrations on as many ideas and concepts as possible, to aid the reader's understanding.

This book examines several important issues:

❑ The basics of market risks and how they affect credit institutions; we will discuss the identification of market risk factors, the modelling of market risks, specific risk models, and finally back-testing and stress testing of market risk exposures.

❑ The basics of credit risk, with analysis of different ways of modelling credit risk. This will include a review of credit risk assessment models that define and estimate credit risks. In addition, an examination of credit risk rating systems and validation techniques will be presented.

❑ How to determine operational risk capital requirements and how to identify, model and assess operational risks and determine loss profiling. It also proposes solutions on the main aspects of operational VAR.

❑ Key concepts of extreme-value theory in the application of risk management. We will also show how to apply the concept of clustering analysis in extreme-value theory.

❑ Characteristics, strengths and weaknesses of the Basel II accord under the framework of market, credit and operational risks.

❑ Integrated risk management frameworks, where the integration of market, credit, operational risk and losses is undertaken. We will also show how to estimate economic and regulatory capital with regards to integration, as well as discussing all the main aspects of integrated VAR.

For those readers who are interested specifically in the Basel II accord, the book also brings together the main key issues of Basel II requirements, providing all the necessary information about market, credit and operational risks (without going into the full technical details), and outlines the basic characteristics, strengths and weaknesses of Basel II.

1

Market Risk

The truth of a theory is in your mind, not in your eyes
— Albert Einstein

INTRODUCTION

According to the "1996 Market Risk Amendment" (see Basel
Committee for Banking Supervision, 1996a) proposed by the Basel
Committee, market risk is defined as "the risk of losses in on and
off balance sheet positions arising from movements in market
prices". Credit and financial institutions attempt to measure losses
on a constant portfolio over a specified period (often the next day
or next ten days) that will be exceeded only on a given fraction of
occasions (typically a probability level of 1%) for internal risk management purposes, using value-at-risk (VAR) models. Except for
the simplifying assumption of constant portfolio synthesis during
the time horizon, VAR models possess some latent, but equally
crucial, weaknesses, arising from the fact that they are tailor-made
models. Often, these are not directly observable, due to the asym-
metry of information between credit institutions and supervisors.
Because of this, the data inputs should be carefully assessed before
the appropriate model is applied. Moreover, the nature of the data
is the key factor that drives the decision about which model is
going to be used.

Risk in financial markets first appeared around 1973, when
the summit in Bretton Woods initiated an era of free, market-
driven, determination of foreign-exchange rates (FX rates). This

fact increased the volatility of FX rates and, consequently, the uncertainty of international transactions. The volatility of FX rates also made an impact on a variety of other financial products that were related to the FX rates through the International Parity Conditions (see Eiteman, Stonehill and Moffett, 2003). The fact that, at that particular point in time, almost all financial products were affected and this invoked risk professionals to construct complex derivative financial products in order to protect investors from the volatile financial environment.

In April 1973, derivative products, namely futures on stocks, started to be traded in the Chicago Board Options Exchange (CBOE). In the same year, the Black–Scholes model (see Black and Scholes, 1973) for options pricing was released and gave a boost to investments that would follow during the eighties. Even though derivative products were created in order to hedge other types of investments from volatility in the financial environment, during the years that followed their origination, they were used for speculative reasons as well.

Although market risk in financial markets existed for several years, its increased severity attracted market participants to be involved with its quantification. The notion of market risk quantification was first captured during the nineties. At that time, a professional team from JP Morgan Bank started to engage themselves with the bank's "morning report". This report was produced early in the morning by the risk management department and it was produced to inform the top management about the perceived market risk for the next day's positions. The market risk was translated in terms of how much money the bank had the possibility of losing by assuming that it retained the previous day's portfolio. In order to evaluate the overall market risk that was assumed to be undertaken by the bank, risk professionals employed by JP Morgan developed three alternative quantitative methods: variance–covariance (VC), historical simulation (HS) and Monte Carlo (MC) simulation methods.

The foremost concern of modern risk management is to estimate VAR. VAR is considered as the maximum loss likely to occur over a pre-specified period of time for a given confidence level. Although the notion of VAR is widely spread as a standard measure for quantifying market risk, most of the techniques involved in measuring market VAR are based on unrealistic or simplified assumptions. The purpose of this chapter is to indicate the proper inputs of market VAR models, to highlight the deficiencies of the techniques involved and to illustrate the exact steps for the estimation of portfolio VAR according to all basic methods, namely, the VC method, the HS method and the MC method. The Basel Committee regulatory framework, described partly in Chapter 2 and detailed in Chapter 5, assigns to every VAR measure a certain multiplication factor according to its estimation efficiency. Furthermore, the accuracy of some of the methodologies according to the Basel II regulatory framework is examined in Chapter 5.

Although the methods are described in more details, later on, it is important for readers to bear in mind that the first and the third methods (VC and MC) are based on parametric estimation while the HC is based on non-parametric estimation. Thus, in order to give the reader sufficient information needed to better understand parametric estimation, the Appendix shows the necessary quantitative tools required.

Capital asset pricing model parameters
The cornerstone theory behind the parametric estimation of the VC and MC methods is the Capital Asset Pricing Model (CAPM) theory. This theory was proposed by Markowitz (1952) and has been the paramount theory for more than five decades in the financial environment.

The parameters underlying the CAPM theory (mainly, return and volatility estimations) will be used throughout the book for the quantification of market risk. When readers use these parameters they should be aware of the miscellaneous simplified assumptions of the model. The validity of these assumptions makes the theory hold universally. These assumptions are as follows.

❑ Investors' beliefs are orthodox. That is, they are risk-averse and return-loving individuals who maximise the expected utility of their end-of-period wealth and have homogeneous expectations, based on the same information, about asset returns. In other words, the model is a one-period model and all investors compete on the same playing field.
❑ Asset returns follow the normal distribution.

❑ Investors may borrow or lend unlimited amounts of this asset at a constant risk-free asset rate. The risk-free asset is available to all investors.

❑ The number of assets under examination and their participation in the portfolio are constant over the period.

❑ All assets are perfectly divisible and priced in a perfectly competitive market.

❑ Asset markets are frictionless and information is costless and simultaneously available to all investors. The implication of this assumption is that there is no spread between bid and offer rates quoted in the marketplace.

❑ There are no market imperfections such as taxes, regulations or restrictions on short selling.

Among the assumptions underlying the CAPM theory is that all assets under examination have stochastic behaviour although nowadays the stochastic behaviour of assets is under discussion and follow normal distribution. Financial analysts have proved that the world of financial returns is not always "normal". Although the distribution of returns can be efficiently described by a more representative density distribution, CAPM theory assumes that asset returns follow normal distribution. The normal distribution can be completely described by only two parameters, namely the location measure, known as mean value (μ), and the dispersion measure, known as variance (σ^2) or standard deviation (σ).

Complex financial products
Equity prices and FX rates can be determined from valuation models. However, it is preferable not to involve these models in the formulation of their prices, because:

❑ the prices can be directly observed in the marketplace and do not exhibit gaps in their returns; and

❑ not all inputs of the models are known or cannot be, somehow, estimated, such as the dividends for equities.

The main drawback for equity models is that it is difficult to quantify the level of dividends on a perpetual basis. On the other hand, there are several microeconomic and macroeconomic factors that cannot be easily modelled and drive the prices of FX rates.

Furthermore, both risk factors, namely equities and FX rates, are liquid traded financial products and their distributions of returns do not exhibit gaps. Thus, instead of using a model for their valuation, it is preferable for the risk manager to use their prices directly from the market.

In the analysis of the risk-measurement methodologies presented throughout this book, several financial products are used because they have both direct and indirect impact on the quantification of market and credit risks. The knowledge of the functions of these products will be helpful in order to quantify their risks. On the other hand, in the absence of crucial risk parameters for the estimation of other products' financial risk, some derivative products can be used in order to derive parameters, as they are embodied in their market values and implied by the market participants.

Furthermore, the two functions of derivative products are not controversial. A bank has the ability to retain in its portfolio an asset for which the risk should be quantified and simultaneously it can use the parameters implied in the market value of the derivative product in order to quantify the risk of other products. In this section, the financial products will be separated according to their use in the forthcoming material of the book. Thus, the products are divided into:

❑ portfolio products; and
❑ products for implying risk parameters, which are discussed in the Appendix.

Portfolio products
As mentioned above, the financial products described in the present subsection will be used as portfolio components for the quantification of a typical banking portfolio. It is worth mentioning that, when "banking portfolio" or simply "portfolio" is referred to in this book, it should be interpreted as the entire portfolio retained by banks or credit institutions.

Furthermore, throughout the book some derivative financial products serve for both portfolio products and products for implying risk parameters. Option contracts are a typical case of this fact, being a basic element of banking portfolios and simultaneously being the reference for deriving implied volatility of the assets underlying them.

Products for implying risk parameters

Apart from the products used for the composition of a banking portfolio, there are financial derivative products that may have dual characteristics, that is, they may also serve as vehicles for the derivation of some hidden parameters. These parameters act as catalysts for the transformation and/or implementation of other risk parameters, not directly observed but necessary for the derivation of financial risk.

Benchmarking

Although traditional financial products, namely equities and FX rates, exhibit time gaps between two consecutive traded prices throughout a typical trading date, usually they regularly exhibit prices on an end-of-day basis. In the following subsections, not only the assembly of time series from actual trading values but also, if it is not always possible, the most efficient alternatives for simulating these values are presented.

Interpolation techniques

Some product values, such as derivative products described in the Appendix, are not observed directly in the marketplace. Therefore, it is essential to find methods for constructing those values from the most relative values observed. The most common is the case of interest rates for different maturities. Data vendors provide only benchmark interest rates, referring to typical maturities. However, portfolios consist of interest rate products that exhibit maturities that do not coincide with the aforementioned maturities of available data. In such a case, several techniques, depending on the nature of the data involved, are employed.

IDENTIFYING MARKET RISK FACTORS
The need for market risk factors

The input of data is the starting point for the implementation of the VAR model. There are two classes of data that should be carefully assessed and imported in the system: market data and position data (see Figure 1). The lack of position data makes the estimation of VAR impossible. On the other hand, without having the necessary market data one needs to produce them. The production of market data is usually done by using either interpolation techniques (see Appendix) or extensive simulation methods (which are discussed later on in this chapter).

After data specification, every VAR mechanism, *implicitly or explicitly*, depends on the selection or estimation of the following components:

❏ individual volatilities and co-movements between or among risk factors;
❏ distribution assumptions;
❏ window length of the data used for parameter estimates;
❏ time horizon of holding the investment, or otherwise named holding period; and
❏ confidence level of the estimation.

The use of return time series is a prerequisite for the estimation of volatilities and co-movements. When the frequency of the data used is very high (such as one week, one day), VAR models assume zero mean return. Nevertheless, the inclusion of the mean of returns in lower-frequency data is suggested when VAR measures are estimated. Figure 1 shows the flow of VAR methodologies.

Apart from the above issue, when constructing VAR methodologies it is essential to define explicitly the major building blocks (for instance, data selection, risk factors, mapping), that characterise their procedures. By doing this, the advantages and the

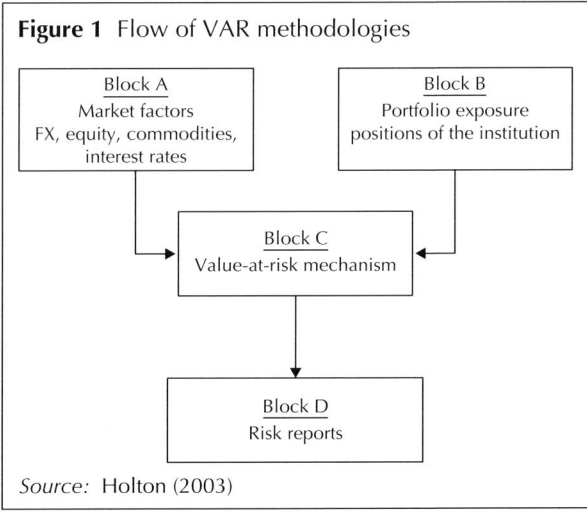

Figure 1 Flow of VAR methodologies

Block A	Block B
Market factors FX, equity, commodities, interest rates	Portfolio exposure positions of the institution

Block C
Value-at-risk mechanism

Block D
Risk reports

Source: Holton (2003)

limitations of every method are more apparent. The comparison of the various methods is carried out throughout the next section.

Position risk and risk factors

Credit and financial institutions' portfolios may contain a wide spectrum of financial products. The infrastructure related to the VAR estimation assumes the combination of market and position data in order to achieve continuous portfolio valuation. Position risk or exposure risk is the risk attributed to a specific position due to the exposure in one or more risk factors. Risk managers assume that the synthesis of the portfolio remains unchanged throughout the holding period. For instance, the estimation of one-day VAR assumes that the portfolio remains steady until the next day. Under the above assumption, the set of market risk factors remains the only source of risk. For example market factors that drive the value:

❏ of commodities are the commodity prices or changes;
❏ of spot FX products are the FX rates or changes;
❏ of equities are the equity prices or changes;
❏ of bonds are the yield level or changes (or zero-coupon yield or changes); and
❏ of options are the underlying asset prices, the volatility of the underlying asset prices and the dividends (dividend schedule or certain dividend yield).

Interest rate risk

The valuation formula of an option-free bond is expressed as follows:

$$P = \sum_{t=1}^{n} \frac{C(t)}{\left(1+\dfrac{y}{m}\right)^t} \tag{1}$$

where, P is the price of the bond, $C(t)$ is cashflow (in €) at time point t, m is the number of coupon payments per year, y is yield to maturity, n is total number of periods expressed in years.

Keeping all other components of the bond valuation constant, the level of cashflows affects the price of the bond according to a non-linear positive relationship. On the other hand, the higher the yield to maturity is, the lower the resulting bond price and vice versa.

Duration approach provides relatively accurate predictions for slight changes in interest rates. However, duration as a sensitivity factor is relatively inaccurate for higher changes. Duration can be interpreted as the relative change of the bond value with respect to a relative change in the interest rate. This is also interpreted as the elasticity of the bond value with respect to the interest rate. The slope of the tangent to the price yield curve became known as "modified duration" or Macaulay duration (see Hicks, 1939; Macaulay, 1938) (modified duration is expressed without the minus sign):

$$\frac{dP}{dy}\frac{1}{P} = -\frac{1}{1+\frac{y}{m}}\left[\sum_{t=1}^{n}\frac{\frac{t}{m}\times C(t)}{\left(1+\frac{y}{m}\right)^t}\right]\frac{1}{P} \qquad (2)$$

The changes in price levels due to changes in interest rates can be linearly approximated by:

$$dP = -MD \times P \times dy \qquad (3)$$

The bond valuation formula assumes that the yield for each point in time appears to be the same until the expiration date. It also assumes that cashflow receivables are reinvested in the same yield for the whole period up to the expiration date. In practice, the above concept implicitly assumes that there is only one interest rate corresponding to the yield to maturity, applicable to a given instrument. The irrationality of this concept is shown by comparing a one-year-to-maturity with a two-year-to-maturity fixed-income instrument. The first-year yield of the two-year-to-maturity instrument may be different from the yield to maturity of the one-year-to-maturity instrument.

In order to overcome this setback, interest rate volatility is measured by using the price value of a basis point (PVBP) method. Instead of expressing the interest rate volatility per product (duration), the PVBP method represents the interest rate volatility per cashflow. Accordingly, sensitivities are calculated for each cashflow instead of each product.

Foreign exchange risk, equity risk and commodity risk
Apparently, the quantification of interest rate risk is difficult due to the complexity of the interrelations among the factors that affect

the valuation of an interest rate product. Instead, FX risk – that is the risk of a value decrease for the credit institution due to a change in FX rates – appears to be less complicated. Every percentage change in FX rates affects the price of the position with the same percentage. Although it applies to the generic case, this does not apply to complex financial derivatives, such as FX options, which exhibit strong non-linear relationships between the inputs of the pricing model and the price of the derivative product (see Appendix for the notion of option pricing).

On the other hand, complex dividend models (see Ross, Westerfield and Jaffe, 1996) describe the derivation of a fair price for equities. However, in reality dividends are not known up front, even for the next year. Most of the dividend models for the valuation of equities assume that dividends are known or can be somehow derived perpetually. The above twofold assumption appears to be unrealistic. Thus, the quantification and management of equity risk should be based on available market prices taken by an organised exchange. Unlike bond prices, equities appear to have quite smooth distributions of returns and they can efficiently substitute for any valuation model. Nevertheless, the image is different when market indexes are used, instead of the data that exactly represent the movement of the equity under examination. In this case there is a market risk by holding the equity, which is not represented by the movement of the index. This risk is known as *specific risk of the equity* and it is examined extensively later.

Finally, commodity risk is the risk arising from movements in commodity prices. The behaviour of commodities is very similar to that of equities, especially in the case of specific risk. For instance, the use of an energy index cannot fully explain the movement of oil because there are specific factors that drive the price of the oil. Similarly, the analysis of the specific risk for equities coincides with the respective analysis for commodities.

Second-order risks

Since many instruments have non-linear terms in their valuation formula, Chew (1994) expressed the view that VAR intends to "translate all instruments into units of risk or potential loss based on certain parameters". Among them, the interest-rate-based products, examined above, exhibit a convex relationship between interest rates (yields) and the price of the asset for large changes in interest rates. However, this relationship cannot be fully captured by the duration measure.

Summing up, the percentage value change of bond-based instruments caused by interest rate changes is based on the Taylor expansion series as follows:

$$\frac{dP}{P} = \frac{1}{P}\frac{dP}{dy}dy + \frac{1}{2}\frac{1}{P}\frac{d^2P}{dy^2}(dy)^2 + \frac{1}{P}error \qquad (4)$$

Convexity introduces a non-linear element (optionally) in the bond valuation. Mathematically expressed, it is the second derivative of the bond price in respect to interest rate changes. Analytically, it is given by:

$$\frac{d^2P}{dy^2} = \sum_{t=1}^{n} \frac{\dfrac{t(t+1)}{m}C(t)}{\left(1+\dfrac{y}{m}\right)^{t+2}} \qquad (5)$$

The impact of duration and convexity is given by the first and the second term of Equation (5), respectively. In line with the above, option values can be approximated from delta and gamma, respectively. The effects from theta, rho and lambda (vega) can also be incorporated in the error term. In the case that all "Greek" effects are included, the VAR is based on the full-valuation method. It is obvious that a higher degree of non-linearity indicates a higher degree of risk (see Group of Thirty, 1993). However, estimation of gamma is a very difficult task to carry out analytically. Thus, it is preferable to employ non-parametric or parametric models.

Transforming the original data and manipulating their weaknesses

A typical portfolio consists of more complex financial products that have multipart payoffs and returns that exhibit huge gaps. Thus, the determination of the desired market risk factors is a much more sophisticated technique. These risk factors may replicate movements in cash products (equity prices, commodity prices and FX rates) or derivatives products (such as implied volatilities and interest rates) and some of them can be easily picked up from organised exchanges. Nevertheless, several risk factors cannot be directly observed in the marketplace and should be calculated by using other sources of information (for instance, zero coupon rates, implied volatilities). Among all cash products, interest rates exhibit this difficulty, which arises from the fact that implied yields to maturity are not unswervingly functional and from the fact that future cashflows are available at different time points from those implied by market benchmarks (see Appendix).

In general, the more complex the synthesis of the portfolio is, the higher the number of risk factors involved and the higher the number of calculations needed. There is a variety of price types that can, potentially, be used as inputs in VAR models, namely:

❑ transaction prices;
❑ conventional prices; and
❑ settlement prices.

Transaction prices are formed in an organised exchange at irregular time points. Conventional prices are quotes that may not be a product of trading, but are publicly available from market makers (bid or ask prices, mid-market prices). Finally, settlement prices are usually non-traded values, but, by some means, they are an average of a large set of transaction prices, which are publicised at the end of each trading day. The task of collecting settlement or closing prices is as easy as recording the daily settlement prices realised at the appropriate organised market.

This selection is not an error-free technique because not all the organised markets close down simultaneously. Moreover, there are organised exchanges that are active for 24 hours a day and do not publicise settlement or closing prices (at least not real-time prices). In such cases, transaction prices should be collected with the condition that the collection time is the same across all products that do not exhibit settlement prices. Ultimately, the problem of non-synchronous data selection is much more apparent when dealing with numerous assets that require transaction prices for the estimation of VAR.

Additionally, there are three possible sources of data errors.

(1) A misplaced digit or a misplaced decimal point. This type of error may lead to an increased volatility when the VAR measure requires its estimation.

(2) A repeated datum. This type of error may lead the volatility estimation to either higher or lower levels depending on the relative level of the datum in relation to the levels of other data involved in the time series.

(3) A missing datum or a datum that is equal to zero, by mistake. This would also affect the volatility estimation. In order to fill up the gap arising from a missing datum, interpolation techniques, as illustrated in the Appendix, are used.

MARKET RISK MODELS

VAR models

The number of different product types – and, consequently, the number of different data types – has a direct effect on the difficulty of VAR estimation, that is to say the higher the number of assets, the higher the time needed for VAR estimation under all three traditional approaches. More specifically, under the VC approach, an increase in the number of positions taken has a direct exponential effect on the number of calculations needed. Under the MC approach, a similar rise causes more significant calculation difficulties. Instead, the magnitude of the effect is lower under the HS approach, although there is also an increased storage need.

Almost all traditional VAR models assume that past and present data contain information about the future behaviour of the underlying portfolio. In this section, two types of VAR are examined: the unitary market risk and, consequently, the portfolio risk.

The unitary market risk refers to the risk an individual asset possesses. On the other hand, the portfolio risk refers to the total risk the portfolio exhibits. The risk of the total portfolio does not arise from just summing up unitary VARs. Instead, not all assets move in the same direction at the same time, resulting in a sub-additive portfolio VAR.

Variance–covariance method

The VC method assumes that risk factors follow a multivariate normal distribution and that they exhibit serial independence. However, the VC method can only be suitable for cash products or derivative products that attain, or are approximated by, linear characteristics. Volatility is a measure that is the key parameter for VAR estimation under the VC method. In order for the volatility to be estimated, it is essential to know the returns time series for each of the products under consideration. Returns can be calculated by using either logarithmic or arithmetic returns, although the former produce smoother measures of volatility. The notion of volatility, according to the VC method, is approximated by the variance or standard deviation of returns. The estimation of the standard deviation can be made by using either equally weighted historical data or unevenly weighted historical data (or simply equally weighted and weighted, respectively). The difference of the latter in relation to the former technique lies in the fact that each of the historical market data receives a different weight when the volatility is estimated.

Except for the standalone volatility estimations, estimations of common movements of risk factors are also the main ingredients in estimating VAR. When the portfolio includes more than one position, the computation of VAR requires an estimation of the entire variance–covariance, or correlation matrix. This matrix creates the sub-additive effect when estimating the portfolio market risk.

Moving from market volatility to market risk

The variability of the risk factors can be transformed into market risk by either linear or non-linear means. The importance of each risk factor exclusively relies on the nature of the market product. Linear relationships between price changes and market risks are depicted by betas, durations and deltas for equity, bonds and options, respectively. On the other hand, non-linear liaisons among them are explained by residual risks, convexities and gammas, for equity, bonds and options, respectively. Additionally, options are affected by the volatilities of the underlying asset (volatility risk), while hedged positions are affected by the difference between hedged position prices and hedging instrument prices ("basis" risk).

For the sake of accuracy, the linear and non-linear effect should be encompassed into a unique measure, called *market sensitivity*. This measure is the main determinant when transforming price variability into market risk. Every change in FX rates, commodity prices and equity prices has an equal quantitative percentage effect on the total position invested in the product (sensitivity of one). However, the interest rate risk measurement is a more complicated task. Its sensitivity, in respect to market volatility, is a non-linear function and usually a difficult one, in terms of the computational power needed. The market risk measurement is given by:

$$\text{Market risk} = \text{Sensitivity} \times \text{Volatility} \qquad (6)$$

The sensitivity factor represents the relationship between the cause from a financial risk factor and its impact on the price of the financial product. The sensitivity factor becomes more important when products with non-linear characteristics are involved in the quantification of market risk.

Equally weighted historical volatility
The volatility of returns R_{is} of the risk factor i, in the time interval between $t - T$ and $t - 1$, is estimated as follows:

$$\sigma_{it} = \sqrt{\frac{1}{T-1} \sum_{s=t-T}^{t-1} (R_{is} - \mu_{it})^2} \qquad (7)$$

where

$$\mu_{it} = \frac{1}{T}(R_{i1} + R_{i2} + \cdots + R_{iT}) \qquad (8)$$

given that T is the time window and t is the time point.

For most financial time series, the true mean is close to zero and any attempt to estimate it will produce statistically insignificant results. Thus, many researchers choose to exclude the mean from the volatility estimation formula. The mean metric can be excluded from the above estimation without significant changes in the volatility estimation.

A reason for applying the above approximation is that regulatory documents of the Bank for International Settlements (BIS) and the European Commission (EC) implicitly support the use of the equally weighted volatility estimation, by stating that the "effective" time window should be no less than one year or, by interpreting the statement, 250 observations (T = 250). The word "effective" may be subject to many and contradictory explanations from the market participants, albeit that the original concept was related to the average life of weights assigned to the observations (see Jorion, 2002). Thus, there is a need for regulatory agents to peg the borders of a common level field over and beyond which the models should not be acceptable.

Weighted schemes

Moving beyond equally weighted schemes, using weighted schemes (see Bollerslev, 1986) suggests that the current volatility depends on the past squared residuals and on short-term and long-term volatility. The generic model is specified as:

$$\sigma_{it} = \sqrt{\gamma V_L + \sum_{s=t-T}^{t-1} a_s (R_{is} - \mu_{it})^2 + \sum_{s=t-T}^{t-1} \beta_s \sigma_{is}^2} \tag{9}$$

where,

$$\gamma + \sum_{s=t-T}^{t-1} a_s + \sum_{s=t-T}^{t-1} \beta_s = 1 \tag{10}$$

V_L is the long-term variance, γ is the weight assigned to V_L, α_s is the positive amount of weight given to residuals at time point s and β_s is the positive amount of weight given to volatility at time point s.

The above approximation of volatility is widely known as the GARCH(s,s) specification. The GARCH(1,1) model has an economic interpretation in the sense that it depends on the most recent financial shock (squared residual) and the prevailing circumstances (most recent estimate of the variance rate). The GARCH(1,1) is given by:

$$\sigma_t = \sqrt{\gamma V_L + a (R_{t-1} - \mu)^2 + \beta \sigma_{t-1}^2} \tag{11}$$

where $\alpha + \beta + \gamma = 1$.

The GARCH(1,1) model carries out relatively good short-run predictions, incorporating the impact of the long-run variance level. However, the model recognises that, over time, the variance tends to get pulled back to a long-run average level of variance (see Hull, 2003). On the other hand, it eliminates the serial correlation from the squared residuals.

Exponentially weighted moving average

A particular case of the GARCH(1,1) model is the *exponentially weighted moving average* model (EWMA) or integrated GARCH

(IGARCH), according to which $\gamma = 0$, $\alpha = 1 - \lambda$ and $\beta = \lambda$. Alternatively viewed, the volatility of T observations according to the EWMA model could also be represented as an integrated GARCH model with no constant term:

$$\sigma_t^2 = (1-\lambda)\varepsilon_t^2 + \lambda\sigma_{t-1}^2 \tag{12}$$

The following formula illustrates the volatility estimation under normal exponential smoothing or, alternatively, exponentially weighted moving average:

$$\sigma_{it} = \sqrt{(1-\lambda) \sum_{s=t-T}^{t-1} \lambda^{t-s-1}(R_{is} - \mu_{it})^2} \tag{13}$$

The mean factor can be excluded from the above formula and it is roughly equivalent to the estimate:

$$\sigma_{it} = \sqrt{(1-\lambda) \sum_{s=t-T}^{t-1} \lambda^{t-s-1}(R_{is})^2} \tag{14}$$

The parameter λ or "decay factor" parameter spans between zero and one and can be externally estimated. Furthermore, the smoothing parameter places less weight on observations as the time distance from the present becomes larger. Additionally, the smaller the value of λ, the less weight is assigned to past observations and the higher the ratio according to which the weights are lowered.

Except for RiskMetrics (1996, 1999) there is no evidence of an optimal decay factor that would be applicable for all financial products at all times (see Alexander and Lee, 1997; Hendricks, 1996; Jackson, Maude and Perraudin, 1998). RiskMetrics proposed a model based on a universal decay factor equal to 0.94 applicable for all categories of risk factors. The specific model, as $T \to \infty$, has an average life of 16.67 days, implying that estimations heavily rely on recent observations. Respectively, the equally weighted model has an average life of weights equal to 125.5 days. Table 1 illustrates the comparison between the average life of alternative models and the average life of the benchmark model.

Table 1 Proportional average life of the sum of weights in relation to the average life of the equally weighted model

"λ"	Observations				
	1 year	2 years	3 years	4 years	5 years
0.94	0.1328	0.1328	0.1328	0.1328	0.1328
0.95	0.1594	0.1594	0.1594	0.1594	0.1594
0.96	0.1991	0.1992	0.1992	0.1992	0.1992
0.97	0.2646	0.2656	0.2656	0.2656	0.2656
0.98	0.3856	0.3982	0.3984	0.3984	0.3984
0.99	0.6211	0.7705	0.7936	0.7965	0.7968
0.991	0.6533	0.8415	0.8786	0.8844	0.8852
0.992	0.6871	0.9229	0.9815	0.9934	0.9956
0.993	0.7224	1.0158	1.1074	1.1312	1.1368
0.994	0.7592	1.1212	1.2618	1.3086	1.3226
0.995	0.7972	1.2398	1.4511	1.5403	1.5746

Following the above theoretical steps and the concept used by the Basel Committee, it can be concluded that only models having values higher than unity in Table 1 (highlighted area) are eligible models. In general, the class of models under discussion does not capture long-term movements in volatility, as the sum of the previous day's residual (or return) coefficient $(1 - \lambda)$ and the previous day's volatility coefficient (λ) result in unity. Nevertheless, the restrictions that the Basel Committee introduces lead to model selection errors. These errors become apparent if the true VAR model is indeed based on a weighted scheme. In that sense, the Basel Committee should have been more flexible and allowed credit institutions to estimate independently the decay factor for each risk factor. Thus, each decay factor would be the best representative for the respective risk factor and the model would be the most suitable for each case.

Variance–covariance matrix

The next step, before fully identifying unitary VAR, is to employ the quantile that corresponds to a given confidence level:

$$VAR = Quantile \times Market\ risk \tag{15}$$

The VC method requires the estimation of possible co-movements among the spectrum of unitary VAR estimates as they are addressed by pairwise correlations:

$$\rho_{ijt} = \frac{\sigma_{ijt}}{\sigma_{it}\sigma_{jt}} \qquad (16)$$

$$\sigma_{ijt} = \frac{1}{T-1} \sum_{s=t-T}^{t-1} (R_{is} - \mu_{it})(R_{js} - \mu_{jt}) \qquad (17)$$

where ρ_{ijt} is the correlation between asset i and j at time t, σ_{ijt} is the covariance between asset i and j at time t.

The estimation of covariances according to the RiskMetrics approach, presented above, is given by:

$$\sigma_{ijt} = (1-\lambda) \sum_{s=t-T}^{t-1} \lambda^{t-s-1}(R_{is} - \mu_{it})(R_{js} - \mu_{jt}) \qquad (18)$$

In turn, the VAR of the portfolio is estimated as:

$$VAR_p = \sqrt{\vec{x}^T C \vec{x}} \qquad (19)$$

$$C = \begin{bmatrix} \rho_{1,1} & \rho_{1,2} & \cdots & \rho_{1,n} \\ \rho_{2,1} & \rho_{2,2} & \cdots & \rho_{2,n} \\ \cdots & \cdots & \cdots & \cdots \\ \rho_{n,1} & \rho_{n,2} & \cdots & \rho_{n,n} \end{bmatrix} \qquad (20)$$

$$\vec{x} = \begin{bmatrix} VAR_1 \\ VAR_2 \\ \cdots \\ VAR_n \end{bmatrix} \qquad (21)$$

Implied volatilities and correlations

In some cases implied volatility estimates, alone or jointly with historical volatility data, are more reliable predictors of future actual volatility (see Campa and Chang, 1998; Duffie and Pan, 1997).

Implied volatility can be obtained by reverting the related options pricing formula (see Appendix) to find the specific risk factor volatility (eg, Black–Scholes model for stocks, Black model for futures and commodities and Garman-Kohlhagen for FX rates). An alternative approximation is the use of stochastic volatility pricing models (see Hull and White, 1987; Scott, 1987; Wiggins, 1987). Under the assumption of independent return and volatility shocks, the volatility is derived from a stochastic volatility model for every day until the day before the expiration date. The average value of the aforementioned volatilities is the input in the BS pricing formula. Finally, implied correlations can be derived only from FX options.

Thus, it is impossible to derive the VAR of the entire portfolio by relying only on implied volatilities and correlations, given that the portfolio consists of more than one (non-FX-rates-related) financial product. Instead, the VAR of FX reserves can entirely rely on implied volatilities and correlation.

Value-at-risk conversions

The results from all the above procedures for estimating VAR depend on the density of available data series. For instance, if daily data are used, daily VAR estimates are produced. However, the need for VAR calculations for different time intervals and the need for size-reduction of cost-increasing databanks stimulate the use of conversion techniques.

The Basel Committee Amendment requires the use of ten-day VAR, but motivates the conversion of the one-day VAR into ten-day VAR, based on the same confidence level as:

$$VAR_{Basel} = VAR_n \times \sqrt{\frac{10}{n}} \qquad (22)$$

where, VAR_{Basel} is the VAR required by the Basel Committee, VAR_n is the internally used VAR for n-days interval.

Moreover, the Basel Committee proposes the use of a 99% confidence level. Nevertheless, it allows the internally used confidence level to be converted into the aforementioned one as:

$$VAR_{Basel} = VAR_{CL} \times \frac{a_{99\%}}{a} \qquad (23)$$

where, VAR_{CL} is the internally used VAR for a particular confidence level, $\alpha_{99\%}$ is the quantile that corresponds to 99% confidence level (approximately 2.33), α is the quantile that corresponds to the internally used confidence level.

Generalising, the desired VAR_d for target quantile a_d and holding period n_d, is given by:

$$VAR_d = VAR_{(CL,n)} \times \frac{a_d}{a} \times \sqrt{\frac{n_d}{n}} \qquad (24)$$

Monte Carlo Simulation

The VC method is not adequately capable of dealing with non-linear products. Within non-linear portfolios, the probability distribution of the changes in portfolio value is (typically) unknown. Even by making assumptions about the distribution of the risk factors, it is not possible to deduce the P&L distribution analytically.

In order to overcome this problem, the MC simulation method is introduced (see Figure 2). Following the assumption that the risk factors (interest rates, volatility, shares and FX rates) follow a geometric Brownian motion (GBM), the method produces numerous changes in the value of the portfolio with the help of a random generator procedure.

Generally, GBM is represented as follows:

$$\Delta \ln P = \mu \Delta t + \varepsilon \sigma \sqrt{\Delta t} \qquad (25)$$

where:

$$\Delta \ln P = \ln P_{i,t+1} - \ln P_{i,t} = \ln \left(\frac{P_{i,t+1}}{P_{i,t}} \right) \qquad (26)$$

Combining Equation (25) and Equation (26) and assuming that for high frequency data the position measure (mean) is zero Equation (27) arises:

$$\ln \left(\frac{P_{i,t+1}}{P_{i,t}} \right) = \varepsilon \sigma \sqrt{\Delta t} \qquad (27)$$

MC simulation implicitly assumes that the probability distribution of the daily logarithmic changes of risk factors is known and the

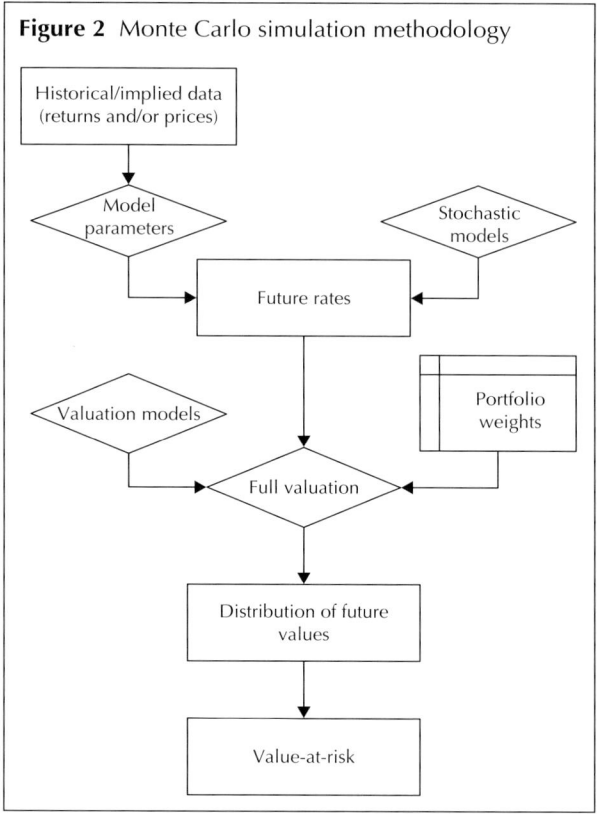

Figure 2 Monte Carlo simulation methodology

daily logarithmic changes of risk factors are multivariate normally distributed.

$$R_{i,t+1} = \ln\left(\frac{P_{i,t+1}}{P_{i,t}}\right) \tag{28}$$

where $R_{i,t+1}$ is the daily logarithmic changes of the risk factor i at time $t + 1$, $P_{i,t+1}$ is the daily price of the risk factor i at time $t + 1$, $P_{i,t}$ is the daily price of the risk factor i at time t.

Otherwise stated, the value of the risk factors of the following day, for high-frequency data (the term μ is dropped out), can be calculated as follows:

$$P_{i,t+1} = P_{i,t} \exp\left(\varepsilon_i \sigma_i \sqrt{\Delta t}\right) \tag{29}$$

Once the variance–covariance matrix of returns (Σ) has been esti-
mated/forecasted (using any one of the methods described above)
the correlation matrix C can be constructed.

$$\Sigma = \begin{bmatrix} \sigma_{1,1} & \sigma_{1,2} & \cdots & \sigma_{1,n} \\ \sigma_{2,1} & \sigma_{2,2} & \cdots & \sigma_{2,n} \\ \cdots & \cdots & \cdots & \cdots \\ \sigma_{n,1} & \sigma_{n,2} & \cdots & \sigma_{n,n} \end{bmatrix} \tag{30}$$

$$C = \begin{bmatrix} \rho_{1,1} & \rho_{1,2} & \cdots & \rho_{1,n} \\ \rho_{2,1} & \rho_{2,2} & \cdots & \rho_{2,n} \\ \cdots & \cdots & \cdots & \cdots \\ \rho_{n,1} & \rho_{n,2} & \cdots & \rho_{n,n} \end{bmatrix} \tag{31}$$

As explicitly shown in Hamilton (1994), the C matrix can be
decomposed into:

$$C = AA^{\mathsf{T}} \tag{32}$$

where:

$$A = \begin{bmatrix} \alpha_{1,1} & \alpha_{1,2} & \cdots & \alpha_{1,n} \\ \alpha_{2,1} & \alpha_{2,2} & \cdots & \alpha_{2,n} \\ \cdots & \cdots & \cdots & \cdots \\ \alpha_{n,1} & \alpha_{n,2} & \cdots & \alpha_{n,n} \end{bmatrix} \tag{33}$$

and,

$$\alpha_{ij} = \begin{cases} 0 & j < i \\[2mm] \sqrt{\sigma_{ii} - \sum_{k=1}^{i-1} a_{ik}^2} & j = i \\[4mm] \dfrac{1}{a_{ii}} \sqrt{\sigma_{ji} - \sum_{k=1}^{i-1} a_{ik} a_{jk}} & j > i \end{cases} \tag{34}$$

Cuthbertson and Nitzsche (2001) showed that a matrix Z of correlated and (randomly) drawn innovations can be produced by:

$$Z = A^{\mathsf{T}} \varepsilon \tag{35}$$

or alternatively,

$$
\begin{bmatrix} z_1 & z_2 & \cdots & z_n \end{bmatrix} = \begin{bmatrix} \alpha_{1,1} & \alpha^*_{2,1} & \cdots & \alpha^*_{n,1} \\ \alpha^*_{1,2} & \alpha_{2,2} & \cdots & \alpha^*_{n,2} \\ \cdots & \cdots & \cdots & \cdots \\ \alpha^*_{1,n} & \alpha^*_{1,n} & \cdots & \alpha_{n,n} \end{bmatrix} \begin{bmatrix} \varepsilon_1 \\ \varepsilon_2 \\ \cdots \\ \varepsilon_n \end{bmatrix} \tag{36}
$$

where the notation "*" represents the change of the position of the specific element when the matrix is transformed from A to A^T. The vector ε ($nx1$) is usually generated 10,000 times and represents the set of randomly drawn standardised normal residuals for all n risk factors. The values of z_i ($i=1, \ldots, n$) are used as inputs, instead of ε_i, in Equation (29) in order to forecast price series (t periods ahead). In turn, the VAR is estimated using the required percentile.

When derivative products are involved, all the risk factors that are used as inputs in the derivatives pricing model are independently estimated. Then the inputs create a new series of derivative prices from which the required order of statistics is taken as the VAR.

Thus, the steps that should be pursued, in order to apply MC simulation, are as follows:

❑ synchronisation of original asset data series (P_i);
❑ convert asset data into return data (R_i);
❑ calculate VC matrix from R_i;
❑ calculate correlation matrix (**C**), which will be used as input in the VAR estimation;
❑ create the matrix P_t ($1 \times n$) for n assets for time t;
❑ the correlation matrix should be decomposed into **A** and A^T;
❑ shock matrix A^T with the column vector ε ($n \times 1$), where n is the dimension of matrix A^T ($n \times n$) and n is the number of assets; the column vector has one random number for each asset (repeat step for 10,000 times);
❑ generate the matrix $\mathbf{Z} = \mathbf{A^T} \, \boldsymbol{\varepsilon}$ ($\boldsymbol{n \times 1}$) 10,000 times;
❑ create 10,000 times a matrix $e\mathbf{Z}$ ($\boldsymbol{n \times 1}$) of which every element $e = 2.71 \ldots$ to the power z_i (e^{z_i});
❑ create 10,000 times the element matrix $\mathbf{P_{t+1}}$ (element) $= \mathbf{P_t}$ ($\boldsymbol{1 \times n}$) x $e\mathbf{Z}$ ($\boldsymbol{n \times 1}$);

❑ the 99th percentile is the VAR for the next day, that is one-day VAR;
❑ ten-day VAR or one-year VAR can be produced by either:
   ❑ multiplying one-day shocks by the square of 10 (10-day VAR) or the square of 365 (one-year VAR); or
   ❑ repeating the procedure for every day of the holding period (very time consuming but the most accurate);
❑ repeat the steps for every $(R_{i,t})$, where i stands for the asset type and t is the time the return of the asset type has appeared. For instance, if the original time series data comprises 750 observations and after the synchronisation 700 return data remain, the procedure is applied to all 700 data; and
❑ report the VAR for every t.

Historical simulation

The historical simulation (HS) method is the most cost-effective and the least time-consuming approach in terms of computational needs. However, it is probably the most costly method in terms of storage requirements. In every case, HS retains the advantage of the straightforward implementation of full valuation.

The underlying methodology consists of going back in time and applying current weights to time series of historical asset returns involved in the computation of VAR. By doing this, a history of a hypothetical portfolio is reconstructed using the current position. Alternatively, the approaches assume that the present portfolio construction is frozen in all time points in the past. According to the HS method, m different scenarios concerning probable future price movements can be applied. Those scenarios are taken from past experiences by utilising all past multivariate returns included in the used time window.

When derivative products with non-linear characteristics are considered, all valuation model inputs (such as interest rates, stock prices, volatilities and FX rates) are required (not only returns), in order to carry out a mark-to-model valuation. The aforementioned inputs are necessary for an independent revaluation of each derivative product for each point in the past, because, in most cases (see options in Appendix etc), there is no or rare historical evidence of derivative market prices. Figure 3 shows this HS methodology.

The new portfolio value, computed from the full set of hypothetical prices, creates the portfolio distribution of returns. VAR is

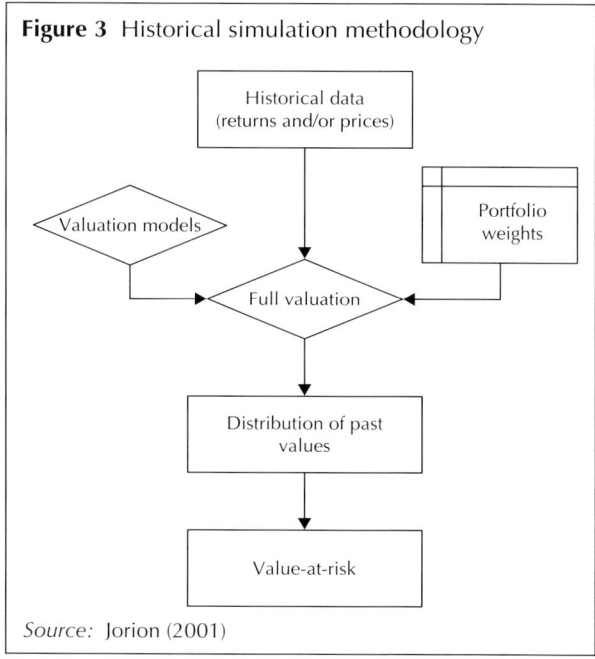

Figure 3 Historical simulation methodology

Source: Jorion (2001)

computed by the $n + 1$-th order statistic that corresponds to the pre-specified confidence level. In other words, VAR is the worst loss observed, after ignoring n negative returns that correspond to the confidence level. The HS method has the ability to incorporate non-linear relationships, to capture gamma and vega risks and to account for fat tails because it refers to the true distribution of returns without assuming any specific distribution.

Hybrid methods

The unconditional HS method does not assume any return distribution but, typically, it is unable to capture conditional heteroscedasticity. In order to overcome this obstacle, several conditional HS methods have been proposed in literature (see Hull and White, 1998; Barone-Adesi, Giannopoulos and Vosper, 1999; Boudoukh, Richardson and Whitelaw, 1998). Barone-Adesi, Giannopoulos and Vosper proposed a variant of the traditional HS methodology referred to as *filtered historical simulation* (FHS). This approach introduces an innovation that captures both conditional heteroscedasticity and non-normality of asset returns within a unique model, improving the performance of classical VC and HS methods that are currently in use.

Originally, the FHS methodology proposes the estimation of an ARMA(1,1) – GARCH(1,1) and, in turn, the construction of residuals and standard deviation series. The VAR value is estimated by selecting the appropriate quantile from the entire future return distribution, which is simulated by repeatedly applying the following sequence of equations.

$$e_t = \frac{\varepsilon_t}{\sigma_t} \tag{37}$$

$$\sigma_{t+1}^2 = \beta_0 + \beta_1 \varepsilon_t^2 + \beta_2 \sigma_t^2 \tag{38}$$

$$z_{t+1} = e_t \sigma_{t+1} \tag{39}$$

$$r_{t+1} = a_0 + a_1 r_t + a_2 \varepsilon_t + z_{t+1} \tag{40}$$

For the remaining σ_{t+s}, until the target time horizon, the ε_t term in the first and the last equations of the sequence is replaced by z_{t+s-1}.

The HS method (see Figure 3) has been criticised because the ability to understand the properties of the VAR model is obfuscated by the simultaneous occurrence of other types of model error, including errors in pricing, errors in GARCH models and other potential flaws in the VAR methodology.

On the other hand, the traditional HS method is considered to be robust, intuitive and not prone to model risk, as the estimation of parameters is not a prerequisite. Another variant of the method, if the distribution of returns on the entire set of the portfolio follows a close-to-normal distribution, would be the VAR estimation to rely on the current variance, resulting from the entire portfolio distribution. However, this variant deviates from the non-parametric concept and can be considered a semi-parametric model.

SPECIFIC MARKET RISK
Specific market risk modelling
The recent modifications of the Basel I framework and the needs of the modern risk management (see Basel Committee on Banking

Supervision, 1996b; Basel Committee on Banking Supervision, 2004; Basel Committee on Banking Supervision and International Organisation of Securities Commissions, 2005), as addressed by the recast of the 2000/12/EU Directive, indicate that banks should treat the specific market risk of their portfolios differently from the way they treat the generic market risk. Some credit institutions use unsophisticated methods for estimating their overall market risk. The estimation of generic market risk is made using a benchmark index and the estimation of specific market risk is made by deriving the portion of the movement of security that is not explained from index movements. Other credit institutions estimate the generic and the specific market risks, jointly. This is achieved by incorporating in the VAR estimation as many risk factors as the open positions in their portfolios. At the end, the selection of the model is based:

❑ on the sole decision of the individual credit institution; and
❑ not only on the accuracy of the model but also on other aspects such as:
  ❑ the time required for the computations;
  ❑ the human resources employed in the implementation of the model;
  ❑ the complexity of the portfolio; and
  ❑ the ability to understand the model from top management.

Although the estimation of the overall VAR value used by the latter class of credit institutions can be considered as more accurate than the traditional simplified methods (see below), it does not provide separate estimations for generic and specific risks. "Generic" is the market risk that is common for all security issuers and it is engendered from economic and non-economic events that affect the marketplace as a whole. Instead, "specific" is the unique market risk for each individual issuer and it is caused from internal events or external views specific for the organisation. Any risk that is common to more than one issuer can be considered as a generic market risk.

The separation of generic and specific market risks is a task that a bank should perform irrespective of the internal model it uses. Thus, one can easily stress that banks have a disincentive to apply the most accurate VAR models because of their time-consuming characteristics. However, this is not the case for the overall risk quantification. A reasonable question is: "Why should a credit institution separately report the specific risk, once it is able to estimate the overall risk?"

Credit institutions should be able, at any time, to address extreme changes in the level of specific risk because they may face instant and severe losses by undertaking high portions of specific risk. Thus, the hidden high portion of specific risk may prove to be harmful to the credit institution's economic status, although the overall VAR does not exhibit such situation.

The challenge of the modern risk manager is to estimate the risk difference between a benchmark risk-free security, or market index, and a risky security. This excess risk is called *specific risk* or *spread risk* for equities and fixed-income securities respectively. The specific or spread risk of a security is caused by factors unique to the security. These factors are rarely specified up to their last increment. However, they usually appear due to default risk, event risk, clientele issues, liquidity preferences, country risk and so on.

Throughout the forthcoming analysis, the default risk of country of residence and the excess default risk of the issuer will be viewed as "spread risk", both caused by different versions of default risk. Generally, specific risk can be identified in two ways:

❑ directly, by estimating a measure of risk for both (risk-free and risky) asset classes and then finding the difference between them; and

❑ indirectly, by analysing the returns of both (risk-free and risky) asset classes, given by or implied by market participants; once the difference between market returns and relying on some benchmark valuation theory is known, the financial analyst can derive an estimation of the excess risk undertaken by investments held in risky assets.

Although the CAPM theory (see Appendix) has been the cornerstone theory for many analysts for many years when assessing the equity risk, it is not the standard approach for assessing excess risk retained by investments held in fixed-income securities. Thus, the following analysis for assessing specific risk for trading and/or banking portfolios will be separated into two parts:

❑ the analysis of equity-specific risk, or simply "specific" risk; and,
❑ the analysis of fixed-income securities specific risk or simply "spread" risk.

Nowadays, the portfolio composition of credit institutions retains some characteristics that force the value of the portfolio to move beyond (positively and/or negatively) that of a risk-free portfolio. These characteristics are partly interpreted by CAPM theoretical background. The CAPM theory stresses, in general terms, that the higher the risk an asset bears – that is, the greater likelihood the security is to move adversely from the expected movement – the higher the return of an asset class should be in order to be attractive for investments. Following this idea, an issuer of a risky asset must set a higher return in order to attract investors for the securities' issuance. The higher return in relation to the return on the risk-free asset will offset the investor for the higher risk undertaken.

The following analysis assumes that the markets for corporate stocks or bonds are perfect and complete, and that trading takes place continuously.

Specific risk

Equities traded in an organised exchange reveal prices that change on a daily basis. These price changes arise from either economic events or non-economic events. In turn, both economic and non-economic events are attributed to either generic events or specific events.

Generic events affect the whole market in a unique way. In other words, they are common for all equities traded to an individual market. On the other hand, specific events affect companies on a standalone basis and, consequently, their equity prices in the marketplace. However, it is very difficult to distinguish between generic and specific events.

The price change y_i of a specific equity i is the sum of the influence of generic factors g_i and the influence of specific factors s_i, where:

$$y_i = g_i + s_i \tag{41}$$

Specific factors may be a number of known or unknown factors, the influence of which is represented by the risk that cannot be represented by common generic factors. The level of the specific risk is a decreasing function of the number of individual stocks included in the portfolio. This means that the greater the number of stocks in the portfolio, the lower the portion of specific risk to the overall risk. The specific risk is alternatively known as:

❏ *idiosyncratic risk*; or
❏ *residual risk*, because it encompasses all known or unknown influences that characterise the behaviour of an individual equity.

As previously mentioned, specific risk can be diversified when trading and investment portfolios (Basel Committee) include a large number of stocks. The specific risk is logarithmically diminished as the number of stocks in the portfolio increases, and it becomes approximately zero when the number of stocks exceeds 20 (see Figure 4).

Irrespective of the manner that the idiosyncratic risk diminishes with the number of individual securities in the portfolio, it is highly significant to assess the speed of specific risk in the portfolio composition. In general, there are two types of internal model that predict the VAR for an equity portfolio:

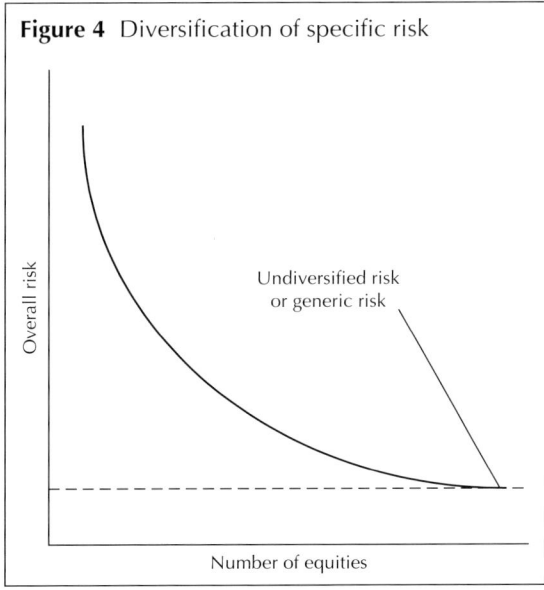

Figure 4 Diversification of specific risk

Undiversified risk or generic risk

Overall risk

Number of equities

❏ single risk factor models; and
❏ multi-risk factor models.

Under the Basel II regulatory framework, credit institutions must distinguish between generic and specific risk in order, separately, to evaluate the accuracy of each part of the applied internal model (see later for backtesting). However, this is directly possible when single risk factor models are involved. The general form of single risk factor models is represented by:

$$r_i = \beta_i \, r_M + \varepsilon_i \qquad (42)$$

where r_i is the return on stock i, r_M is the return on the market index, β_i is the beta of the stock i on the market index and ε_i is the issuer-specific return on stock i. The beta coefficient represents the response of stock return on market index changes. Although beta coefficient may differ from stock to stock, it represents the sensitivity of an individual stock on market index turbulences.

In order to include the effect of market index changes on all equity-based financial products, it is essential to introduce the meaning of the product price sensitivity against changes in market index prices. This can be approximated:

❏ first, by interpreting market index changes into stock changes using beta coefficient; and
❏ consequently, by translating the stock changes into product prices using the appropriate valuation model sensitivity of the product's price against the price of the stock used as an underlying asset (ie, the first-order sensitivity factor of option prices against the underlying asset is the delta coefficient that indicates the quantity that option premium changes due to changes in the underlying asset).

Mathematically, the above relationship is represented as follows:

$$r_i \equiv d_i \beta_i r_M + d_i \varepsilon_i \qquad (43)$$

where r_i is the return on product i, r_M is the return on the market index, β_i is the beta of the stock i on the market index, d_i is the sensitivity coefficient of value change in product i in relation to the value change ($\beta_i r_M$) of the stock (eg, delta) and ε_i is the issuer-specific return on stock i as it is represented in the premium of the financial product. The generalisation can also be extended to calibrate changes for the total portfolio of equities. This extension is represented as follows:

$$r_p \equiv \sum_{i=1}^{N} d_i \beta_i r_M + \sum_{i=1}^{N} d_i \varepsilon_i \qquad (44)$$

where r_p is the return on a given portfolio p composed of equity-based securities.

The above-mentioned equations estimate the portion of stock return attributed to either generic or specific events. However, this estimation is not explicitly attributed to each kind of events. In order to account for the level of risk, the variability of portfolio returns should be calculated and, consequently, they should be attributed to generic and specific risk factors. The variability is represented by the variance of portfolio returns and is given by:

$$\sigma_p^2 = gr + \sum_{i=1}^{N} (d_i^2 \sigma_{\varepsilon_i}^2) \qquad (45)$$

where, gr stands for generic risk, σ_p^2 is the variance of portfolio returns and $\sigma_{\varepsilon_i}^2$ is the residual variance of issuer i.

On the other hand, multi-risk factor models hold the characteristic of modelling the behaviour of each risk factor instead of linking each one of them to a general market index (single risk factor models). This characteristic results in better predictions of the future portfolio changes than the predictions made by single risk factor models because it closely imitates the behaviour of individual risk factors. Nevertheless, the specific class of model does not provide separate and independent estimations of the generic and specific risk. The general form of multi-risk factor models that gives the return on a portfolio of assets is represented as follows:

$$r_p \equiv \sum_{i=1}^{N} w_i r_i \qquad (46)$$

where r_p is again the return on a given portfolio p, r_i is the return on an individual risk factor i that corresponds to an individual security and w_i is the participation of security i in the total capitalisation of the portfolio p.

Once the sequence of returns has been constructed, the VAR value is estimated using one of the methods presented earlier, under "Market risk models". The modern risk manager has to examine whether the internal model used by credit institutions covers both types of risk, namely generic and specific. As previously mentioned, the main drawback of the multi-risk factor methods is that they do not distinguish between generic and specific risk. In order to overcome this drawback, risk managers should conduct the following two actions:

❏ estimate the VAR of the portfolio using individual risk factors; and
❏ estimate the VAR of the portfolio using the corresponding risk-free benchmark index with which every individual risk factor is linked.

When conducting the above two actions, the risk managers have, respectively, an overview of the following figures:

❏ the VAR corresponding to the total risk of the portfolio (generic and specific); and
❏ the VAR corresponding to the generic risk.

By gathering the above information, it is easy to estimate the portion of the specific risk in the total portfolio VAR. This is made by subtracting the VAR of generic risk from the VAR corresponding to the total risk of the portfolio. The information concerning the level of specific risk is worthless without having the information about the accuracy of the model for both generic and specific risk. For this purpose the backtesting technique proposed by the Amendment to Basel I should be used.

In order to backtest the performance of the internal model for both generic and specific risk, an estimation of the following information is needed when multi-risk factor models are involved:

❏ time series corresponding to total VAR;
❏ time series corresponding to generic VAR; and
❏ time series corresponding to actual changes of the portfolio.

Once the full set of time series is available the following must be calculated:

❑ by how many times actual portfolio changes exceed the total VAR; and
❑ by how many times actual portfolio changes exceed the generic VAR.

If the events corresponding to the second case do not exceed four, then the internal model can be considered efficient for covering generic risk. If the events corresponding to the first case do not exceed four, then the internal model can also be considered efficient for covering both generic and specific risks. This happens because there are no extra events arising from the fact that individual risk factors that contain specific risk are used.

However, the more interesting cases are those that exhibit more events using the first approach than using the second approach. Under these circumstances, the excess number of events can be attributed to the capture or not of the portfolio-specific risk. Thus, the excess number can be used in order to formulate the multiplication factor for the calculation of capital requirements corresponding to the specific risk of the trading portfolio as mentioned previously.

Fix-income specific risk

In order to separate equity-specific risk from fixed-income-specific risk, the latter will be referred to as *spread risk*. Spread risk is the risk exhibited by both corporate bonds and non-risk-free government bonds beyond that of a benchmark risk-free bond. The use of the widely known terminology of corporate credit spreads is rather vague for the forthcoming analysis, mainly, for two reasons:

❑ the term *corporate credit spreads* does not include spreads arising from the comparison of risk-free government bonds and non-risk-free government bonds; and
❑ the aforementioned term does not include specific risk arising from factors not related to the default risk of an organisation.

Fixed-income securities are characterised by specific risk that arises from default risk (see Chapter 2) or event risk. The specific risk is reflected in the excess spread over a benchmark, risk-free, fixed-income security. The excess spread, and hence the overall risk, is split among all the above-mentioned risk categories. This approximation implies that interest rate risk of fixed-income securities is characterised by changes in interest rates due both to market risk and to:

❑ credit risk;
❑ operational difficulties;
❑ regulatory constraints; and
❑ various clientele issues.

Distinguishing among and identifying each of the above-mentioned causes of interest rate changes is a very difficult task for the risk professional. However, some of them may be ignored in the quantification of market risk because they are quantified independently in another source of risk. Changes in interest rates due to market risk are a common source of influence for both government and corporate fixed-income securities. Furthermore, interest rates of corporate fixed-income securities are additionally influenced by other factors of risk such as default risk, liquidity risk and event risk. The common factor for changes in interest rates can be considered as the generic risk of a bond portfolio, while the remaining factors can be considered as specific risk factors.

The equation that gives the overall interest rate changes y_i, for a given corporate fixed-income security i, is defined as:

$$y_i = g_i + d_i + s_i \qquad (47)$$

where g_i is the part of the overall interest rate level that results from the influence of generic market risk, d_i is the part of the overall interest rate level that results from the existence of default risk for the credit standing of securities that the specific security belongs to, and s_i is the part of the overall interest rate level that results from the influence of other risk factors.

When government bonds with credit rating AAA are involved in the analysis, the last two elements of the second part of the above equation (Equation (47)) are eliminated, while, when government bonds with credit ratings below AAA are involved, the last element of the second part of the above Equation (Equation (47)) is eliminated. Figure 5 shows the decomposition of corporate yields.

Figure 5 Decomposition of corporate yields

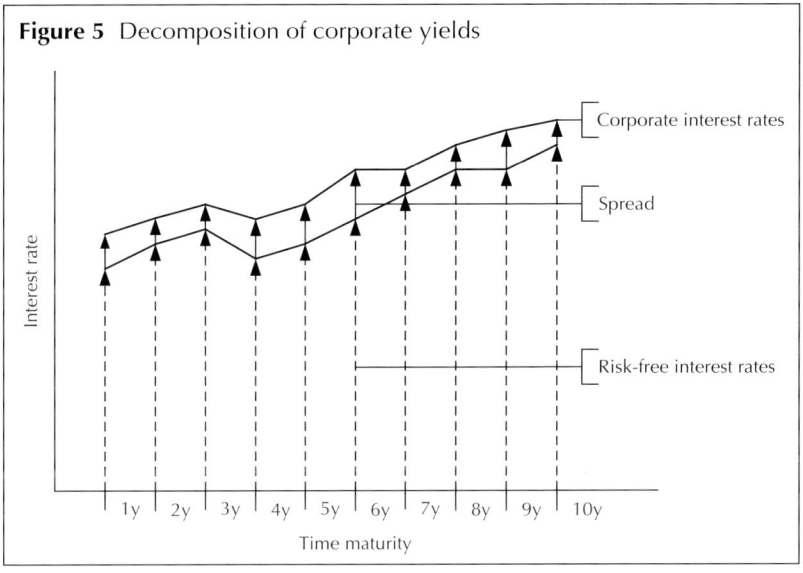

Default risk

Some companies issue fixed-income securities in order to finance their activities. However, the credit quality of these companies is not always the best available in the market. In order to make the issuance of the securities attractive, they offer, to potential investors, more return than the companies offering the best credit quality. The difference between the returns reflects the fact that all fixed-income securities with lower credit ratings possess higher default risk. Credit spreads reflect potential losses caused by default risk and a risk premium for bearing this risk. Some of the spread risk is specific to the issuer, but the remaining can be attributed to common credit risk factors (usually macroeconomic factors) that cannot be diversified away within a large credit portfolio. Thus, when the macroeconomic conditions provide prosperity to the society, credit spreads are low. Instead, when macroeconomic conditions suffer a slowdown, credit spreads are high. According to the first case, companies are more likely to default while according to the second case companies are less likely to default. In other words, economic conditions are negatively correlated with default spreads. The opposite case represents a market inefficiency that would be corrected by market participants.

To initiate the analysis concerning default risk, that is one of the components of spread risk, it is essential to refer to what will happen to a zero-coupon risky bond with a maturity of one year. A zero-coupon risky bond is assumed to pay its par value at its maturity. However, due to the fact that the bond under investigation is risky, it may or it may not pay the promised amount. In other words, the bond may or may not default. If it does not default, the bond will pay the full par value, or otherwise it will pay the amount recovered from default. The second case is assigned to the probability of default of the rating corresponding to the bond, while the first case is assigned to the remaining probability.

The current price of the corporate bond should be the weighted average of the alternative states, that is:

$$\frac{V_{t+1,T}}{1+r_{t,t+1}^{C}} = \left(\frac{V_{t+1,T}}{1+r_{t,t+1}^{G}}\right) \times \left(1-\pi_{t+1}\right) + \left(\frac{aV_{t+1,T}}{1+r_{t,t+1}^{G}}\right) \times \pi_{t+1} \qquad (48)$$

where, π_{t+1} is the probability of default in period $t+1$, given that no default will occur up to $t+1$; $r_{t,t+1}^{C}$ is the yield rate from t to $t+1$ for corporate bonds; $r_{t,t+1}^{G}$ is the yield rate from t to $t+1$ for government bonds; a is the recovery rate assumed constant in each period; $V_{t+1,T}$ is the value of a T period bond at time $t+1$, given that no bankruptcy will occur up to $t+1$.

After solving π_{t+1}, which is the implied probability of default, the above equation is transformed to the following form:

$$\pi_{t+1} = \frac{1}{1-a} \times \left(1 - \frac{1+r_{t,t+1}^{G}}{1+r_{t,t+1}^{C}}\right) \qquad (49)$$

Then, if less than one year's compounding is ignored and continuously compounding interest rates are assumed, the above equation takes the following form:

$$\pi_{t+1} = \frac{1}{1-a} \times \left[1 - e^{-\left(r_{t,t+1}^{C} - r_{t,t+1}^{G}\right)}\right] \qquad (50)$$

Finally, the spread due to default risk, after incorporating the coupon rate C, is given by:

$$e^{-\left(r_{t,t+1}^{C}-r_{t,t+1}^{G}\right)} = (1-\pi_{t+1}) + \frac{a\pi_{t+1}}{V_{t+1,T}+C} \tag{51}$$

In order to perform the estimation proposed above, it is essential to estimate coupons, recovery rates and default probabilities (for a detailed description of recovery rates and default probabilities see Chapter 2).

Event risk

The spread is caused not only by excess default risk. An additional component of it is the event risk related to the risk of unfavourable changes in an economic and/or non-economic-changes environment that will affect the position of a fixed-income security on a one-off basis. The set of such changes may consist of:

❏ a radical change in the legislation that affects the interests of the issuer;
❏ a fraud detection that forces the issuer to make a large jump towards default; or
❏ even a change in the taxation that affects the issuer's ability to distribute its profits.

So, when both government and corporate bonds of the same credit rating are subject to different taxation, the issuer of a corporate fixed-income security is inclined to increase the level of coupon payments in order to equal the disposable revenue from the corporate bond with the disposable revenue from the government bond.

Apart from the above-mentioned cases, there are a number of alternative economic events that affect the excess spread. Even though default risk is incorporated in the specific risk, other credit events comprise the set of event risks. The rationale behind this is that the default risk is related only to the possibility that the security will default on its obligations to investors, while there is always a risk that a rating agency will downgrade the credit quality of the security to a lower level, but not necessarily to the default level.

Another component of the spread composition over a benchmark yield is the appearance of an embedded option in the valuation of a particular bond. Embedded options usually harm investors' interests because issuers choose to exercise their right only when economic or non-economic conditions move adversely for issuers' interests. For example, if there is a step-up and call option in an issue of an asset-backed security, the issuer is obliged to step up (increase) their payments to the investor at regular or irregular time points. The step-up provision requires the issuer to increase their payments to the investor and, consequently, the investor to receive more from such an investment when the step-up becomes valid.

The step-up makes the investment on such security more favourable for the investor and, instead, more unfavourable for the issuer. The investor has the opportunity to call back the security, protecting themselves from extra cash outflows. On the other hand, the investor is missing extra cash inflows from the step-up provision. In order to be protected by a similar provision, the investor requires more frequent coupon payments, and discounts their expected capital inflows using a higher yield.

The event risk observed in market spreads may also be the result of operational risk quantification for an individual issuer. Event spread usually reflects the impression that investors have of the generic operational conditions (such as the complexity of procedures and/or systems and the quality of human capital) of an individual company. This impression may be the result of either an advanced model for the quantification of operational risk or a set of publicised information concerning the malfunction of an organisation's department. This implies that an issuer with higher operational risk should assign more spread to their securities while an issuer with lower operational risk should assign less event spread to their securities.

Other risks

The last component of excess spread of risky fixed-income securities is idiosyncratic risk that is due to other fuzzy and ill-defined factors. The most apparent reason for the idiosyncratic risk is based on liquidity privileges or preferences of an individual security in relation to other securities. Liquidity privileges mean that investors have better access to the security in relation to other securities. On the other hand, the term *"liquidity preferences"* explains the tendency of investors to prefer a specific security. In the latter case, there is an inner driving force for the existence of liquidity preferences that is connected to other unidentifiable components. By further analysing the driving forces behind liquidity preferences, one may come to the conclusion that it is due to a slight difference in the credit standing of the security. In turn, this conclusion leads to the fact that liquidity preferences are somehow correlated with the default risk.

Moving one step forward, one can say that liquidity in the equity markets is closely and inversely related to the liquidity observed in the markets of corporate fixed-income securities. The liquidity in bond markets is usually affected by or correlated with the level of equity prices. Moreover, the market value of equities can inversely affect the credit standing of fixed-income securities. For example, when stock prices rise, default risk goes down, and, when stock prices fall, default risk goes up. In other words, this fact introduces a systematic factor that relates the level of default risk with the level of the excess spread due to other reasons except for default risk and taxation.

If the effects of taxation and of other factors on credit spreads are ignored, the part of excess spread due to default risk can be estimated. In order to estimate the magnitude of the credit spread, it is essential to assume that the act of discounting the expected cash-flows from a government bond at the government spot rates will produce the same present value as discounting the expected cash-flows from a corporate bond at the corporate spot rates.

Properties of spreads

The spread of privately owned or governmental companies over a benchmark risk-free government bond retains some major properties:

❏ the change of risk-free yields inversely affects spreads;
❏ the spread curve is upward-sloping; and
❏ the spreads are lower for higher credit-rated bonds.

In order to understand the first property, it is essential to mention some preliminary characteristics of credit risk. In general terms, credit risk is assessed by the expected and/or unexpected credit loss that is estimated to appear throughout a prespecified period. Using the method of internal estimates, the constituents of expected credit loss (more analysis is provided in Chapter 2) are:

❏ the probability of default;
❏ the loss given default; and
❏ the exposure.

Assuming that the first and last constituents remain stable, an increase in risk-free yields will decrease the level of credit risk. This will happen because the increased yields will accordingly decrease the discount factors to be applied in the expected cash outflows of the defaulted amount, resulting in a diminished loss given default. In turn, the diminished loss given default will lower the credit loss and the credit risk, respectively. Finally, the lower credit risk will provide the investors with lower spreads. The opposite happens when the risk-free yields are decreased.

It is obvious that, when yields of the benchmark, risk-free, fixed-income security are increased, the level of spread that is due to default risk is diminished. The reason is very simple and lies in the approach according to which banks calculate the expected loss in cases of default. The expected loss is affected by the probability of default, the loss given default and the exposure at default (see Chapter 2). An increase in benchmark interest rates and thus in yields would result in lower loss given defaults because the discount factor would be lower. Once loss given default decreases, expected loss becomes lower (lower credit risk), given that the probability of default and exposure remains unchanged. Changes in expected loss for two similar securities become more apparent for the security with a longer recovery period, and less apparent for the security with a shorter recovery period.

The upward slope of the spread curve (See Figures 6, 7 and 8) is a feature coming from the fact that bonds, with higher effective maturity, represented by either duration measure or other more detailed measures, possess higher risk. In turn, the higher risk is apparent because the same change in the level of yields affects more the bond with the highest effective maturity. Moreover, investors are compensated for the excess risk they bear by correspondingly possessing higher levels of expected returns. The opposite consists a market inefficiency that market participants tend to, promptly, correct.

Last, but not least, spreads are a decreasing function of the credit quality of a bond. Thus, a higher credit rated bond will be expected to have lower spread, while a lower credit rated bond will be

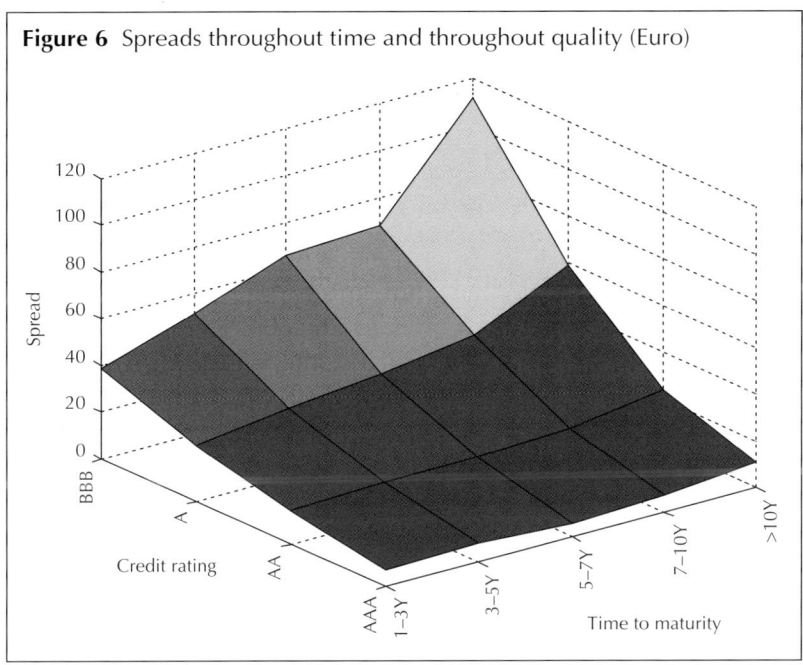

Figure 6 Spreads throughout time and throughout quality (Euro)

expected to have higher spreads. The relationship of bonds with different effective times to maturity and different credit ratings are shown in Figure 6 for EUR, Figure 7 for USD and Figure 8 for GBP.

Trading on spread inefficiencies

The decomposition of spreads is essential for risk managers in order to better manage the associated risks. Moreover, it is useful for internal auditors in order to identify and classify risk types and for traders who need to estimate the spread in order to exploit potential market inefficiencies. These market inefficiencies arise due to spread mispricings for various risk factors, such as credit standing, liquidity and optionality, for all bonds with the same maturity.

When bonds with the same credit standing but different credit spreads appear in the market, then traders have the opportunity to exploit this market inefficiency. By purchasing the bond with the lower credit spread and/or selling (or short-selling) the bond with the higher credit spread, the trader takes a position that will produce profits when the market restores equilibrium. However, this

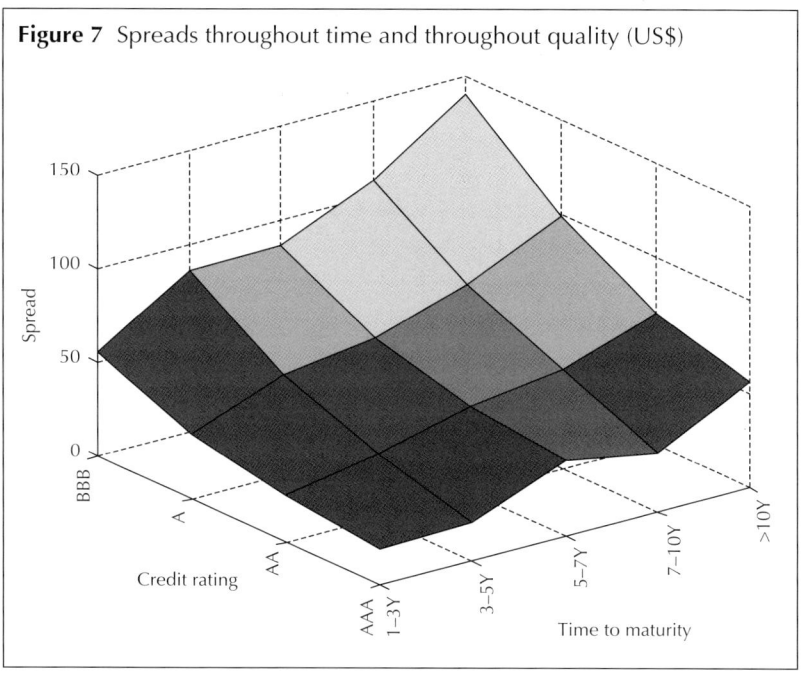

Figure 7 Spreads throughout time and throughout quality (US$)

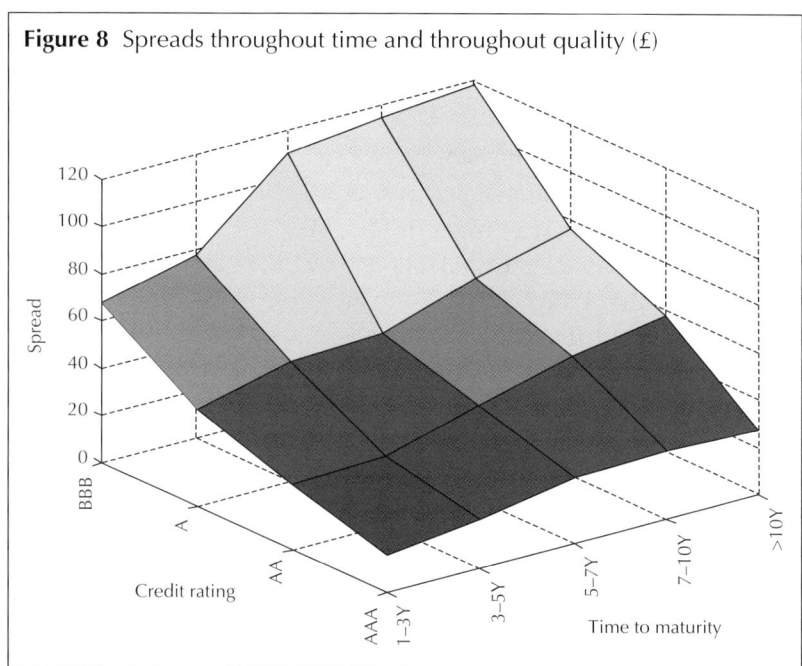

Figure 8 Spreads throughout time and throughout quality (£)

case assumes that both bonds have the same liquidity. Instead, if bonds exhibit different levels of liquidity, the trader may not be able to profit from such trading.

When bonds with the same liquidity but different liquidity spreads appear in the market, traders also have the opportunity to exploit this kind of market inefficiency by purchasing the bond with the lower liquidity spread and/or selling (or short-selling) the bond with the higher liquidity spread. This technique assumes that credit spreads are the same among different yields of the same maturity.

As mentioned above, several adjustments should be made when comparing bond yields without embedded options with bond yields *with* embedded options. These adjustments have to do with the construction of option-adjusted yields for bonds with the same or similar maturity. The manipulation of these yields leads to the construction of credit spreads. If these credit spreads are of the same magnitude, the investor should choose the bond that is free of embedded options. Alternatively, the investor may take their investment decision by investing on the lowest option-adjusted spread after constructing the cross-sectional structure of option-adjusted spreads.

Case studies

Case I

For example, an Indonesian corporate bond denominated in Indonesian currency (rupiah, or Rp) retains an excess specific risk portion in relation to the corresponding US Treasury Note arising from the credit standing of Indonesia in the global financial environment (country risk), from the relatively lower liquidity, from events relative to the sector of the corporate (event risk) and a potential excess default risk over the governmental Indonesian default risk (default risk).

Case II

For example, if a corporate bond with a credit rating AA+ pays a coupon of Libor + 2 basis points (henceforth "bp") while a US Treasury Bill with a credit rating AAA and the same characteristics with the corporate bond pays a coupon of Libor + 3 bp, no investor has the incentive to purchase the corporate bond. On the other

Table 2 Credit spreads as of 01/08/2005

Euro	1–3 Y	3–5 Y	5–7 Y	7–10 Y	>10 Y	All-euro
AAA	7.8	9.1	6	8.5	12.1	8.5
AA	14.8	16.7	16.5	17.7	24	17.2
A	25.4	29.8	32.7	39	58.7	32.7
BBB	37.1	52.3	66.2	68	112.6	55.6
US$	**1–3 Y**	**3–5 Y**	**5–7 Y**	**7–10 Y**	**>10 Y**	**All-US$**
AAA	19.6	22.1	42.8	33.6	59	26.2
AA	26.1	37.2	52.7	57.5	66.9	37.1
A	39	57.8	63.7	80	103.4	63.6
BBB	57	89.3	91.9	112.3	146.7	99.9
£	**1–3 Y**	**3–5 Y**	**5–7 Y**	**7–10 Y**	**>10 Y**	**All-£**
AAA	14.2	20.7	28.7	29.6	26.8	23.6
AA	26.4	30.1	40.7	49.9	57.5	42.3
A	41	50.7	53.1	65.8	76.4	62.9
BBB	68	78.2	109.8	114.6	118.7	103.8
Yen	**1–3 Y**	**3–5 Y**	**5–7 Y**	**7–10 Y**	**>10 Y**	**All-Yen**
AAA	1	−3.7	1.5	4.2	0.8	−0.7
AA	4.7	6.4	5.3	3.1	−3.2	4.7
A	10.5	14.7	35.7	33.8	0	15.5
BBB	0	0	0	35.2	0	35.2

Source: Reuters

hand if both bonds have the same coupon and the lower-rated bond exhibits lower risk (measured by either the probability of default or any other statistical measure), market participants have incentives to purchase the lower-rated bond (see Elton *et al*, 2001). The obligation for a modern risk analyst is to address and quantify similar market inefficiencies concerning the default risk premium and, consequently, the obligation of a trader is to exploit these market inefficiencies.

Case III

In Table 2 the spreads are attributed to four credit-rating categories. The spreads presented are for investment-grade credit ratings that are AAA, AA, A and BBB for the Euro zone, US, UK and Japan.

On the other hand, the exact maturities for each category of credit rating and maturity bands are presented in Table 3.

Bearing in mind the theory described and Tables 2 and 3, it is essential, in order to exploit them, for the risk manager to investigate:

Table 3 Average time to maturity

Euro	1–3 Y	3–5 Y	5–7 Y	7–10 Y	>10 Y	All-Euro
AAA	2.169	4.029	5.741	8.412	19.491	5.96
AA	2.182	4.034	5.979	8.343	15.536	5.927
A	2.152	4.049	5.952	8.193	17.192	5.425
BBB	1.992	3.966	5.98	8.377	19.378	5.091
US$	1–3 Y	3–5 Y	5–7 Y	7–10 Y	>10 Y	All-US$
AAA	1.942	3.863	6.02	8.133	23.412	4.476
AA	1.967	3.713	5.93	8.297	27.45	4.018
A	1.973	3.925	5.958	8.042	24.435	6.499
BBB	2.09	4.005	6.157	8.604	24.732	8.476
£	1–3 Y	3–5 Y	5–7 Y	7–10 Y	>10 Y	All-£
AAA	1.801	3.796	5.886	8.576	23.065	12.573
AA	1.848	3.797	5.992	8.349	22.004	10.186
A	2.145	4.12	5.662	8.019	19.599	11.217
BBB	1.956	3.78	6.355	8.123	16.693	8.95
Yen	1–3 Y	3–5 Y	5–7 Y	7–10 Y	>10 Y	All-yen
AAA	2.012	4.156	5.973	7.392	15.746	5.172
AA	2.03	4.117	6.12	8.181	17.246	5.674
A	1.975	3.807	6.118	8.164	0	3.315
BBB	0	0	0	7.897	0	7.897

Source: Reuters

❑ possible implicit and/or explicit inefficiencies in the valuation or trading of the corporate fixed income; and
❑ whether the spread of the corporate bonds over the benchmark government bonds fully corresponds to default risk.

Initially, the negative Japanese 3–5 Y spread consists of an explicit inefficiency by itself. This happens for two reasons: first, because the AAA corporate bond appears to yield lower income for the bearer than the corresponding government bond does; and, second, because, as mentioned above, the longer the maturity of fixed-income security of a certain credit rating, the higher the spread should be. Instead, in the case examined here, exactly the opposite happens: the Japanese 3–5 Y spread is lower than the Japanese 1–3 Y spread.

There are two approaches in order to investigate whether the second case holds.

(1) To take into account the historical realised probabilities of default (PDs) that correspond to each of the credit-rating

Table 4 Cumulative average historical PDs

Euro	1–3Y (%)	3–5Y (%)	5–7Y (%)	7–10Y (%)	>10 Y	ALL-Euro (%)
AAA	0.00	0.05	0.24	0.40	–	0.24
AA	0.00	0.15	0.40	0.68	–	0.40
A	0.09	0.48	0.89	1.73	–	0.89
BBB	0.46	1.56	2.89	4.61	–	2.89

categories given by a rating agency, and convert them into spreads. If constructed spreads are lower than those observed by comparing corporate and government market yields, then the spread does not fully correspond to default risk.

(2) To take into account observed spreads that correspond to each of the credit-rating categories and convert them into probabilities of default. If the constructed PDs do not correspond to the respective PDs given by the rating agency, being higher than them, again the spreads do not only allow for default risk.

Although the first approach is more straightforward, the following case study will focus on the second approach. The realised probabilities of default were derived from Moody's KMV (see Moody's KMV, 2003) and were assigned to the corresponding rating categories of the Standard & Poor's. Consequently, the probabilities of default reported for multiple maturities were averaged in order to keep up a correspondence with the maturity bands. Table 4 shows the cumulative average historical PDs.

Once again, there are two alternatives from which one has to choose in order to compare the historical probability of default with the implied probability of default derived from market spreads. They are:

❑ to compare the cumulative probabilities of default; and
❑ to compare the annual average probabilities of default.

In the present case study the second approach was followed. For this reason, the cumulative average probability of default was converted into annual average probability of default using the methodology presented in Chapter 2.

BACKTESTING AND STRESS-TESTING MARKET RISK EXPOSURES

The need for backtesting and stress testing

Credit institutions should not apply VAR models randomly or unconditionally. Credit institutions should test the efficiency of the models. The efficiency test should be made on portfolios held by the specific credit institution, as credit institutions may possess different financial products and may follow different investment policies. On the other hand, credit institutions must maintain the efficiency of the VAR model used by conducting continual tests when structural changes are taking place in the nature of their portfolios. For these reasons credit institutions should periodically perform backtests. Backtests check whether the VAR predictions correspond to observed market changes.

Moreover, credit institutions should check their vulnerability in extreme circumstances that conventional VAR measures fail to predict. Extreme market events should be taken into consideration because one of them may prove catastrophic for the institution. For this reason, credit institutions should conduct regular stress tests along with the results produced by VAR models.

The Basel Committee has set the regulatory framework that supports the implementation of backtesting and stress testing in the portfolios of credit institutions. The present section presents the theoretical and, occasionally the practical aspects of backtesting and stress testing.

Backtesting – the absolute framework

The tests that are related to the efficiency of the models have to do with two perspectives. First, models should be tested according to whether they fulfil the criteria set by the confidence levels. Second, they should be tested in relation to other models that are candidates to be introduced as internal models in the credit institution. According to the first perspective, two characteristics of the model should be used in order to evaluate its performance:

❑ the confidence level that is implied by the model; and
❑ the ratio of the number of times that the model underestimates the actual portfolio change to the total number of predictions made.

If the above ratio exceeds the confidence level set by the VAR model, the model is considered to be insufficient to represent reality. However, the phenomenon could appear occasionally. The number of failures may sporadically deviate from the aforementioned confidence level. For this reason the Basel Committee introduced a matrix that assigns the number of failures to a multiplication factor. The multiplication factor increases as the number of failures increases because the possibility that the failure ratio deviates from the confidence level ratio becomes more certain.

Backtesting – the Basel II framework

Far beyond the standardised approach (not examined here) introduced by the Basel Committee in 1988, credit and financial institutions turned their attention to the internal model approach for the calculation of regulatory capital requirements. The internal model approach relies on VAR estimates produced by sophisticated tailor-made models, assuming a 10-day holding period and a 99% confidence level.

The capital requirement for generic market risk, with which a financial institution is charged for the next trading day, is given by the maximum amount of either the current one-day VAR or three times the average VAR of the last 60 days:

$$C_{t+1} = \max\left(VAR_t^{(10 \text{ days, } 99\%)}, M_t \frac{1}{60} \sum_{i=0}^{60} VAR_{t-i}^{(10 \text{ days, } 99\%)} \right) + SR_t \qquad (52)$$

where, C_{t+1} is capital requirement, $VAR_t^{(10 \text{ days, } 99\%)}$ represents 10-day VAR with 99% confidence level. M_t is multiplier arising from backtesting, SR_t is the capital requirement assigned to specific risk.

The determination of regulatory capital requirements assigned to specific risk is not part of the scope of this book, although it is an attention-grabbing topic.

The multiplier M_t adjusts the VAR estimations to the expectations of the competent authorities for the minimum capital requirement that includes the model error risk. The withstanding regulatory framework defines the multiplier according to the economic (not the statistical) precision of VAR estimates. According to the existing regulatory framework, the multiplier M_t should not be

Table 5 Multiplier generation in accordance with realised overshootings

Zone	Overshootings	Multiplier
Green	1	3.00
	2	3.00
	3	3.00
	4	3.00
Yellow	5	3.40
	6	3.50
	7	3.65
	8	3.75
	9	3.85
Red	10 or more	4.00

lower than three. The number of exceptions (or overshootings) during the previous year is distributed within three "traffic light" zones as shown in Table 5.

When the number of exceptions, during the last year falls in the green zone, it is indicated that the internal model is appropriate and the lower multiplier (3) is assigned to the VAR estimates. Alternatively, when the number of exceptions, during the last year, ranges from 5 to 9 the internal model is still considered appropriate, but the multiplier gets higher than 3 and increases in conjunction with the number of exceptions. Finally, when the number of exceptions, during the last year, falls in the red zone, it is indicated that the internal model is either inappropriate or needs major corrections and the higher multiplier (4) is assigned to the VAR estimates.

Stress testing

The term "stress testing" is common among credit and financial institutions and regulatory entities. It is an attempt to assess the risk that will appear under extreme circumstances. Their need came up in order to fill a gap in the concept of VAR methodology. VAR is used to provide a probabilistic prediction on losses that are likely to happen for a prespecified holding period and confidence level (the most widespread combination of the two is the maximum loss that is likely to happen over a 10-day holding period with a 99% confidence level).

VAR by itself is a source of a model error risk because nobody is able to find a universally applied, error-free VAR model. Even if such a model existed, it would still be an estimation of an "all-in-one" figure of the overall risk of the credit institution. However, both credit institutions and regulatory entities need to know specific aspects of extreme risk events arising from either individual business lines of the organisation or individual position types of trading and/or banking portfolios.

Supervisory authorities introduced stress testing as a complementary, but obligatory, test to VAR estimations, in order to assess the vulnerability of credit and financial institutions to exceptionally unexpected, but plausible, usually non-probabilistic, financial events. Generally, stress tests can be either scenario-based or sensitivity-based.

The supervisor and/or the relevant executive in the institution is responsible for the determination of these moves. By moving one step backwards, the motivation for market risk factor moves can be based on either recent news or consensus estimations by market participants or estimations made by actual market risk factor changes that happened in the past.

Although professionals involved in stress testing may have a different test for each risk factor, risk factors are usually grouped into limited categories (such as equity prices, interest rates, FX rates, commodity prices) according to their nature, for the sake of time and simplicity.

Scenario-based tests assume that changes in risk factors happen simultaneously on all categories of risk factor. This assumption reflects the consensus of risk professionals that the aforementioned spectrum of events will happen instantaneously in the near future. Although it has been mentioned that the scenarios can be chosen from either a historical or hypothetical event, risk professionals should feel free to establish a scenario that consists of a combination of both. This category of tests usually involves one direction move of risk factors that has to do with the position that is common for the majority of credit and financial institutions.

Sensitivity-based tests try to evaluate the impact of price changes on the value of a portfolio. Because credit institutions exhibit a variety of portfolios, the tests are made for both directions, that is for both negative and positive changes. This is made in order for the stress test to capture the nature of different portfolios. The nature of a portfolio may differ due to either the variety of products contained in the portfolio or the net long or short position of the portfolio.

Except for bidirectional changes in market risk factors, it is essential to stress-test the links between the related positions of a portfolio. The most common related positions are those that hedge each other. These positions are usually taken according to a sensitivity factor and/or a correlation estimator. Credit institutions should be in the position:

❑ to identify what kind of change in each sensitivity factor and/or each correlation estimator would adversely change the value of the portfolio; and
❑ to set the exact test for each one of them.

It is somewhat unavoidable to distinguish between scenario-based tests and sensitivity-based tests, in the sense that some scenario-based tests implicitly assume some scenarios for sensitivity or correlation estimators. The most apparent paradigm is the case of the simultaneous adverse change on all market risk factors. In practice, this technique assumes a unique unity correlation for all bilateral product co-movements.

Ad hoc stress tests
Basel Committee guidelines
The Basel Committee relates the integrity of every risk management internal model to the existence of a reliable stress-testing mechanism. Most of the risk management models heavily rely on the assumption of continuous distribution of market risk factors. The necessity of the stress-testing mechanism lies in the fact that it is able to capture market movements that are prone to discrete price jumps. Price jumps appear mainly due to positions in the following risk factors:

❑ non-linearity; and
❑ emerging markets (debt or equity).

Moreover, stress tests have been employed in order to determine the "loss tolerance" limits of two kinds:

Table 6 Stress-testing approaches

Market risk factors

Equities	Interest rates	Commodities	Other
Stress event or hypothesis			
Black Monday (1987)	Historical interest rate increases /declines	Middle East crisis (1990)	Volatility disruptions
Hypothetical Stock market crash	Bond market crash (1994) and related changes	Commodity stress (prices and volatilities)	
New Economy crash	Global tightening US tightening		

Source: Committee on the Global Financial System (2001)

❑ trading limits for one-off deals; and
❑ cumulative-position limits.

The method for calculating both trading and cumulative-position limits is shown in the following paragraphs of this section. Table 6 shows an overview of potential stress tests that are proposed by the Committee on the Global Financial System.

Tests directed to stress the FX rates are not shown in Table 6 because they appear to be as a result of other market shocks. However, the tests proposed are shown below and sometimes are harsher than the sources (interest rates shock, for example) that cause them.

The hypothetical stock market crash simulates closely the "Black Monday" scenario, but it contains a characteristic of subjectivity in the sense that it assumes that the scenario is extreme enough. The "New Economy" scenario distinguishes between the stocks of "old" and "new" economies. However, the test should be based on both macro and micro stress testing and should be based on the knowledge of specialised professionals because this kind of stock ("new"-economy stock) is not easy to analyse.

The most common stress tests for commodities are those related to adverse market movements in oil prices. These movements were apparent during the periods of oil crises (for instance, 1974, 1978, 1990, 2005). Because the majority of crises were produced by war outbreaks or governmental disturbances, these crises can also be considered as political crises. The most common scenario is the Middle East crisis in 1990. Moreover, credit institutions that have invested in other products are required to run stress tests for these products. This kind of stress test involves the stress in both their prices and volatilities and they are more historical than hypothetical scenarios.

Finally, shocks in volatility and correlation levels can be extensively used for parametric and semi-parametric internal models, but they are not very good with non-parametric internal models. Generally, they are very useful for the valuation of derivative products. Particularly, correlation shocks are not of much use because the pairwise correlation inherent in the risk factors participating in the stress testing is assumed to be one.

Miscellaneous suggestions

The Basel Committee set both a qualitative and a quantitative framework for the determination of stress-testing techniques by exploiting the experience of a number of large credit institutions that already stress-test their portfolios. However, it has not provided explicit quantitative standards for hypothetical scenarios that would be required by supervisors or regulators. The regulators should not require banks only to apply the stress tests they determine, but also to apply "tailor-made" stress tests that are appropriate for the nature of their portfolios. In that sense, credit institutions should, by themselves, define the optimal mixture of stress-testing scenarios given that they have already analysed the nature of their portfolios.

The experience of the International Monetary Fund (see Blaschke *et al*, 2001) directs the determination of stress-testing framework to the determination of the following characteristics:

❏ type of risk (interest rate risk, exchange rate risk, commodities risk, etc);
❏ type of stress test to perform (sensitivity, scenario, extreme value, maximum loss);
❏ type of shock to apply (historical, hypothetical, MC simulation;
❏ type of assets to be shocked (cash products, derivative products, etc);
❏ the magnitude of the shock; and
❏ the holding period.

Credit institutions usually use stress testing in order to examine the vulnerability of all products in their trading portfolios because they are sensitive to market price changes. However, stress testing should be performed for both trading and banking portfolios in order to retain the element of aggregation. On the other hand, extensive datasets for market price changes are not always available to risk analysts. Thus, the historical scenarios cannot always be applied. In order to overcome this drawback, hypothetical scenarios should be used instead. Thus, the only variable to be defined is the magnitude of the shock of the hypothetical scenario.

The Derivatives Policy Group (1995) suggests the use of a concrete framework for stress testing defined as the capital that exceeds the confidence level set by the internal method used, which is 99%. Thus, any shock above that level constitutes a stress test. The changes in risk factors that are suggested are as follows:

❑ an increase/decrease in equity index values by 10%;
❑ an increase/decrease in equity index volatilities by 10%;
❑ an increase/decrease in the exchange value (relative to the US$) of foreign currencies by 6%, in the case of major currencies, and 20%, in the case of other currencies;
❑ an increase/decrease in FX rate volatilities by 20%; and
❑ an increase/decrease in swap spreads by 20 basis points.

All shocks should be applied on the risk factor relevant to the position and, if it is not possible, they should be applied on the risk factor that exhibits high correlation in relation to the risk factor of the position examined. The aforementioned guidelines do not refer to commodities but, given that the Basel Committee suggests as a broad benchmark for non-stress situations, the change of 15% level, stress tests should take into account scenarios that assume more extreme jumps.

Finally, the holding period that the stress test assumes should be in accordance with the holding period that internal models use. As presented earlier in the section "Market risk models", the Basel Committee proposes a holding period of 10 trading days to serve as a basis point for the calculation of capital requirements for the trading book. However, the different nature of the banking book requires the above-mentioned holding not to serve as the global benchmark. In order to overcome that obstacle, it is essential to use the holding period that corresponds to the internal method used to calculate the capital requirements for a specific class of investment.

Non-probabilistic scenarios
Non-probabilistic scenarios are based on risk analysts' self-estimations or historical estimations about the moves in market factors that are assumed to prevail in the near future. The scenarios, mainly, involve moves in the following categories of risk factors:

❑ equity;
❑ interest rates;
❑ FX rates;
❑ commodities;
❑ volatilities; and
❑ correlations.

These scenarios should be made for all types of currencies, separating the emerging countries from the developed countries, or, even better, making the separation according to the geographical territory where the investment is made. In the following paragraph, the proposed, ad hoc, scenarios are presented.

The Basel Committee on Banking Supervision (1996a) stresses the need that

> Banks that use internal model approaches for meeting market risk capital requirements must have in place a rigorous and comprehensive stress testing ... To identify events or influences that could greatly impact banks is a key component of a bank's assessment of its capital position.

Although in 1995 the generic guidelines set by the Derivatives Policy Group were of high importance, since then financial conditions have changed and new products have arrived in the global financial environment. Thus, the validity of the scenarios of stress testing has more or less expired and the necessity for new and more conservative scenarios has arisen. Table 7 presents the full set of stress testing for all market risk factors.

Historically based stress tests
Probabilistic scenarios
As mentioned in the section "Market risk models" above, traditional HS is one of the alternative approaches in order to estimate

Table 7 Revised stress-testing framework

Market risk factors

Equities	Interest rates	Foreign exchange rates	Commodities	Other
Stress hypothesis				
(+/−) 20% for developed market indexes	(+/−) basis points (bp)) 200 parallel shift for yield curve	(+/−) 30% for major currencies	(+/−) 30% for energy commodities	+30% on all volatilities
(+/−) 40% for emerging market indexes	(+/−) bp) steepening 50 (<3 m), 100 (3 m−2 y), 150 (2 y−5 y), 200 (>5 y)	(+/−) 50% for other currencies	(+/−) 20% for other commodities	
(+/−) 30% for developed markets stocks	(+/−) bp) flattening 200 (<3 m), 150 (3 m−2 y), 100 (2 y−5 y), 50 (>5 y)			
(+/−) 50% for emerging markets stocks				

the VAR. Moreover, it is the only approach that does not assume the estimation of any risk parameter. The only prerequisite is the upfront knowledge of the desired confidence level and time horizon. Due to these characteristics, the HS approach is the easiest method to estimate VAR. If the risk professional involved with the risk assessment of the credit institution simply increases the confidence level, the HS method is able to estimate the figure for the VAR for that confidence level.

The most widespread confidence level parameter in order to estimate VAR for credit institutions is 99%. Thus, any level above 99% automatically consists of a test that extends beyond the velocity of VAR. In that sense, any VAR estimated for a confidence level above the aforementioned level can potentially correspond to a stress test. Thus, HS is a natural stress-testing mechanism according to which the risk professional can arbitrarily choose the confidence level. Under extreme scenarios using a confidence level of:

$$cl = 100 - \frac{1}{n} \qquad (53)$$

where cl is the confidence level and n is the total available observations, the most extreme historically appeared scenario is used.

Scenario analysis
An alternative evaluation of the impact arising from stress events is the analysis of simultaneous stress events with different probabilities assigned to them. The most appropriate technique that serves as a basis for the application of scenario analysis is a special case of the MC simulation approach presented in the section "Market risk models". According to this approximation, the stress-testing impact cannot be expressed in a unique number. Instead, scenario analysis implies that there would be multiple results corresponding to a different magnitude of changes for different market risk factors. Thus, risk analysts have to evaluate each scenario separately and then apply a probability to each result. The ultimate stress impact is given by adding the participation of each scenario, after assigning probabilities to each one of them.

Extreme value theory
Stress tests can also be carried out using extreme value theory (EVT). The notion according to which the stress test is made is that risk managers/analysts should find the value that would prevail once the threshold of VAR is exceeded. This notion corresponds to the expected shortfall of EVT.

Aspects of institution-wide integration

Stress testing is not an isolated statistical examination of the financial conditions that prevail in the credit or financial institution. Instead, it is a supplementary examination of the risk undertaken by the institution and usually it is simpler than the internal models used to quantify market risk. Stress-testing technique is generally used for the following purposes:

❑ to set limits;
❑ to conduct contingency planning for adverse market movements; and
❑ to allocate capital within the institution.

The character of stress testing, which supposes a detailed investigation of the impact of extreme events on the financial condition of the institution and that the purposes implicitly set are fulfilled, does not need to be conducted at high frequency. Alongside the fact that stress testing is simple to understand, it is a useful tool for senior management. Although risk managers are able to have an adequate view of the institution's risk profile by simply applying VAR, they may also use stress testing in order to report the institution's risk profile to senior management.

The reporting of stress-testing results should take place according to a frequency that corresponds to the frequency of decision making among senior management. The reporting of stress-testing results should be reported in accordance with the meetings held by senior management. Thus, if decisions for the limits or for the allocation of capital are determined every month, limits should be reported accordingly.

Limits in the capitalisation of trading and/or position taking are part of the risk management strategy of a modern credit institution. They are used in order for credit institutions to avoid a systematic and simultaneous loss realisation. Although limits can be used for all types of risk, namely market risk, credit risk and operational risk, the reference made in this section is solely to market risk. Credit or financial institutions set the limits arising from stress-testing exercises according to the loss that they are able to incur without having an undesirable impact on their functionality. Alternatively, they can use, as a reference of functionality, a threshold for the capital adequacy ratio in order to set the aforementioned limits.

The starting point for the quantification of limits is the strategic decision of a "risk committee" on the maximum level of deterioration tolerance of the capital adequacy ratio. If the aim of this risk committee is not to exceed the lower boundary set by the Basel Committee for the capital adequacy ratio, then the limit is determined by the following equation:

$$L = \frac{(CAR - 8\%)}{ST} \times ROF \qquad \textbf{(54)}$$

where, L is the limit, CAR is the capital adequacy ratio, ST is the amount corresponding to the loss arising from the stress-testing exercise and ROF is the variable for the regulatory capital. Alternatively, the risk committee can set the "deterioration tolerance" to lower levels according to the risk appetite of the credit institution.

Additionally, credit institutions exploit the results to conduct prudential contingency planning for adverse market movements. This happens by introducing a hedge strategy that is optimal for the nature of their portfolios. The hedge strategy should have a long-term horizon because institutions are not able to anticipate the exact timing of the stress event. Alternatively, banks can avoid the impact of the stress event if they simply liquidate their position where they maintain excess risk. The liquidation of the position may also take place in order for the institution to eliminate or reduce the liquidity risk related to market risk.

Instead of just liquidating the position, a credit or financial institution may use the stress testing in order to allocate better the capital among various business lines. Thus, if the stress testing conducted by an institution indicates that a business line retains more risk than another does, a proper action would be the exchange of positions between these two business lines. The exchange of position should take place from the business line that retains more market risk towards the business line that retains less market risk. This action effectively retains the aggregate level of the open position of the credit or financial institution.

The empirical properties of the traditional VAR models and the comparison evidenced by the superiority of the HS method in terms of total exceptions realised are examined in Chapter 6. However, the management of financial institutions should implement, improve and evaluate tailor-made models that best fit their specific needs, their outstanding portfolio composition and their cost–benefit trade-offs. The risk manager should compare the level of capital requirements with the level of operational cost arising from a certain VAR model. The model that produces the best trade-offs is the most suitable for implementation by the credit institution.

SUMMARY

The present chapter, which consists of four sections plus Introduction and this Summary, has presented the theoretical background necessary for the quantification of market risk. The material of the chapter has demonstrated the properties of the parameters employed in CAPM for the parametric estimation of financial risks (see the section "Market risk models") and introduced the reader to:

❑ the use of the essential financial derivative products that act as components of a banking portfolio;
❑ the understanding of their properties; and
❑ the mathematical theory behind their valuation.

The above three elements will be presented in the Appendix, along with the discussion about benchmarking and interpolation techniques. Moreover, financial derivative products, for the derivation of implied risk parameters, were presented, irrespectively of their use as portfolio components. The fact that data, for some financial products, are not always available was taken into consideration. In order to overcome the lack of data, especially for products for which data are not readily available (options, futures, for instance), benchmarking was introduced.

Benchmarking is separated into two broad approaches: the mark-to-market and the mark-to-model. The former approach uses benchmark product prices while the latter uses benchmark valuation models for the derivation of product prices using as inputs parameters taken from the marketplace. Finally, when the bench-marking of product prices does not yield reliable results, it is of high importance for the risk manager to use interpolation tech-niques. Techniques employed involve linear, exponential and poly-nomial interpolation. Interpolation techniques depend on the type of financial data and financial products.

The first section presented the major risk factors that influence the value of the assets held by a credit or financial institution. The risk factors are separated into four categories: interest rate risk, FX risk, equity risk and commodity risk. The most concern is given to the interest rate risk because of the complexity of its estimation and the existence of non-linear relationships between interest rates for different cashflows and the value of the interest rate asset. It also demonstrated which data are needed to represent each of the risk factors. However, this section did not examine the impact of each risk factor on the valuation of derivative products with non-linear characteristics such as options which is examined in the Appendix.

The purpose of the second section ("Market risk models") was to introduce the reader to the widespread methods for estimating VAR and to provide evidence of possible superiority of one method against all others. The delta-normal model uses parameters based on historical data, such as those implemented by traditional esti-mation procedures or by RiskMetrics, or on implied volatilities derived from heavily traded over-the-counter (OTC) or exchange-traded options. Both approximations generate a covariance matrix over which the linear or quasi-linear positions are applied in order to calculate the portfolio VAR.

Among full valuation models, HS is the easiest to implement, but it is criticised for the single, past-related path that it provides. This path may miss time periods during which the volatility changes may be significant. On the other hand, the MC simulation is the most comprehensive model because it provides simulations of numerous different paths, but also the most difficult to imple-ment. For portfolios that do not contain options or embedded options in their synthesis, the delta-normal method may well be the best choice. However, for portfolios containing option posi-tions, this method is not appropriate. As an alternative, the man-agement of financial institutions prefer to turn to historical or MC simulations.

Apart from the generic market risk, most credit and financial institutions face a significant amount of specific market risk, which was discussed in the section "Specific market risk". This type of risk is very important, especially for banks that do not utilise the full and exact dataset of market risk factors relevant to the nature of the portfolio. The quantification of specific risk is very difficult in terms of available data and storage costs for the data. That section concentrated on the quantification of specific risk on fixed-income securities. Corporate, or non-risk-free, fixed-income securities retain an excess level of risk that is reflected in the market price and represented by interest rate spreads. However, interest rate spreads are not fully attributed to market risk factors. Instead, other risk factors attributed to credit and operational risks and reflected in the price of fixed-income securities may also be attributed to interest rate spread. These risks may be analysed either from data derived by the marketplace or from internal data provided by credit institutions. The section referred to and analysed the various risk factors that drive the level of interest rate spread. The quantification of these risk factors are extensively analysed in Chapters 2 and 3.

The soundness of the models should be proved by their statistical accuracy as examined in the section "Backtesting and stress-testing market risk exposures". On the other hand, the Basel Committee on Banking Supervision (1996a), implicitly supports that a model is valid for internal use if its predictions are more conservative than the actual VAR. The amendment of Basel I (see Basal Committee for Banking Supervision, 1996a), along with the forthcoming changes in its context (rules related to market risk are expected to remain unchanged) not only allows but also stimulates credit and financial institutions to apply their own internal models. Furthermore, the Basel Committee proposes a test of appropriateness in economic terms. In this context, the Basel Committee provides credit institutions with the appropriate tools to evaluate every method within the same financial environment. More analytically, the Basel Committee encourages credit institutions to use alternative models for the same portfolio composition (positions), using the same type of data (risk factors), in order to evaluate their appropriateness. Having in mind the exact methodology for the determination of capital requirements, the only task that competent authorities and credit institutions have to carry out is to define the regulatory parameters for capital requirements.

REFERENCES

Alexander C. O. and C. T. Leigh, 1997, "On the Covariance Matrices used in Value-at-Risk Models", *Journal of Derivatives* **4(3)**, pp 50–62.

Barone-Adesi, G., K. Giannopoulos, and L. Vosper, 1999, "VAR without Correlations for Portfolios of Derivative Securities", *Journal of Futures Markets* **19**, pp 583–602.

Basel Committee on Banking Supervision, 1996a, "Amendment to the Capital Accord to Incorporate Market Risks", updated November 2005.

Basel Committee on Banking Supervision, 1996b, "The Textual Changes of the Market Risk Amendment to the Basel Capital Accord", January.

Basel Committee on Banking Supervision, 2004, "The International Convergence of Capital Measurement and Capital Standards: a Revised Framework", June.

Basel Committee on Banking Supervision and International Organisation of Securities Commissions, 2005, "The Application of Basel II to Trading Activities and the Treatment of Double Default Effects", June.

Basel Committee on Banking Supervision, 2005, "Amendment to the Capital Accord to incorporate market risks", updated November.

Black, F. and M. Scholes, 1973, "The Pricing of Options and Corporate Liabilities", *Journal of Political Economy* **81**, pp 637–654.

Blaschke, W., *et al,* 2001, "Stress Testing of Financial Systems: An Overview of Issues, Methodologies, and FSAP Experiences", International Monetary Fund working paper, URL: http://www.imf.org/external/pubs/ft/wp/2001/wp0188.pdf, June.

Bollerslev, T., 1986, "Generalized Autoregressive Conditional Heteroskedasticity", *Journal of Econometrics* **31**, pp 307–327.

Boudoukh, J., M. Richardson, and R. Whitelaw, 1998, "The Best of Both Worlds", *Risk* **11**, pp 64–67.

Campa, J. and P. K. Chang, 1998, "The Forecasting Ability of Correlations Implied in Foreign Exchange Options", *Journal of International Money and Finance* **17**, pp 855–880.

Chew, L., 1994, "Shock treatment", *Risk* **7(9)**, pp 63–70.

Committee on the Global Financial System, 2001, "A Survey of Stress Tests and Current Practice at Major Financial Institutions", April.

Cuthbertson, K. and D. Nitzsche, 2001, *Financial Engineering: Derivatives and Risk Management* (New York: John Wiley & Sons).

Derivatives Policy Group, 1995, "A Framework for Voluntary Oversight of the OTC Derivatives Activities of Securities Firm Affiliates to Promote Confidence and Stability in Financial Markets", URL: http://newrisk.ifci.ch/137790.htm, March.

Duffie, D. and J. Pan, 1997, "An Overview of Value at Risk", *Journal of Derivatives* **4(3)**, pp 7–49.

Eiteman, D. K., A. I. Stonehill, and H. H. Moffett, 2004, *Multinational Business Finance,* 10th edn (Addison Wesley).

Elton, E. J., *et al,* 2001, "Explaining the Rate Spread on Corporate Bonds", *Journal of Finance* LVI(1), February 2001.

Group of Thirty, 1993, "Special Report on Global Derivatives, Derivatives: Practices & Principles".

Hamilton, J. D., 1994, *Time Series Analysis* (NJ: Princeton University Press).

Hendricks, D., 1996, "Evaluation of Value-at-Risk models using historical data", *Economy Policy Review*, Federal Reserve Bank of New York.

Hicks, J. R., 1939, *Value and Capital* (Oxford, UK: Clarendon Press).

Holton, G. A., 2003, *Value at Risk: Theory and Practice* (San Diego, California, USA: Academic Press).

Hull, J. and A. White, 1998, "Incorporating Volatility Updating into the Historical Simulation Method for Value at Risk", *Journal of Risk* **1(1)**, pp 5–19.

Hull, J. and A. White, 1987, "The Pricing of Options on Assets with Stochastic Volatilities", *Journal of Finance* **42**, pp 281–300.

Hull, J., 2003, *Options, Futures and Other Derivatives* (Saddle River, NJ: Prentice Hall).

Jackson, P., D. J. Maude, and W. Perraudin, 1998, "Bank Capital and Value at Risk", working paper, Bank of England.

Jorion, P., 2001, *Financial Risk Manager Handbook* (New York: John Wiley & Sons).

Jorion, P., 2002, "Fallacies About the Effects of Market Risk Management Systems", *Financial Stability Review*, pp 115–127.

Macaulay, F. R., 1938, "The Movement of Interest Rates, Bond Yields, and Stock Prices in the United States Since 1856", National Bureau of Economic Research, New York.

Markowitz, H. M., 1952, "Portfolio Selection", *Journal of Finance* **7(1)**, pp 77–91.

Moody's – KMV, 2003, "Default & Corporate Rates of Corporate Bond Issuers, 1920–2002", February, p 39.

RiskMetrics, 1999, Risk Management: A Practical Guide, RiskMetrics Group.

RiskMetrics, 1996, *Technical Document*. J.P. Morgan/RiskMetrics, 4th Edition, New York.

Ross, S. A., R. W. Westerfield, and J. Jaffe, 2002, *Corporate Finance* (New York: McGraw Hill).

Scott, L. O., 1987, "Option Pricing When the Variance Changes Randomly: Theory, Estimation and an Application", *Journal of Financial and Quantitative Analysis* **22**, pp 419–438.

Wiggins, J. B., 1987, "Option Values Under Stochastic Volatility: Theory and Empirical Estimates", *Journal of Financial Economics* **19**, pp 351–372.

2

Credit Risk

Risk comes from not knowing what you're doing
— Warren Buffett

INTRODUCTION

Given several factors, such as a country's economic conditions, globalisation of financial markets and the wide variety of financial products, credit institutions have to deal with credit, market, liquidity, operational and other risks. Credit risk is probably the most popular type of risk in financial institutions.

Despite the methodologies adopted to measure credit risk and predict bankruptcy, everyone agrees that credit risk measurement has become a very important issue. The increasing number of bankruptcies internationally, the competitive spreads in loans and the risk-adjusted credit policies are some of the reasons that make the assessment of credit risk more important than ever before.

In the past, the majority of financial analysts used their subjective analysis for the assessment of credit risk. They used information from different obligor characteristics and the result was the subjective opinion of an expert to approve (or not) a loan.

Nowadays, credit institutions are not so much based on the relationship with their customers, but are basically using the technology and are developing sophisticated models in order to upgrade their credit risk management systems and approve or reject a loan in an objective way. Therefore, a wide variety of credit models have been built in order to measure credit risk and provide reliable estimates for the credit risk parameters such as the probability of default and loss given default. This chapter consists of three sections that deal with credit risk assessment models, credit risk parameters and credit rating systems and validation.

CREDIT RISK ASSESSMENT MODELS
Commonly used credit assessment models

In the last decades of the 20th century, several studies have been made in relation to bankruptcy. As a result, the possibility of predicting bankruptcy symptoms before they become obvious is a very interesting process. The first attempts in the US to use various statistical techniques for the prediction of a company's bankruptcy were made by Beaver and Altman in 1968 (see Beaver, 1966; Altman, 1968). Credit risk modelling is managed through different methodologies. In this section, there is a description of different methods in model development and the assumptions of each method, as well as their advantages and disadvantages.

Qualitative methods – expert systems

Expert systems are based on the judgement of experts who are involved in the credit-approval process and take into consideration their experience, knowledge and education on credit assessment. The results of an expert system combine the analysis of the creditworthiness of the obligor, with the practical experience and observations of the experts who apply the analysis. Therefore, the quality of empirical models (or expert systems) depends on how accurately they depict the subjective experience of credit experts. The factors that assess the creditworthiness analysis of the obligor are determined empirically, and also, their influence and weight in overall assessments are based on subjective experiences.

Expert systems take into consideration the experience of experts and produce rules with regard to a specific problem. For example, credit officers assign ratings that are based on financial ratios, opinions on management quality and other data. The expert systems codify the rules of successful credit officers. The aim of the rules is to be able to recreate the "expert" behaviour and judgement as accurately as possible. What usually happens is that the experts first predefine several creditworthiness characteristics that, from their experience, play an essential role in the future credit behaviour

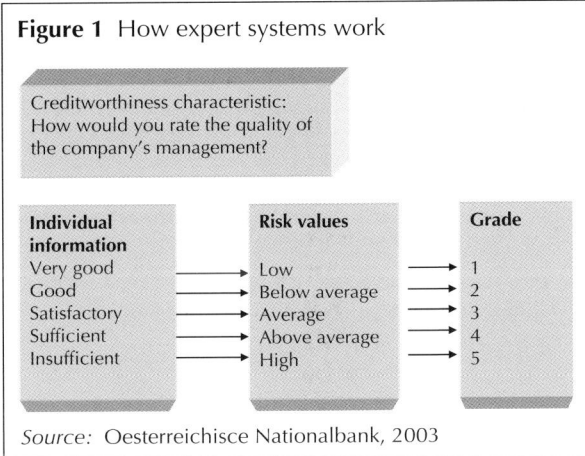

Figure 1 How expert systems work

Creditworthiness characteristic:
How would you rate the quality of
the company's management?

Individual information	Risk values	Grade
Very good	Low	1
Good	Below average	2
Satisfactory	Average	3
Sufficient	Above average	4
Insufficient	High	5

Source: Oesterreichisce Nationalbank, 2003

of the obligor. Then, the creditworthiness characteristics are rated from a predefined rating scale, according to the experts' opinion on the specific obligor (that means that the rating scale is based on individual information of the obligor). Each rating is then linked to a risk value and a corresponding grade. As a result, each creditworthiness factor is linked to a risk grade as shown in Figure 1.

In Figure 1, the individual information of the obligor is linked to a risk value and then to a risk grade. The individual factors' grades are combined to produce an overall assessment grade. So, the assessment involves the following steps.

1. The individual information is linked to a level of risk (risk value), which is determined by the experts' experience.
2. The level of risk is linked to a risk grade.
3. The individual grades are aggregated to generate an overall assessment.
4. The aggregation process uses the expert system's aggregation rules, which cannot be influenced by the credit analysts.

Quantitative methods
Quantitative methods are based either on statistical models or on causal models. Each model is built under several assumptions. So, it is only logical to say that there is a level of uncertainty that can influence the model results. There is uncertainty for the factors that might not be predicted, uncertainty for the correctness of the

estimation of parameters and uncertainty of how close the model is to reality. All of the above play an important role in the correct development of a model. Wrong assumptions, or wrong explanations of the assumptions, may lead to wrong decisions.

Statistical models

The process of building models should follow certain steps. Each step should be discrete and adequately validated so as to avoid a "black-box" nature of the model. The steps are as follows:

1. *Data availability/data selection/data clearance.* The accuracy, efficiency and appropriateness of data are very important issues, so that the model is built not only upon a sufficient number of data but also upon real and representative data of the population. It is crucial that the model is not built upon a poor number of "bad" (defaulted) obligors. "Bad" indicates the obligors defaulted on their obligations. The percentage of "bad" obligors should be at least 25% of the sample (because what happens in reality is that the bank usually has low-defaulted portfolios and a big number of non-defaulted clients). The remaining 75% of the sample is the percentage of "good" clients, meaning that they have not defaulted on their obligations.

2. *Determination of model methodology.* The model can be based upon empirical or statistical methodologies or a combination of the two (hybrid forms). Without regard to the methodology adopted, the functional relationship of the model should be well defined.

3. *Assessment of the parameters of the model.* The assessment of the model parameters should be scientifically established and ensure a good predictive power of the model and the stability of the parameters.

4. *Qualitative and quantitative validation.* The performance of the model and the stability of the parameters should be validated on an ongoing basis. There are a number of quantitative and qualitative validation methods, which are discussed later.

5. *Conclusions.* The conclusions should be very carefully extracted and based upon the appropriateness of the model, the application of the parameter assumptions and the proper choice of the confidence levels. The model should be assessed by human

judgement, so as to ensure that it performs well and has good predictive power (forward-looking model). The human judgement should take into consideration all other relevant information that cannot be considered by the model.

Univariate analysis

Univariate analysis explores each variable in a dataset separately. It looks at the central tendency of the values (mean, median) as well as at the dispersion. It has two goals: to analyse individual variables or to be used as the first step for multivariable analysis. Therefore, the first goal is to identify creditworthiness characteristics that are important in the business context and that show high discriminatory power (eg, when the purpose is to discriminate solvent from distressed obligors). The preselection of the creditworthiness characteristics reduces the complexity of the ensuing multivariate analysis.

Univariate analysis includes tests that compare samples from different groups. It evaluates one variable at a time: the variable of interest. It is simple to compare for example the value of the variable of interest with the mean value calculated for another group (such as the group mean value). The means, distributions and variances from the two samples can be compared.

There are a number of tests that allow the comparison of either the means of the two groups, or the variances, or the overall shape of the distribution. For example, a *t*-test is appropriate for a two-sample comparison if the data is distributed approximately normally. If not, the comparison of the two samples is fulfilled through the non-parametric test, the Mann–Whitney U-test. Furthermore, there are also tests mathematically equivalent to the above tests in order to compare two samples, such as the chi-square test and the Kolmogorov–Smirnov test, which are non-parametric.

Discriminant analysis

In its basic form, discriminant analysis seeks for a linear function of variables that best distinguishes between two or more predefined groups of obligors. If two groups are predefined – for example, good and bad debtors – then we seek the function of financial ratios that best distinguishes between solvent and distressed obligors. To come to such a conclusion there should be an analysis of an extensive number of financial ratios, so as to choose those ratios that maximise the variance between the two groups, while at the same time minimising the variance within each group.

Discriminant analysis is the multidimensional method that seeks the linear function of "i" variables X_i that best separates two (or more) groups. Using the procedure for the analysis of variables X_i, as mentioned before, the weights of the discriminant function Z are determine by:

$$Z = a_1 X_1 + a_2 X_2 + \cdots + a_p X_p \tag{1}$$

where a_i are the coefficients for the independent variables X_i, $i = 1, 2, ..., p$.

The above function leads to a Z-score for each observation of the population. In this section we are mostly trying to analyse methods that best distinguish between solvent and distressed obligors and for that reason we will deal with the case of two populations – "good" obligors (population Π_1) and "bad" obligors (population Π_2). The definition of "good" and "bad" obligors depends on the financial institution's strategy.

Discriminant analysis was invented by Fisher (1936) and used broadly (see Altman 1968; Altman et al, 1977). Fisher's linear discriminant function is also called *classification function*, because it is used in classifying observations into two (or more) groups. By this method a classification score for the observations of each group is calculated. The observation is then classified into the group with the highest classification score.

Fisher's idea was to transform multivariate variables x into univariate variables z, in such a way that the two populations Π_1 and Π_2 are best distinguished by their mean values ($\bar{z}_1$ and $\bar{z}_2$). Fisher's procedure does not assume multivariate normality of the populations, but it assumes that the variance–covariance matrices for the two groups are equal ($\Sigma_1 = \Sigma_2$). Still, it should be pointed out that data that do not meet the multivariate normality assumption may cause problems in the estimation of the discriminant function, meaning that the method will not distinguish in a good, acceptable way between the two populations. So, the method works better under the assumption of normality.

Assume that μ_1 is the mean value vector of the population Π_1 and the covariance matrix is Σ_1, μ_2 is the mean value vector of the population Π_2 and the covariance matrix is Σ_2, and that the covariance matrices are equal. Therefore we have:

$$\Sigma_1 = \Sigma_2 = \Sigma \tag{2}$$

Assume n_1 observations from the multivariate random variable $X' = [X_1, X_2, \dots, X_p]$ for the population Π_1 and n_2 observations for the population Π_2, where $n_1 + n_2 - 2 \geq p$, then:

$$X_1 = \begin{pmatrix} x'_{11} \\ x'_{12} \\ \vdots \\ x'_{1n_1} \end{pmatrix}_{(n_1 \times p)} \tag{3}$$

and

$$X_2 = \begin{pmatrix} x'_{21} \\ x'_{22} \\ \vdots \\ x'_{2n_2} \end{pmatrix}_{(n_2 \times p)} \tag{4}$$

where x_{ij} is the j observation of the population i (vector of p variables)

$$j = 1, 2, \dots, n_i \quad \text{and} \quad i = 1, 2.$$

Then the sample mean vectors and the sample covariance matrices are respectively for each of the two populations:

$$\bar{x}_1 \atop (p \times 1) = \frac{1}{n_1} \sum_{j=1}^{n_1} x_{1j} \tag{5}$$

$$\underset{(p \times p)}{S_1} = \frac{1}{n_1 - 1} \sum_{j=1}^{n_1} (x_{1j} - \bar{x}_1)(x_{1j} - \bar{x}_1)' \tag{6}$$

$$\bar{x}_2 \atop (p \times 1) = \frac{1}{n_2} \sum_{j=1}^{n_2} x'_{2j} \tag{7}$$

$$S_2 \atop (pxp) = \frac{1}{n_2 - 1} \sum_{j=1}^{n_2} (x_{2j} - \bar{x}_2)(x_{2j} - \bar{x}_2) \qquad (8)$$

Because of the assumption $\Sigma_1 = \Sigma_2 = \Sigma$, the sample covariance matrices S_1 and S_2 are pooled in order to give an unbiased estimate of Σ:

$$S_{pooled} = \left[\frac{n_1 - 1}{(n_1 - 1) + (n_2 - 1)} \right] S_1 + \left[\frac{n_2 - 1}{(n_1 - 1) + (n_2 - 1)} \right] S_2 \qquad (9)$$

The S_{pooled} is an unbiased estimate of Σ if the data matrices X_1 and X_2 contain random samples from Π_1 and Π_2 respectively.

The discriminant function of each observation for each of the two populations, Π_1 and Π_2, is:

$$z_{1j} = \hat{\alpha}'x_{1j} = \alpha_1 x_{1j1} + \alpha_2 x_{1j2} + \cdots + \alpha_p x_{1jp} \qquad (10)$$

where $j = 1, 2, \ldots, n_1$

$$z_{2j} = \hat{\alpha}'x_{2j} = \alpha_1 x_{2j1} + \alpha_2 x_{2j2} + \cdots + \alpha_p x_{2jp} \qquad (11)$$

where $j = 1, 2, \ldots, n_2$.

Then,

$$\bar{z}_1 = \sum_{j=1}^{n_1} z_{1j}/n_1 = \hat{\alpha}'\bar{x}_1 \qquad (12)$$

$$\bar{z}_2 = \sum_{j=1}^{n_2} z_{2j}/n_2 = \hat{\alpha}'\bar{x}_2 \qquad (13)$$

We are searching for the vector $\hat{\alpha}$ that maximises the ratio: $\bar{z}_1 - \bar{z}_2 / s_{\hat{z}}$ or the ratio $(\bar{z}_1 - \bar{z}_2)^2 / s_{\hat{z}}^2$ (because $\bar{z}_1 - \bar{z}_2 / s_{\hat{z}}$ can be negative).

Then:

$$\hat{\lambda} = \frac{(\bar{z}_1 - \bar{z}_2)^2}{s_{\hat{z}}^2} = \frac{[\hat{\alpha}'(\bar{x}_1 - \bar{x}_2)]^2}{\hat{\alpha}'S_{pooled}\hat{\alpha}} = \frac{(\hat{\alpha}'\bar{x}_1 - \hat{\alpha}'\bar{x}_2)^2}{\hat{\alpha}'S_{pooled}\hat{\alpha}} = \frac{(\hat{\alpha}'d)^2}{\hat{\alpha}'S_{pooled}\hat{\alpha}} \qquad (14)$$

where $d = \bar{x}_1 - \bar{x}_2$.

The maximum is produced if

$$\hat{a} = S_{pooled}^{-1}(\bar{x}_1 - \bar{x}_2) \tag{15}$$

The vector $\hat{\alpha}$ is not unique, since the maximum is produced for all multiples of $S_{pooled}^{-1}(\bar{x}_1 - \bar{x}_2)$, but it is important to stress that it is unique by direction.

The basic aim is to predict whether a new observation should be classified in group Π_1 or Π_2, that is, whether a new obligor will end up as a solvent or distressed one.

Under Fisher's assumptions, we try to decide whether a new observation x_0 (vector of p variables) belongs to the first or the second population.

We measure the vectors $\bar{x}_1, \bar{x}_2$ as well as S_{pooled}. Then,

$$z = \hat{\alpha}'x_0 = (\bar{x}_1 - \bar{x}_2)'S_{pooled}^{-1}x_0 \tag{16}$$

For the population Π_1 we measure

$$\bar{z}_1 = \sum_{j=1}^{n_1} z_{1j}/n_1 = \hat{\alpha}'\bar{x}_1 = (\bar{x}_1 - \bar{x}_2)'S_{pooled}^{-1}\bar{x}_1 \tag{17}$$

and for Π_2:

$$\bar{z}_2 = \hat{\alpha}'\bar{x}_2 = (\bar{x}_1 - \bar{x}_2)'S_{pooled}^{-1}\bar{x}_2 \tag{18}$$

According to Fisher's classification method, the observation x_0 is classified in the population Π_1, when $z = \hat{\alpha}'x_0$ is closer to $\bar{z}_1$ (than it is from $\bar{z}_2$). In the same way, x_0 is classified in the population Π_2 if z is closer to $\bar{z}_2$. So it is obvious that z is closer to $\bar{z}_1$ if:

$$z > \frac{1}{2}(\bar{z}_1 + \bar{z}_2) \tag{19}$$

We come up with Fisher's function for the classification of the new observations.

Because:

$$\frac{1}{2}(\bar{z}_1 + \bar{z}_2) = \frac{1}{2}(\bar{x}_1 - \bar{x}_2)'S_{pooled}^{-1}(\bar{x}_1 + \bar{x}_2) \tag{20}$$

Fisher's classification rule becomes:

The observation x_0 is classified in the population Π_1 if:

$$\bar{z}_0 = (\bar{x}_1 - \bar{x}_2)' S_{pooled}^{-1} x_0 \geq m = \frac{1}{2}(\bar{x}_1 - \bar{x}_2)' S_{pooled}^{-1}(\bar{x}_1 + \bar{x}_2) \qquad (21)$$

or

$$z_0 - m \geq 0 \qquad (22)$$

The observation x_0 is classified in the population Π_2 if:

$$z_0 < m \text{ or } z_0 - m < 0 \qquad (23)$$

In the Fisher's classification function the a-priori probabilities p_1 *and* p_2 *are assumed to be equal, but what happens in reality is that the a-priori probabilities are not expected to be equal.* For example, it is obvious that, in the case of the two populations that are characterised as *good* (for the good debtors) and *bad* (for the bad debtors), we expect that a new applicant is more likely to be characterised as a good client than a bad one ($p_1 > p_2$). So, if the *a priori* probabilities p_1 *and* p_2 *(where* $p_1 + p_2 = 1$*)* are known for the two populations, then the classification rule is different. In such a case we have to be aware of the density functions of the two populations: $f(x_0 \mid \Pi_1)$, $f(x_0 \mid \Pi_2)$. Then the optimum classification rule that minimises the probability of classification error is (see Welch, 1939):

The observation x_0 is classified in the population Π_1 if

$$p_1 = f(x_0 \mid \Pi_1) > p_2 = f(x_0 \mid \Pi_2) \qquad (24)$$

or, otherwise, it is classified in Π_2.

As for the density functions, if we assume that $f(x_0 \mid \Pi_1) = N_p(\mu_1, \Sigma)$ and $f(x_0 \mid \Pi_2) = N_p(\mu_2, \Sigma)$, then we have the result:

The observation x_0 is classified in the population Π_1 if

$$\hat{\alpha}' x_0 = (\bar{x}_1 - \bar{x}_2)' S_{pooled}^{-1} x_0 > \frac{1}{2}(\bar{x}_1 - \bar{x}_2)' S_{pooled}^{-1}(\bar{x}_1 + \bar{x}_2) + \ln \frac{p_2}{p_1} \qquad (25)$$

or, otherwise, it is classified in Π_2.

In the above rule, if $p_1 = p_2$, we end up with Fisher's function again.

Logistic regression models

Binomial (or *binary*) *logistic regression* is a form of regression that is used when the dependent variable is a dichotomy and the independents are of any type. *Multinomial logistic regression* exists to handle the case of dependents with more classes than two. When multiple classes of the dependent variable can be ranked, then *ordinal logistic regression* is preferred to multinomial logistic regression.

If we assume that the response variable (the regressand) can take only two values, 1 and 0, then it means that the regressand is a binary or a dichotomous variable (in the general case we can have a polychotomous or multiple-category response variable).

Let us assume that a multiple regression model is:

$$y = a_1 x_1 + a_2 x_2 + \cdots + a_k x_k + e \tag{26}$$

where y is the dependent variable or explained variable, $x_1, x_2, \ldots, x_k$ are the independent or explanatory variables and $a_1, a_2, \ldots, a_k$ are the coefficients of the independent variables. In this setting, y is the regressand, $x_j, j = 1, 2, \ldots, k$ are the regressors and e is the random disturbance (because it disturbs an otherwise stable relationship). We assume that each of the i observation in sample $(y_i, x_{i1}, \ldots, x_{ik})$ $i = 1, 2, \ldots, n$, is generated by an underlying process described by:

$$y_i = a_1 x_{i1} + a_2 x_{i2} + \cdots + a_k x_{ik} + e_i \tag{27}$$

Our objective is to estimate the unknown parameters of the model and predict the variable y.

The regressand y can either be quantitative or qualitative. In models where y is qualitative, the objective is to find the probability of something's happening and that is why these qualitative regression models are usually known as *probability models*.

For a binary dependent variable y, the regression model becomes:

$$y = p(x) = a_0 + a_i x_i \tag{28}$$

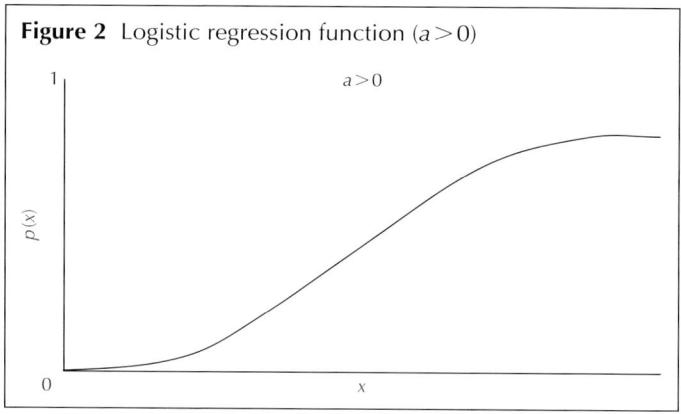

Figure 2 Logistic regression function $(a>0)$

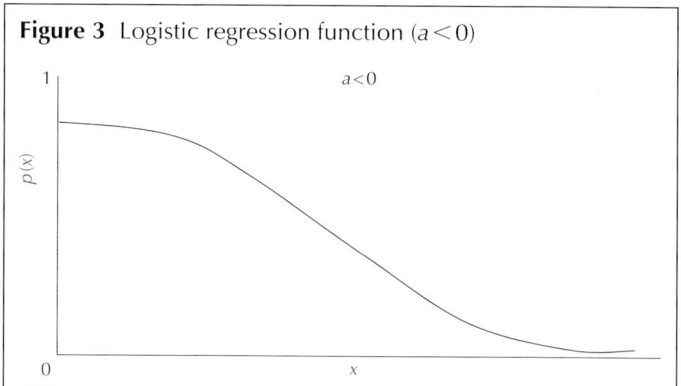

Figure 3 Logistic regression function $(a<0)$

where p is the probability of an event to occur, x_i are the independent variables, a_i are the coefficients of the independent variables and a_0 is the constant. This is called a *linear probability model*. Probabilities fall between 0 and 1 (but the linear function takes values over the entire real line). The model is suitable over a limited range of x values. But, when it is plausible, it has a great advantage: it is easy to interpret: a is the change in $p(x)$ for one unit increase in x. But, what happens in practice is that binary data result from a non-linear relationship between $p(x)$ and x. Non-linear relationships between $p(x)$ and x are often monotonic, with $p(x)$ increasing continuously as x increases.

The curves shown in Figures 2 and 3 are typical S-shaped curves (selecting an S-shaped logistic function curve ensures that the *p* values fall between 0 and 1 and can thus be interpreted as actual probabilities).

The most important curve with the above shape has the model formula:

$$y = p(x) = \frac{\exp(a_0 + a_i x_i)}{1 + \exp(a_0 + a_i x_i)} \tag{29}$$

The above ratio can also be written as:

$$y = p(x) = \frac{1}{1 + \exp[-(a_0 + a_i x_i)]} \tag{30}$$

This is the logistic regression model. When $a < 0$ and $x \to \infty$, then $p(x) \downarrow 0$. If $a > 0$ then $p(x) \uparrow 1$. The function that links the logistic regression with a generalised linear model is found by using the odds ratio. The odds ratio of is:

$$\frac{p(x)}{1 - p(x)} = \exp(a_0 + a_i x_i) \tag{31}$$

So, the log odds has the linear relationship:

$$\log \frac{p(x)}{1 - p(x)} = a_0 + a_i x_i \tag{32}$$

The coefficient estimates a_i are obtained through maximum-likelihood estimation techniques. By substituting the estimates a_0 and a_i in Equation (32), we can estimate the logarithm of the probability of an event to occur and then estimate the probability itself. Therefore, the appropriate link function for which logistic regression is a generalised linear model is the log odds transformation, the *logit*. Logistic regression models are generalised linear models with binomial random component and logit link function. Logistic regression models are also called *logit models*.

The logit is the natural parameter of the binomial distribution, so, whereas $p(x)$ must fall between the range (0,1), the logit can be any real number.

If the general definition of regression models is applied to credit-assessment procedures, the objective is to use certain creditworthiness characteristics (independent variables) to determine whether borrowers are classified as solvent or distressed (dependent binary variable). According to the analysis mentioned above, in binary logistic regression (in the general case), the probability p that a borrower is classified as solvent or distressed, is measured according to the following formula:

$$p = \frac{1}{1 + \exp[-(a_0 + a_1 x_1 + a_2 x_2 + \cdots + a_n x_n)]} \tag{33}$$

where n is the number of criteria included in the scoring function, $a_i, i = 1, 2, \ldots, n$ are the coefficients of the indicators within the scoring function, x_i stands for the specific value of each creditworthiness criterion and a_0 is the constant.

An alternative methodology for binary models is to use the cumulative standard normal distribution F (it is the distribution with mean value 0 and variance 1). If we substitute the normal distribution for the logistic distribution, we have a probit model.

First of all, let's assume the linear function of the parameters x_i:

$$Z = p(x) = a_0 + a_1 x_1 + a_2 x_2 + \cdots + a_n x_n \tag{34}$$

then the cumulative standard normal distribution $F(Z)$ gives the probability of a credit event to occur (for every value of Z):

$$p_i = F(z_i) \tag{35}$$

Then we have:

$$p_{Logit} = \frac{1}{1 + \exp(-Z)} \tag{36}$$

and

$$p_{Probit} = F(Z) \tag{37}$$

Both model functions can be adjusted to give almost identical results. The results of the two models are for that reason not significantly different.

Causal models

Causal models derive credit ratings using a theoretical business-based model and use only a few (exclusively quantitative) input parameters without explicitly taking qualitative data into account. The information relevant to creditworthiness is therefore complete only in certain segments (such as large corporates).

The most prevailing class of causal models is option-pricing models. Merton (1974) and Black and Scholes (1973) proposed a simple model of a firm that provides a way of relating credit risk to the capital structure of the firm. The firm has issued two classes of securities: equity and debt. The equity receives no dividends, while the debt is a pure discount bond where a payment of D is promised at the time T. If at time T the firm's asset value exceeds the promised payment D, the lenders are paid the promised amount and the shareholders receive the residual asset value. If the asset value is less than the promised payment, the firm defaults, the lenders receive a payment equal to the asset value and the shareholders do not get anything.

If E is defined as the value of the firm's equity and A as the value of its assets, and if E_0 and A_0 are the values of E and A today and E_T and A_T the values at time T, then in the Merton framework the payment to the shareholders at time T, is given by:

$$E_T = \max[A_T - D, 0] \qquad (38)$$

The equity value of the firm, E, can be treated as a call option written on the value of assets, A, where the strike price, B, is given by all the short-term liabilities, B_s, plus half of the long-term ones, B_L.

The isomorphism between the market value position of equity holders and the position of holders of a call option on the firm's assets leads us to the following set of equations:

$$E = f(A, \sigma_A, r, B, T) \qquad (39)$$

$$\sigma_E = g(\sigma_A) \qquad (40)$$

where σ_A, σ_E are asset and equity volatility respectively, r is the risk-free interest rate and T is the time horizon of the option holder.

From the above equations it is possible to obtain asset value and volatility, otherwise, unobservable quantities on a regular, short-term basis, from equity value and volatility, which are easily available from stock market data. Once the asset value and its volatility are obtained, a distance to default, DD, can be determined as a multiple of asset volatility as:

$$DD = \frac{A - \left(B_S + \frac{1}{2}B_L\right)}{\sigma_A} \qquad (41)$$

It is obvious from Equation (41) that a default situation is approached when the expected value of assets becomes closer and closer to the expected value of liabilities and when the asset volatility is large, therefore making it possible, from a statistical point of view, to have insufficient assets backing liabilities.

The implementation of Merton's model has received commercial attention in recent years: for example, Moody's KMV uses it to estimate relative probabilities of default.

Hybrid models

The hybrid forms of credit-assessment models are combinations of empirical (or expert) models and one of the other two model types – statistical and causal. In practice, the use of only empirical or only quantitative models does not lead to conclusions with adequate forward-looking results. On the other hand, the objectivity of quantitative systems in the elaboration of quantitative data combined with the superiority of empirical systems in the incorporation and analysis of qualitative criteria leads to a better classification of risk.

Overall, this approach can generally be seen as favourable: statistical or causal models have the great advantage of finding rules in an objective way and can also perform better than empirical models when trying to predict the creditworthiness of obligors. But, at the same time, statistical or causal models cannot take into consideration all the creditworthiness factors, and so very important information on the borrowers' characteristics would be lost in individual cases without the empirical help of credit experts.

Three different types of hybrid forms are usually met.

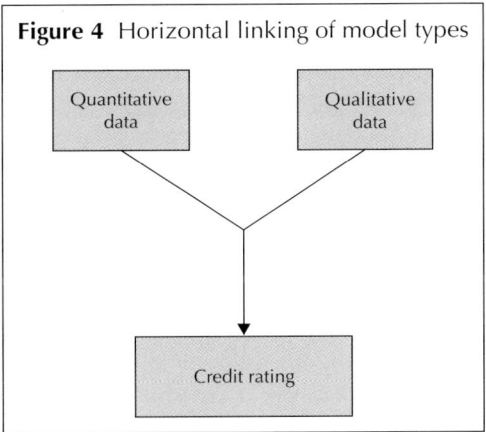

Figure 4 Horizontal linking of model types

Horizontal linking of model types

The results of a statistical or a causal model are supplemented with additional qualitative criteria used by credit analysts. Then, IT systems can possibly combine the output by these two modules, in order to come up with an overall credit assessment as seen in Figure 4.

Overrides

The experts in charge of the credit-approval process modify the proposed classification by a mathematical model. Such modifications are known as *empirical overrides*. Both positive and negative overrides are met, in the meaning that a mathematical model may result in a credit rejection of an obligor and the credit expert approves the loan (positive override) or the opposite may occur (negative override).

When the overrides are rare, the system is assumed to be quantitative, while, when the overrides are frequent, the system is assumed to be qualitative. Especially in the latter case, it is very important to define precisely the cases and the range in which overrides can be used. The range can change according to the type of portfolio for example, the maximum permitted percentage of overrides for the corporate portfolio can be 1.5% and for the retail portfolio 3%. This is highly recommended in order to avoid ending up with an empirical system having the subjectivity problems mentioned before (see Figure 5).

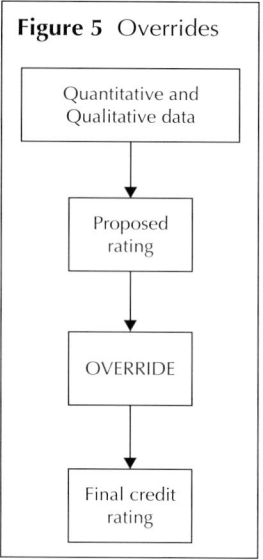

Figure 5 Overrides

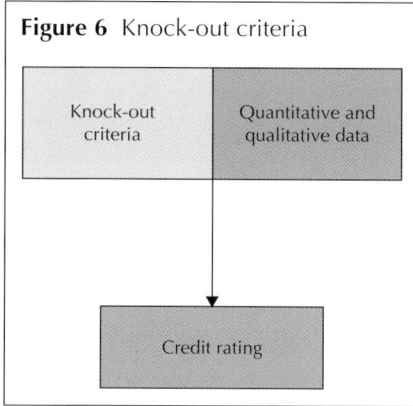

Figure 6 Knock-out criteria

Knock-out criteria

These systems are based first of all on several knockout criteria defined by the credit experts and the credit institutions' policy and then on a mathematical model. If a credit application fulfils one of the knockout criteria, then it is rejected without determining the mathematical model. This process is also known as *pre-screening*. If the credit application is not "knocked out", then, it is rated according to the results of the mathematical model (see Figure 6).

Institution-based *versus* market-based models

A number of institution-based models, such as expert models, regression and discriminant analysis models, have been described in this section. At the same time, market-based models were analysed through causal models and the Merton model. The basic advantages and disadvantages of each model are analysed, to enable the risk analysts to determine which methodology fits their data better, as well as the weaknesses that they are going to face. Let us recap on the various discussed methodologies. First of all, expert systems are systems that are easy to apply and are very flexible. They have a great openness to further development and a rigorous structure. On the other hand, the factors relevant to creditworthiness are determined empirically and their influence and weight in the overall assessment are based on subjective experience.

Concerning the univariate method, it is one of the simplest methods in the prediction of the obligor's creditworthiness. However, the method has poor predictive powers, as the decision of the credit analyst for approving a loan or not, depends on the "one-by-one" comparison of financial ratios with team rules, branches, etc. Although univariate analysis is still in use in several credit institutions, most academics and experts seem to disapprove of the use of such models and favour the development of statistical methodologies. But it should be pointed out that univariate analysis is an appropriate method to analyse individual variables as the first step for multivariate analysis.

When using the discriminant analysis methodology, one should be aware of the following points:

❑ The method is easy to understand and easy to use and apply.
❑ It transforms the different values of the independent variables into only a discriminant score z. Therefore, instead of analysing the independent variables one by one, we have to analyse only z.
❑ It can produce very good results under certain circumstances. For example, it has much better results under the assumption of the multivariate normal distribution of the variables (although normality is not an assumption for the use of the method).
❑ Assumptions of multivariate analysis are not easily satisfied (normality, equal variance–covariance matrices), which can cause problems to the soundness of the method.

❏ Categorical variables are not evaluated by this method (that means qualitative data are not included in the analysis).
❏ The result of the method is the scoring of the examined customer, but it does not produce probability of defaults.

Logistic regression has advantages over multivariate discriminant analysis, for the following reasons.

❏ Logistic regression does not require normal distribution as input indicators (independent variables). This allows logistic regression models to process qualitative creditworthiness characteristics without previous transformation.
❏ The result of logistic regression can be interpreted directly as the probability of group membership. This allows assigning a one-year default rate to each result (eg, by rescaling the value p).
❏ Logistic regression models are often characterised by more robust and accurate results and have very important predictive powers.

As for the market-based model, the Merton model, it takes into consideration general conditions that are expected to rule the market, in the way that these conditions are expressed by the market participants. On the other hand, the Merton model faces a basic weakness, in that it can be applied only for firms exchanged in the stock market. The model could end up with misleading results in the case of insufficient liquidity of the market, where exchange securities of the firm under evaluation are being traded.

CREDIT RISK PARAMETERS: DEFINITIONS AND ESTIMATIONS
Credit value-at-risk, expected loss and unexpected loss
When market risk is quantified as discussed in Chapter 1, the notion of maximum loss for a certain confidence level and a prespecified holding period was introduced. This notion is identical to the value-at-risk (VAR) measure. Similarly, when trying to estimate credit risk, the respective measure is to estimate VAR for the credit portfolio. In the course of dealing with market risk, returns on assets were used in order to construct the returns' distribution of a specific product, or the returns' distribution of a portfolio of products. The assumption that usually underlines the distribution in the market risk portfolio is that it follows multivariate normal distribution.

On the other hand, credit risk portfolios are less likely to exhibit characteristics attributed to normal distribution, although in the same cases the actual distribution is very close to normal or, more often, close to lognormal. This is one of the main drawbacks attributed to the Basel Committee approximation to credit risk: capital requirements (see Chapter 5) are calculated according to the assumption that losses follow normal distribution. When dealing with economic capital, credit VAR is estimated according to the actual distribution of losses. Credit VAR comprises two components: the expected loss and the unexpected loss.

Expected loss is related to the loss that a credit institution may incur during its ordinary business. Therefore, credit institutions are able to continue their operations by simultaneously having a certain level of losses. In the Basel II Committee framework, this level of losses is related to the level of provisions that a bank should set aside in order to cover them. On the other hand, unexpected loss is the loss that a credit institution may face under extreme circumstances that lie beyond the level of expected losses. Credit VAR is visually presented in Figure 7.

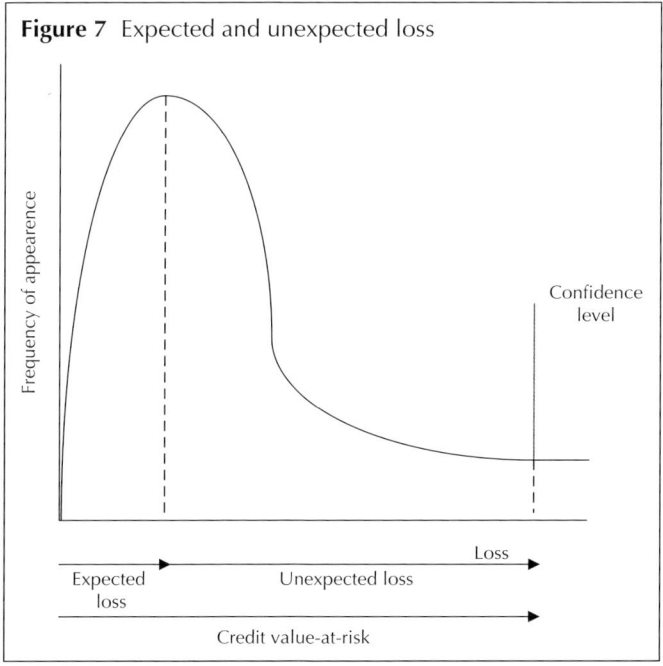

Figure 7 Expected and unexpected loss

The credit VAR measure is heavily based on the distribution of losses observed in a credit portfolio. However, the expected and unexpected losses can be further broken down into other components, namely the probability of default (PD), the loss given default (LGD) and the exposure at default (EAD). Assuming that the EAD depends on the culture of the individual credit institution, whenever its appearance is implied in the forthcoming analysis, it is assumed to be one currency unit. Based on this assumption, expected loss is calculated as follows:

$$EL = PD \times LGD \times EAD \qquad (42)$$

or, by adopting the assumption that $EAD = 1$ currency unit, Equation (42) becomes:

$$EL = PD \times LGD \qquad (43)$$

On the other hand, the unexpected loss, in fully parametric approaches, can be represented as follows:

$$UL = \sigma_{credit} \times m \qquad (44)$$

where m is the appropriate quantile of the credit loss distribution, in order for the model to reach the credit VAR confidence level given by:

$$m = \frac{VAR_{credit}^{(1year,\ 99.9\%)} - EL}{\sigma_{credit}} = \frac{UL}{\sigma_{credit}} \qquad (45)$$

where $VAR_{credit}^{(1\ year,\ 99.9\%)}$ is the credit VAR measure for 1 year confidence level and holding period and 99.9%, $UL^{(1\ year,\ 99.9\%)}$ is the unexpected loss and σ_{credit} is the volatility of the individual asset expressed in terms of the volatility of PD and LGD as follows:

$$\sigma_{credit} = \sqrt{PD \times \sigma_{LGD}^2 + LGD^2 \times \sigma_{PD}^2} \qquad (46)$$

Given Equation (45), the relationship among credit VAR, expected and unexpected loss is demonstrated as follows:

$$VAR_{credit}^{(1year,\ 99.9\%)} - EL = UL \qquad (47)$$

All equations from Equation (43) to Equation (47) refer to the unitary credit VAR that is the VAR used to quantify the risk of a unique credit element (such as a loan). However, in reality, there are multiple assets in a credit portfolio. The values of these assets are correlated in a similar way to the returns in the market risk. These correlations are named *asset correlations* and they are particularly useful for the estimation of the LGD of a credit portfolio. On the other hand, there may be a correlation between defaults that have occurred on different assets. In other words, a default in one asset may or may not cause another asset to become defaulted. This type of correlation is named *default correlation* and it is extremely useful for the estimation of the PD of a portfolio with multiple assets. In turn, default correlations are used to estimate the standard deviation and the unexpected loss of a credit portfolio. The standard deviation (σ_p, *credit*) of the portfolio that is used as an input for the estimation of unexpected loss is derived as follows:

$$\sigma_{p,credit} = \sqrt{\sum_{i=1}^{n}\sum_{j=1}^{n}\rho_{ij}UL_iUL_j} \qquad (48)$$

where ρ_{ij} is the correlation coefficient for assets i and j, and it is given by:

$$\rho_{ij} = \frac{P(D_i \times D_j) - PD_i \times PD_j}{\sqrt{PD_i \times (1 - PD_i)}\sqrt{PD_j \times (1 - PD_j)}} \qquad (49)$$

where $P(D_i \times D_j)$ is the joint probability of default.

In the case of parametric models, the unexpected loss of the credit portfolio – assuming that it follows the same probability distribution as the individual asset does – is given by:

$$UL_p = \sigma_{p,credit} \times m \qquad (50)$$

where UL_p and $\sigma_{p,credit}$ stand for the unexpected loss and the volatility of the credit portfolio, respectively.

The construction of the correlation matrix can be inferred from the corresponding matrix calculated in Chapter 1 for the market risk. Similarly, with market risk, the expected loss of the portfolio of credit assets consists of the sum of the expected losses of the individual assets that the portfolio comprises. The entire modelling of credit risk is based on the estimation of the probability of default and the loss given default. The estimation of these two components of expected loss can be performed by two means:

❑ implied derivation; and
❑ internal estimation.

Consequently, implied derivation of the parameters can be carried out by two approximations:

❑ implying credit risk parameters by exploiting the information contained in credit derivative products; and
❑ implying credit risk parameters by exploiting the information provided by the credit VAR model.

Implying parameters from credit default swaps
The first derivation of the above-mentioned parameters can be made by using traded credit derivative products, such as credit default swaps. In its traded price, a credit default swap implies an expected loss for the reference asset (underlying asset), hence a combination of PDs and LGDs (PD x LGD). However, there are infinite combinations of PDs and LGDs that may lead to the same expected loss. In order to come up with an exact value for each of the two parameters, the other parameter should be kept invariant. Alternatively, both parameters can be estimated simultaneously by utilising optimisation techniques applied to a sufficient number of credit default swaps with the same reference asset. In order for this optimisation to be stable, the bounds for the estimation of each parameter should be set in advance. Thus, the method is subject to a value selection error because the bounds of both PDs and LGDs are not known upfront. The reader who is interested in the valuation of these products and the consequent derivation of the parameters can refer to the Appendix.

Implying parameters and constructing credit loss distributions from credit risk models
The second derivation needs the use of a valid credit risk model applied to internal data concerning credit products. This model

estimates expected and unexpected losses. Once the credit VAR (ie, the sum of expected and unexpected losses) has been estimated it is effortless to attribute the contribution of each component of loss to the total credit VAR. Between the two independent parameters, presented in Equation (42), LGD is the most problematic in terms of available reliable data. Among all known methodologies for estimating credit VAR, the majority is drawn from the corresponding methodologies used for the quantification of market risk. However, the suitability of the methodologies used for producing efficient estimations should be assessed within the context of the availability of historical data.

Fully available historical loss data
If historical loss data are fully available, the following methodologies are the natural candidates for the estimation of credit VAR:

❏ historical simulation; and
❏ the variance–covariance method applied to historical losses.

If historical loss data are available for many years (say 20), the entire distribution of losses can be generated for both:

❏ loss data over the entire observation period; and
❏ loss data over a specific year.

Respectively, the credit VAR can be estimated by two different approximations:

❏ inter-temporal credit VAR estimated over the entire observation period; and
❏ year-in-time credit VAR estimated for an individual year.

In the first case, data may be collected in large quantities for each year attributing each loss to the respective credit asset. The sequence of annual credit losses comprises time series of credit losses. These time series can be used in order to:

❏ estimate long-term annual credit VARs; and/or
❏ estimate regressions for the forward-looking credit VAR and/or EL and UL and, thus, make predictions for them.

In the second case, where only one year is considered, the credit loss observed should be attributed to each asset or each asset class.

The loss for each asset should be accounted for in the year in which it appears. According to the optimal case in constructing credit loss distributions, for each day and each asset class the loss that has appeared during the past year (365 days) should be registered. Consequently, there would be daily observations for annual losses for every year and every asset class. Thus, credit VAR is estimated by using either historical simulation or the variance–covariance method for all available data. On the other hand, the expected loss is independently estimated by the means of the loss distribution, and the difference between credit VAR and expected loss would be the unexpected loss.

Partly available historical loss data

If historical data are partly available, which means there is no adequate historical database, the most appropriate methodology to model credit losses should be based on both:

❏ historical data; and
❏ Monte Carlo simulation.

Most credit institutions do not have adequate historical data for the construction of the entire probability distribution over the entire period of time. Instead, when only scattered and scarce data of asset losses exist for each year, the distribution of the loss data can be constructed by using Monte Carlo simulation. The credit institution should start by constructing the loss distribution for each single year. In turn, Monte Carlo simulation should be applied on each asset or asset loss for multiple years. Thus, the credit loss evolution is constructed. After the construction of the loss evolution, yearly losses should be attributed to each corresponding year in order to construct the loss distribution for each individual year.

Lack of historical data

If the credit institution lacks historical loss data, only Monte Carlo simulation can be used in order to estimate the loss distribution. In order to infer the loss distribution the value of the asset of the credit portfolio should be known. In turn, the asset value is shocked by applying Monte Carlo simulation. When Monte Carlo simulation is used for the estimation of credit VAR, an assumption should be made about the distribution from which random numbers are drawn (see

Chapter 1). The assumption should be based on the anticipated shape of the distribution of credit losses.

Expected loss
Whatever the availability of data, expected loss should be exploited for the implication of its determinants, namely PD and LGD. Once:

❑ the determinants of the expected loss are two; and
❑ the expected loss is already known.

One of the determinants should be estimated independently and be kept invariant and the other should be implied from the estimation of expected loss. The estimation of expected loss can be made by using various techniques, models or products.

It is preferable that the estimation of PD should be carried out independently, since it is the most straightforward parameter to estimate using data available from the credit institution. Given that the PD is known, the derivation of LGD can be carried out by either:

❑ estimating it by using the available historical data; or
❑ implying it from credit default swaps (see Appendix).

The estimation by using available data is very difficult because it is assumed that the credit institution will keep reliable records about the behaviours of the credit assets and to efficiently estimate some other parameters necessary for its estimation (see below). Conversely, the credit institution can potentially be in a position to infer LGD from available credit default swap prices. In this case, the PD parameter is considered to be invariant and the estimation of the LGD parameter is carried out by inverting the valuation formula of credit default swaps that appears in the Appendix.

Forward-looking expected loss
The use of any of the above methods provides yearly estimates for both expected and unexpected loss. However, the basic requirement of the Basel II Committee, along with the through-the-cycle estimation of PD, is the estimation of forward-looking PDs. In order for this to be feasible according to the above approaches, the forward-looking expected loss should be predicted. The time series

corresponding to expected losses can be used as inputs in an econometric model that is designed to predict the future expected loss. Usually, the model has the form of an autoregressive model [AR(1)] represented as:

$$EL_{t+1} = a_0 + \sum_{i=1}^{n} a_i EL_{t+1-i} + \varepsilon_t \qquad (51)$$

where EL_{t+1} is the forward looking expected loss, EL_{t+1-i} is the past expected loss of the year $t+1-i$, a_0 is the constant coefficient that stands for the minimum value of expected loss every year irrespective of recessions or accessions, a_i is the coefficient that stands for the influence of the past expected loss (EL_{t+1-i}) on the future expected loss and ε_t is the error term of the estimation.

The validity of the above-mentioned econometric model should be tested for both in-sample estimations and out-of-sample estimations before it is used for the estimation of forward-looking expected loss. Consequently, PDs and LGDs are derived from the forward-looking expected loss in a similar way to the one described above.

Independent approximations of risk parameters

A credit granted to an entity or individual can be characterised as either defaulted or active. The loan is "in default" when one of the conditions described in the remaining section is fulfilled, while it is considered "active" if the scheduled instalments are paid regularly or any past due appearance does not conflict with the definition of default. The internal derivation of PD and LGD is described, analytically, below.

Probability of default

There are two sets of criteria in order for a credit asset to be characterised as "in default". Thus, the estimation of probability of default involves two sets of criteria as well:

❑ quantitative criteria; and
❑ qualitative criteria.

In most cases both sets of criteria are complementary in the sense that a quantitative criterion should be assessed after using a qualitative criterion (eg, the "unlikeliness-to-pay" clause in the Basel II document (see Basel Committee on Banking Supervision, 2005) should be first assessed qualitatively and then quantitatively).

Quantitative criteria

The probability of default (PD) for a specified class of loans is defined as the number of loans that were defaulted during a certain period of time. Thus, the annual default rate or probability of default is the percentage rate of the loans that were defaulted in relation to the total portfolio of loans during the period of one year, while the biannual default rate is the same measure for a period of two years. Mathematically expressed, the annual probability of default is represented as follows:

$$PD_{annual} = \frac{DL_{annual}}{TL} \times 100 \tag{52}$$

where PD_{annual} is the annual percentage probability of default, DL_{annual} is the number of defaulted loans during the year under examination and TL is the total number of loans of the examined loan class.

The probability of default for loans is rather a difficult task for the risk manager, but not as much as the LGD. The main difficulties are the:

❑ criteria set to form a quantitative definition of default; and
❑ criteria set to form a qualitative definition of default.

However, not all loans exhibit the same difficulties. According to the Basel II Committee, the probability of default, concerning mortgages, is the inability or insufficiency of debtors to pay a substantial portion of their loan for three months (or 90 days) as it has been scheduled. The probability of default for mortgages based on the six-month-period quantitative definition of default, although not mentioned in the original draft of the Basel Accord II, is a common practice in the European banking system. This definition is relaxed in relation to the three-months definition of default, originally mentioned in the Basel II document. However, in North America the quantitative definition of default for the same category of credit is related to three months (or 90 days) past due loans.

The "materiality" is another point that must be clarified in order to provide a concrete definition of the probability of default. The "materiality" notion coincides with the meaning of "substantiality". The most common implied definitions of materiality are the following:

❏ some banks consider as "material" the fact that the debtor is unable or unwilling to pay three or six (in the case of mortgage loans assessed by European banks) consecutive monthly instalments; while

❏ other banks have tightened the definition mentioned above by considering as "material" by imposing either:

    ❏ three or six (in the case of mortgage loans assessed by European banks) months' equivalent additive instalments of the loan, including both principal and interest amount overdue, that was supposed to be paid; or

    ❏ the level after which the "road" to default, according to any of its definitions, is irreversible for a certain confidence level.

All approximations assume that the single measure of PD is estimated by averaging a number of annual estimations of PD realised during different past years. The averaging should be extended to a sufficient number of years in order to cover a full economic cycle. Nonetheless, the estimation of PD should contain a forward-looking element in order to protect the credit institution from anticipated future loses arising from credit risk.

The definition of default may vary depending on the different characteristics of the category of credit. All credits granted by a credit institution can be attributed to two main categories:

❏ scheduled instalments; and
❏ revolving credit.

The definitions of default that can be used for the former category are the following.

❏ Standard three months past due. If the DL_{annual}, in Equation (52), is replaced by $\sum_{i=1}^{n} d_i$, where d_i is either 0 if the loan is "active" or 1 if the loan is "in default", the probability of default is found as follows:

$$PD_{annual} = \left[\left(\frac{\sum_{i=1}^{n} d_i}{TL} \right) \times 100 \, \middle| \, d_i = 1, \, \forall \left(\frac{TPDAI_i}{CAI_i} \times \frac{12}{AIF_i} \right) > 3 \right] \quad (53)$$

where $TPDAI_i$ is the total past due amount of instalments for the loan i, CAI_i is the contractual amount of instalments that had to be paid since the first past due amount had appeared, AIF_i is the annual instalments frequency.

❑ Standard six months past due. Similarly, Equation (53) is transformed for default definition that is linked to six months past due as follows:

$$PD_{annual} = \left[\left(\frac{\sum_{i=1}^{n} d_i}{TL} \right) \times 100 \;\middle|\; d_i = 1, \; \forall \left(\frac{TPDAI_i}{CAI_i} \times \frac{12}{AIF_i} \right) > 6 \right] \quad (54)$$

❑ Default definition encompassing interest overdue in the standard three-months definition. Here Equation (53) is slightly transformed, in order to encompass the term ODI_i, which stands for any overdue interest on the past due instalments for asset i, as follows:

$$PD_{annual} = \left[\left(\frac{\sum_{i=1}^{n} d_i}{TL} \right) \times 100 \;\middle|\; d_i = 1, \; \forall \left(\frac{TPDAI_i + ODI_i}{CAI_i} \times \frac{12}{AIF_i} \right) > 3 \right] \quad (55)$$

According to this definition of default and, consequently, probability of default, the default appears before it would appear under the standard definition.

❑ Default definition encompasses interest overdue in the standard six-months definition. Similarly, Equation (54) becomes:

$$PD_{annual} = \left[\left(\frac{\sum_{i=1}^{n} d_i}{TL} \right) \times 100 \;\middle|\; d_i = 1, \; \forall \left(\frac{TPDAI_i + ODI_i}{CAI_i} \times \frac{12}{AIF_i} \right) > 6 \right] \quad (56)$$

❑ Default definition encompassing interest overdue and the static materiality notion in the standard three-months definition. The static materiality notion can be related to either:

❑ materiality in relation to the amount of the instalment; or
❑ materiality in relation to the remaining outstanding amount of the loan.

The materiality notion can be based on historical observation of the behaviour of similar loans. It can be easily derived, from either an econometric model or a neural network, for a certain confidence level that if the past due amount of instalments exceeds a benchmark level then the default is irreversible. This is expressed in mathematical terms by imposing a *materiality haircut* (MH_i) that takes values from 0.5 to 1 as follows:

$$PD_{annual} = \left[\left(\frac{\sum_{i=1}^{n} d_i}{TL} \right) \times 100 \middle| d_i = 1, \forall \left(\frac{TPDAI_i + ODI_i}{CAI_i \times MH_i} \times \frac{12}{AIF_i} \right) > 6 \right] \quad (57)$$

❑ Default definition encompassing interest overdue and dynamic materiality notion in the standard three-months definition. This definition is very similar to the latter version of the estimation of PD but it differs in the estimation of MH_i that should be estimated continuously and individually in order to reflect the changing behaviour of a loan and the specific nature of a loan, respectively.

The definitions of default that can be used for the latter category are the following:

❑ standard three months past due;
❑ standard six months past due;
❑ default definition encompassing static materiality notion in the standard three-months definition;
❑ default definition encompassing static materiality notion in the standard six-months definition; and
❑ default definition based on the structural behavioural change of the payments; in order for this definition to be efficient it should contain the volume of the past credit and the number of past transactions – in this case, default heavily relies on the performance of present payments in relation to the performance of past payments made by the same obligor on the same credit.

In contrast to the definitions given for loans with prespecified instalments, revolving credits are characterised by the absence or limited existence of scheduled payments. For this reason, the definition of default should be based on the definitions given for loans with prespecified instalments and should also focus on the fuzzy nature of these products.

Qualitative criteria

It is obvious that, in many cases, the above-mentioned definitions do not effectively describe the credit standing of the debtor. This is why the Basel Committee introduced the unlikeliness-to-pay clause in order to capture events according to which unlikeliness to pay is observed before the six-months period. "Unlikeliness to pay" is a qualitative criterion that refers to cases where the debtor, albeit that it did not exceed the threshold of six months, is observed to be unlikely to pay its obligations to the bank.

Bearing in mind the quantitative (the period after which the loan is considered as defaulted) and the qualitative ("unlikeliness to pay") parts of the definition of default, its definition is yet unclear. The former part of the definition is still the "materiality" of the instalments. The modern view on "materiality" is the aspect that concentrates on the behaviour of the same loan or similar loans when the debtor was unable to pay a certain amount of loan instalments.

In other words and going backwards, the risk manager should proceed to the following tasks:

❏ separate all loans that were defaulted according to the first or second definition of default; and
❏ establish the aforementioned level as the "materiality" that the risk manager is pursuing.

Although the estimation of PD for mortgages retains some characteristics that to some extent have been examined, the estimation of the PD for consumer loans, credit cards and other types of credit lines exhibits a higher level of difficulty. This is generated by the nature of those products. Credit lines are loans that give debtors the right, but not the obligation, to pay as often as they like provided that they pay, frequently, a certain minimum amount.

According to Basel II, the default is defined as the inability or insufficiency of the debtor to pay a material portion of their loan for three months (or 90 days) as it has been scheduled (although US and Canada have deviated from that definition by imposing a six-month delay of payments). However, the schedule may not account for payments within three-month periods. The challenge for the risk manager is to invent an efficient, but not subjective, methodological, but not strict, quantitative approximation for a PD estimation based on the past behaviour of the loan under examination or the behaviour of other similar loans.

Case Study I

Suppose that a loan assumes monthly instalments, to be paid on the last day of each month, equal to €200 and its past behaviour in relation to the past year is examined on 31 August every year. The loan was paid on the scheduled dates from 31 August 2004, until 31 December 2004. However, on 31 January, the instalment was not paid in full, as shown in Table 1.

Given that the overdue interest is 12%, the behaviour of the obligor is assessed according to approximations described above. According to the approximation that the default is observed by adding up only monthly instalments, no default was observed during the last year. The total amount of the delayed instalments equals €1,170, while each monthly instalment equals €200. Thus, the inability of the debtor is translated into €1,170/€200 = 5.85 months' delay of payments. This definition does not lead to labelling the loan as defaulted. On the other hand, if overdue interest is taken into account the situation is slightly different. After

Table 1 Comparison between two approximations of materiality

	January	February	March	May	June	July
Scheduled instalments (principal and interest)	€200	€200	€200	€200	€200	€200
Realised instalments (principal and interest)	€30	–	–	–	–	–
Scheduled and realised instalments' difference	€170	€200	€200	€200	€200	€200
Overdue interest on 31 August	€10.2	€10	€8	€6	€4	€2
Months delayed	6	5	4	3	2	1

accounting for overdue interest, the total amount of the delayed instalments equals €1,170 + €40.2 = €1,210.2. The latter definition leads to characterising the loan as defaulted because the inability of the debtor is translated into €1,210.2/€200 = 6.05 months' delay in payments.

In the first case the loan is not accounted for as defaulted and is not measured in the probability of default, while in the latter case the loan is accounted for as a defaulted loan. Thus, it is obvious that marginal differences in the definition of default may lead to different levels of probability of default.

Case Study II

The approximation for estimating PD can be illustrated by the following example concerning fixed monthly repayment instalments. Suppose that a credit institution faces the following facts during the last three years:

❏ on 31 August 2002, the portfolio consisted of 8,500 loans, from which 40 were defaulted during the next year;
❏ on 31 August 2003, the portfolio consisted of 9,000 loans, from which 50 were defaulted during the next year; and
❏ on 31 August 2004, the portfolio consisted of 10,000 loans, from which 70 were defaulted during the next year.

Probability of default for every year is estimated by applying Equation (52). Thus, the PD for the first composition of loan portfolio is:

$$PD_{2003} = \frac{DL_{2003}}{TL_{2002}} \times 100 = 0.47\%$$

The PD for the second composition of the portfolio is estimated by, first, subtracting the already defaulted loans from the total number of loans. The remaining number of outstanding, "healthy", loans is 9,000 – 40 = 8,960 loans, given that none of the defaulted loans during the last period have not returned into "healthy" ones. In that case, only loans that have remained defaulted should be subtracted from the total portfolio. As a result, the PD is given by:

$$PD_{2004} = \frac{DL_{2004}}{TL_{2003}} \times 100 = 0.56\%$$

Accordingly, the PD for the next year is calculated as:

$$PD_{2005} = \frac{DL_{2005}}{TL_{2004}} \times 100 = 0.71\%$$

In this case, all loans defaulted during previous years that remained in the same situation during 2005 are subtracted from the loan portfolio.

Finally, if the three-year period from 2003 to 2005 is conceived as a full economic cycle period, the PD, applied in the forthcoming calculations for the estimation of credit risk, is the average value of the above-mentioned separate annual PDs. Hence, the PD is given by:

$$PD_{AVG} = \frac{PD_{2005} + PD_{2004} + PD_{2003}}{3} = 0.58\%$$

Loss given default

Loss given default is the loss conditional to the appearance of a default. After a default realisation, credit institutions that have granted a credit to an obligor are trying to recover the outstanding amount at the default event. If a credit institution fully recovers the outstanding amount (exposure at default), the resulting loss would be zero. However, the procedure usually takes many years and many elements should be taken into account.

❏ The long-term procedure, by itself, implies that all cashflows are shifted at an unknown future date. In this case, the same payment received at a future date is worth less than if it were received according to the original schedule. A discount factor that is based on a relative interest rate should form the basis for the calculation of the recovered amount.

❏ The procedure for collecting the outstanding amount assumes some administrative costs. These costs are in addition to the exposure at default. They may vary from operational costs, such as collection phone calls to legal costs, such as those of suing the obligor and the costs of lawyers. Although administrative costs may add to the exposure at default, at a future time they should be discounted as well in order to express them in present terms.

If the EAD is expressed in absolute terms, that is, in its nominal value at the time of default, the recovery rate (RR) is expressed, in percentage terms, as follows:

$$RR = \frac{\sum_{i=1}^{T} \left[\frac{(\omega_i + \psi_i - \varphi_i)}{(1+r_i)^i} \right]}{EAD} \times 100 \tag{58}$$

where ω_i is the variable attributed to the recovered part of the asset paid in cash by the obligor at time interval i, ψ_i is the variable attributed to the recovered part of the potential collateral, related to the asset, at time interval i, φ_i is the variable attributed to all administrative costs realised at time interval i, r_i is the zero-coupon interest rate assigned to time interval i.

Since it is extremely difficult to assign costs or receivables to a specific time point, credit institutions should be permitted to assign them to time intervals. The cash inflows and cash outflows are assumed to be realised at the end of the time interval. These time intervals may be as long as one year or much shorter. The shorter the time interval, the higher the accuracy of recovery rate.

The recovery rate is related to the LGD by the following relationship:

$$LGD = 1 - RR \tag{59}$$

The LGD parameter relies heavily on the nature of the asset. If the asset is not backed by a collateral asset, the LGD will be high; if the asset *is* backed by a collateral asset, the LGD will be lower. In any case the LGD is very difficult to estimate internally and universally because of the following:

❑ the legal regime for collections before or after the obligor declares themselves bankrupt may differ from country to country;
❑ the legal regime for collections before or after the obligor declares themselves bankrupt may differ from time to time throughout the collection period;
❑ the priority of payments in relation to other payments the obligor is past due;
❑ the continuous change in zero-coupon rates that are directly applied in Equation (58); and
❑ the uncertainty of the duration of payments in cash made by the obligor.

CREDIT RATING SYSTEMS AND VALIDATION

Modelling credit risk is usually the first step for building a rating system. A rating system consists of several credit rating grades that rank the creditworthiness of the obligors. In other words, the credit ratings are summary indicators of the relative risk on a credit exposure. There are different types of credit rating systems according to the rating dimensions, the rating assignment techniques and the historical data used to produce the ratings. But, regardless of the type of rating system, it should be well validated in order to give confidence in the rating system's suitability for the specific credit institution and in order that it depicts the pragmatic creditworthiness of the obligors. Therefore, validation is the internal assessment of the credit institutions' rating system and it involves (or, at least, it should involve) regular reviews of the rating system's quality and suitability on the basis of ongoing operations.

Credit rating systems

A rating system, in its most widely known form, might be either expressed as letters (public agency ratings are usually expressed in such a way) or as whole numbers, for instance from 1 to 10 or from 1 to 8 (bank internal ratings tend to be expressed in such a way). The larger the number of grades, the better, because it means better discrimination of credit risk and, at the same time, avoids granularity. Regardless of the form in which the rating system is expressed, meaningful credit ratings share two characteristics:

❏ they group credits to discriminate among possible outcomes; and
❏ they rank the perceived levels of credit risk.

The process for building quantitative models, as a first step in order to come up with a credit rating system should follow certain steps that were discussed in the section "Credit risk assessment models" above.

Rating systems' categories
One- and two-dimensional rating systems
There are two ratings dimensions:

❏ obligor ratings; and
❏ loss severity ratings.

If the rating system classifies risk depending on obligor characteristics, then it is assumed to be one-dimensional. If it considers characteristics of the transaction (facility), then it is two-dimensional. Obligor and loss severity ratings must be calibrated to values of the PD and the LGD, respectively. So, credit institutions may assign obligor ratings, which will be associated with a PD. Also, they can either assign a loss severity rating, which will be associated with LGD values, or directly assign LGD values to each transaction (facility).

Point-in-time and through-the-cycle
For point-in-time rating systems, obligors are assigned certain ratings, according to the relevant information at the time of the rating, so the obligors' default frequency concerns a particular year. Point-in-time ratings change from year to year as borrowers' circumstances change, including changes according to the economic conditions.

In through-the-cycle rating systems, the obligors' ratings take into consideration their attitude through all the phases of the cycle, as well as distressed circumstances that might influence the obligors' creditworthiness in the long term. In these systems common risks are supposed to have been included in the analysis of credit risk, while the monitoring of obligors' creditworthiness takes place whenever there are firm-specific risks. Like point-in-time ratings, through-the-cycle ratings will change from year to year due to changes in a borrower's conditions. However, since through-the-cycle rating systems take into consideration downturns in the economy and consider stress circumstances, year-to-year ratings will be less influenced by changes in the economic environment. Ratings agencies are commonly believed to use through-the-cycle rating approaches.

Point-in-time rating systems are more appropriate when determining the economic capital, for identifying the credit behaviour of a loan or calculating provisions. On the other hand, for decision making on loans at a long notice or for investment purposes, through-the-cycle rating systems are more appropriate.

Qualitative and quantitative rating assignment techniques
Rating systems that are used by the credit institutions to assess credit risk are based on different rating methodologies. The different rating techniques are basically the judgemental, the quantitative or

a combination of the two. The best technique to be chosen in every case depends on the risk philosophy of each credit institution as well as on the availability of data.

The quantitative rating systems demonstrate the results of a mathematical rating model. The mathematical models of this type can be categorised into statistical and causal models (as described in the section "Credit risk assessment models" above). For more analysis, we can summarise credit risk classification techniques into two major categories:

❑ parametric; and
❑ non-parametric.

The first category involves statistical models such as discriminant analysis and the probit and logit models that were discussed earlier.

The category of non-parametric involves advanced techniques for the estimation and forecasting of credit risk and its components, such as the PD and LGD. These are models that are based on neural networks, expert systems, fuzzy logic systems and multi-criteria analysis. All of these methods are flexible (more flexible than the statistical ones because they can handle more variables) and they are free from statistical bias (because they are not based upon certain statistical hypotheses). However, these techniques are more complex than the parametric ones.

The qualitative rating systems demonstrate the results of an empirical rating model. Empirical models are based on the experts' judgement and experience (as discussed in the section "Credit risk assessment models" above).

Validation of credit rating systems

For the validation of the results of a rating system, we must first examine the performance of several qualitative criteria and then of quantitative criteria. The diagrammatic depiction of the two steps of validation, qualitative and quantitative, is described in Figure 8.

The two aspects of validation complement each other. It has to be stressed that, on its own, the quantitative validation of the results is not enough and it should not be the most critical point for the rejection of the rating procedure. This is mostly because statistical estimates are subject to random fluctuations and so there is a certain degree of freedom when interpreting the results. The greater

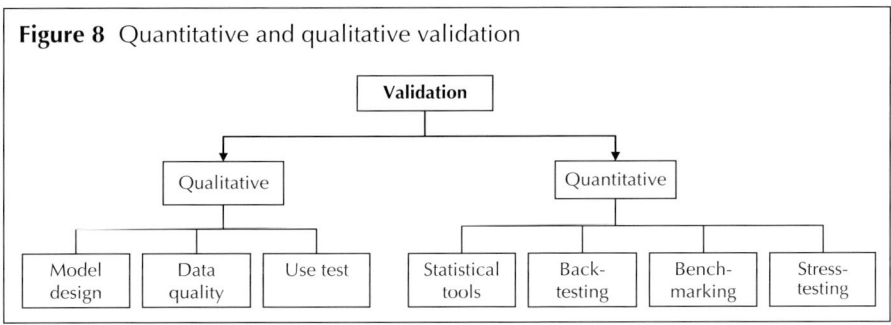

Figure 8 Quantitative and qualitative validation

emphasis should be put on qualitative validation. Insufficient qualitative validation could lead to the rejection of the appropriateness of the rating system for the credit institution, while, on the other hand, insufficient quantitative validation could be overcome by detecting the causes and trying to do the appropriate adjustments.

The above allegations are described in Figure 9.

Qualitative validation
The qualitative validation of the results is achieved with the examination of the model design and development, the quality of the data and the internal use of the rating system in the credit institution's credit approval process (use test).

Model design. The examination of the model design should be followed by an articulate documentation of the model development process. The documentation should be transparent, consistent and complete. To be more specific, credit institutions should at least document:

❑ the description of the rating method and the type of the model;
❑ the dataset used in the rating development;
❑ the way that the rating criteria had been chosen;
❑ validation during the model development;
❑ all model functions;
❑ the definitions of the obligor's default and of the loss; and
❑ the calibration of the model output to the default probabilities.

Data integrity. The data integrity and the systematic collection of data are basic assumptions for the development of a trustworthy

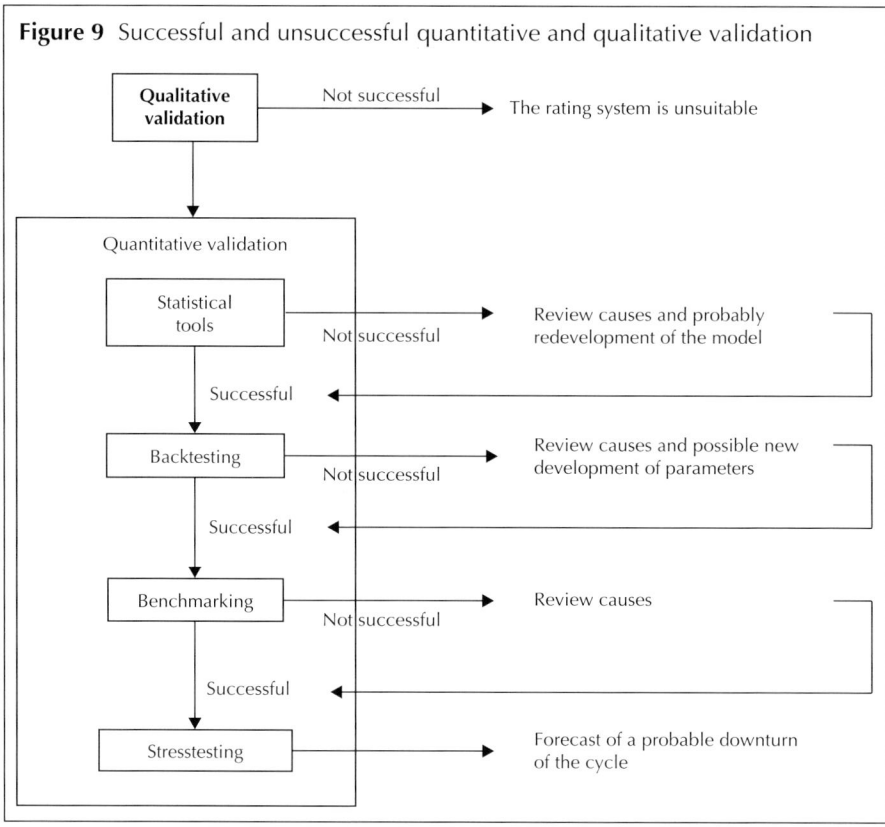

Figure 9 Successful and unsuccessful quantitative and qualitative validation

database with adequate historical data. This is essential for the development of a rating system that is built on adequate and reliable history and that leads to accurate estimates of the parameters of credit risk – such as the PD, LGD and EAD. The basic requirements for the data that credit institutions should collect are (data according to the EU Directive for the minimum capital requirements):

A. For the corporate portfolio –

❏ complete rating histories on obligors and guarantors;
❏ the dates the ratings were assigned;
❏ key data and methodology used to derive the rating;
❏ the identity of obligors and exposures that defaulted;
❏ the dates and circumstances of such defaults;
❏ data on the PDs associated with rating grades; and

❏ if credit institutions use their own estimates of LGDs and/or conversion factors, then they should collect complete histories of data on the facility ratings and LGD together with the conversion factor estimates associated with each rating scale, the dates the estimates were done, the methodology used to derive the facility ratings and LGD, convention factor estimates and data on the estimated and realised LGDs and conversion factors associated with each defaulted exposure.

B. For the retail portfolio –

❏ data used in the process of allocating exposures to grades or pools (groups with common characteristics);
❏ data on the estimated PDs, LGDs and conversion factors associated with grades or pools of exposures;
❏ the identity of obligors and exposures that defaulted; and
❏ for the defaulted exposures, data on the grades or pools to which the exposure was assigned over the year prior to default and the realised outcomes on LGD and conversion factor.

Use test. The *use test* is the internal use of the rating system in the credit institution's approval process. The consistent development of the rating system should be followed by the internal use of the system in the credit approval process, the setting of the limit strategy, the pricing of the loans and the credit institution's policy concerning credit risk in general.

Quantitative validation
The basic concern of the quantitative validation is the ability of the rating system to discriminate effectively between solvent and distressed obligors and to categorise them according to the appropriate classes. Furthermore, the stability of the produced results is a very important issue. The accuracy of the estimates is achieved through the following.

Backtesting. Backtesting is the comparison of the model estimates, with the realised historical data of the credit institution. At least once every year, credit institutions should check whether the realised default rates are between (or beyond) the estimated PD range of each rating class. The same test should be performed for the LGD parameter as well, in the case that is built on the credit institution's internal estimates. In the case that the estimated parameters differ significantly from the credit institution's history, the causes of the problem should be detected and the appropriate adjustments should be made to the model. These comparisons in the backtesting process should be clearly documented.

It is often alleged that backtesting the results of the *parameters* of credit risk (PD, LGD) is not the most accurate way of validating the results. This allegation concerns mostly low-default portfolios. In general, credit institutions, should perform statistical tests on backtesting and define (as a policy) the allowable deviations between realised and estimated data.

Benchmarking. Benchmarking is the comparison of the model estimates with the results of external assessment institutions and prestigious and broadly known models. The comparison of the results is achieved through quantitative analysis and is an extremely useful methodology when backtesting cannot give credible results. It is extremely beneficial for credit institutions to develop a system of benchmarking that will be interpreted in relation with the results from backtesting.

Statistical tools. There are a number of different statistical tools that test the ability of a rating system to discriminate between solvent obligors and the ones with a higher probability of default. Such statistical tools include the Gini coefficient, the Kolmogorov–Smirnov test, the CAP and ROC curves.

The different statistical tests all measure the integrity of a rating system, regarding the allocation of risk between the obligors. A common concern is whether there is a benchmark for the statistical tests that helps one to be confident about the model's discriminatory power and results. Unfortunately, no perfect value exists, since it depends on the type and the synthesis of the portfolio. The experts who analyse the results should never rely upon one statistical test, but should perform a number of different tests and explain the results accordingly and in relation to each other. Furthermore, the discriminatory power and the stability of a rating system (or model) seem to be satisfactory when the results produced by the system are satisfactory, according to the:

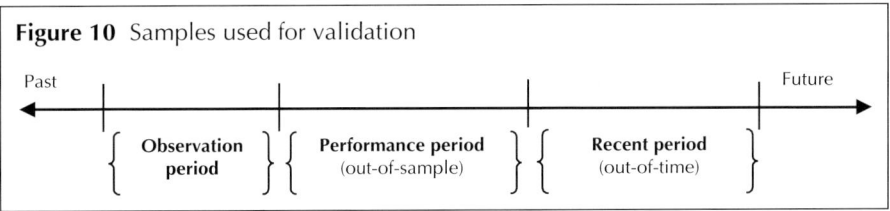

Figure 10 Samples used for validation

□ in-sample validation;
□ out-of-sample validation; and
□ out-of-time validation.

Two-thirds (approximately 66.66%) of the sample is the "training sample", which is the base for the in-sample validation and is used for model building, feature selection and model fitting. The remaining 33.33% of the development sample is the "test sample", which should be used for the out-of-sample validation. Furthermore, the importance of out-of-time validation should be stressed here. After the observation period (usually a year of data collection from accounts booked during this period) and the performance period (usually 12–18 months after the observation end date) of the accounts observed, analysts should test the behaviour of the model with a sample from a more recent period, which is usually the period after the performance date. Figure 10 refers to the samples for in-sample, out-of-sample and out-of-time validation.

Stability of a rating system. The stability of a rating system should be tested according to the recent profile of the obligors, which might have changed from the initial population, the maturity of the portfolio and the strategy adopted by the credit institution. One way to achieve this stability test is by monitoring the migration matrices' stability.

Moreover, the *stability* of a rating system should be tested according to the phases of the economic cycle. In most cases, historical data from a full economic cycle are not available. As a result, credit institutions cannot measure the consequences of a downturn of the economic cycle. For that reason, it is recommended when building models to take into consideration not only microeconomic variables but also macroeconomic variables, which could be stressed in order to give results in the case of an economic recession. The stress scenarios of the macroeconomic variables could concern the GDP growth, the unemployment rate, the Consumer Price Index, etc.

Stress testing. Stress-testing scenarios ensure the forward-looking ability of a model. Such scenarios take into consideration the phases of a downturn in the economic cycle. Credit institutions should put stress-testing exercises into their internal ongoing processes as a tool for the management of risks, and measure the influence on the capital adequacy. For that reason, they should form stress-testing scenarios that are representative of the credit institution's history and experience, and also take into consideration the economic conditions. After the stress-testing scenarios are formed, they should be repeated on an ongoing basis (at least once every year) and also be taken into consideration at the assessment of the capital adequacy and the overall strategy of the credit institution.

The assumptions made about risk scenarios raise the issue of subjectivity entering into the stress tests. Under the Basel II, banks have to hold capital amounting to at least 8% of their risk weighted assets in order to cover their credit risks. One crucial parameter in determining the risk weighting under Basel II is the probability of default by the individual borrower. One idea when conducting credit risk scenarios is to increase the probability of default by 30% and 60%. Such an increase will lead to a stress-expected loss. The two scenarios (30% and 60%) might roughly correspond to one or two downgrades in the rating scale of the loan portfolio.

Another idea is to use statistical methods to select the appropriate scenarios. The risk parameters are estimated from historical data, and then scenarios representing the extreme events of the probability distribution are selected.

Another scenario option is the model-based analysis. This is especially the case if macro stress tests are to be applied. This method is based on an econometric model, in which the interrelationships of the relevant risk factors can be shown.

SUMMARY

Credit institutions face a variety of risks, but credit risk is probably the most popular one. There are a number of models and techniques that aim to capture credit risk and provide reliable estimates of the credit risk parameters. Credit institutions are upgrading their risk management systems by increasing the level of sophistication of the techniques they use in their effort to predict the creditworthiness of obligors. The existing models as well as new promising ones appear to be powerful in the estimation and prediction of credit risk. The appropriate methodology for each credit institution is based on the type of the portfolio, the profile of obligors, the credit policy adopted by each institution, the business cycle, etc. That is why model developers should take into consideration the purpose of the model development, the phase of the economic cycle and the assumptions of each method, as well as its advantages and disadvantages, before deciding on the appropriate model.

In this last section the estimation of fundamental parameters were examined. Their estimation was carried out by either implying them from widely traded credit products or using the internal data of the credit institution. Credit default swaps are proposed as the optimal products, in order to imply the parameters of credit risk. However, it is complicated, or even impossible, to estimate simultaneously PD and LGD from credit default swaps. For this reason one of the two parameters should be estimated independently. On the other hand, fully parametric models, which use the internal information about the behaviour of loans incorporated in a portfolio, should carefully evaluate the available information and incorporate the prerequisites set by top management concerning the notion of risk. Thus, the section proposes various quantification techniques for the independent quantification of probability of default in order for every credit institution to find its own risk attitudes and articulate them into these techniques.

Credit ratings are summary indicators of the credit risk on a credit exposure. There are many forms of credit rating systems. Regardless of the form, meaningful credit ratings should group credits in order to discriminate between possible outcomes of the credit analysis and at the same time should rank the perceived levels of credit risk. The integrity of a credit rating system is checked through qualitative and quantitative validation. Great focus should be put on the qualitative validation process. In the case of unsuccessful results in the qualitative validation the system should be regarded as inappropriate for the assessment of credit risk. In the quantitative validation process it is important to transact all three validations: in-sample, out-of-sample and out-of-time. At the same time, stress tests allow for a forward-looking analysis and help to identify potential risks to the banking system as a whole. Therefore, continuous performance and development of stress tests are needed.

REFERENCES

Altman, E. I., 1968, "Financial Ratios, Discriminant Analysis and the Prediction of Corporate Bankruptcy", *Journal of Finance* **23**, pp 589–609.

Altman, E., R. Halderman, and P. Narayanan, 1977, "Zeta Analysis: A New Model to Identify Bankruptcy Risk of Corporations", *Journal of Banking and Finance*, June.

Basel Committee on Banking Supervision, 2005, "International Convergence of Capital Measurements and Capital Standards, A Revised Framework", November.

Beaver, W., 1966, "Financial Ratios as Predictors of Failure", *Journal of Accounting Research* **4**, pp 71–111.

Black, F. and M. Scholes, 1973, "The Pricing of Options and Corporate Liabilities", *Journal of Political Economy* **81**(3), pp 637–654.

Fisher, R. A., 1936, "The Use of Multiple Measurements in Taxonomic Problems", *Annals of Eugenics* **7**(2), pp 179–188.

Merton, R. C., 1974, "On the Pricing of Corporate Debt: The Risk Structure of Interest Rates", *Journal of Finance* **29**, pp 449–470, May.

Oesterreichisce Nationalbank, 2003, Guidelines on credit risk management, "Rating models and validation".

Welch, B. L., 1939, "Note on Discriminant Functions", *Biometrika*, **31**(1/2), pp 218–220.

OTHER READINGS

Johnson, R. A. and D. W. Winchern, 2002, *Applied Multivariate Statistical Analysis*, 5th edition (New Jersey: Prentice Hall).

Rencher, A. C., 2002, *Methods of Multivariate Analysis*, 2nd edition (New York: John Wiley & Sons).

Fisher, R. A., 1938, "The Statistical Utilization of Multiple Measurements", *Annals of Eugenics* **8**.

Agresti, A., 2002, *Categorical Data Analysis*, 2nd edition (New York: John Wiley & Sons).

John H., I. Nelken, and A. White, 2004, "Merton's Model, Credit Risk and Volatility Skews", working paper, version September.

Hull, J., 2005, *Options, Futures and Other Derivatives*, 6th edition (New York: McGraw-Hill).

Galati, R., 2003, *Risk Management and Capital Adequacy* (New Jersey: Prentice Hall).

3

Operational Risk

*There are two kinds of people, those who say what to do and those who do
what they say*

— Ioannis Akkizidis

INTRODUCTION

The Basel II Accord presents three pillars (see Figure 1 in Chapter 5)
for credit institutions to provide the foundation for a sound risk
management framework. Under Pillar I, institutions need to implement systems and procedures to develop robust risk measures to calculate the minimum regulatory capital requirements. Under Pillar II,
supervisors will check whether the information from Pillar I is cor-
rectly put together, and used not only for regulatory compliance but
also for internal risk management. Therefore, Pillar II concerns the
supervisory review process. Pillar III addresses market disclosure
requirements and ensures that risks are not only measured accurately, but are reported to the outside world accordingly.

According to Basel II, internationally active banks and banks with
significant operational risk exposures are expected to use an
approach that is appropriate for their risk profile and level of sophistication. This seems to indicate that, for example, the basic approaches
would be suitable only for smaller, local banks with low risk profiles
and the more advanced approaches are used for bigger more complex
and international credit institutions. Market analysts and rating agencies are likely to place increasing importance on a bank's response to
Basel II, so banks that aim for the more sophisticated approaches are

likely to be rewarded with strong market confidence and a maintained or improved credit rating. Obviously, banks that choose simpler approaches will not have to provide a lot of information about their risk situation to comply with Basel II's basic requirements.

This chapter consists of three sections. The next section, "Operational risk capital requirements", discusses, as its title suggests, the capital requirements of operational risk. It deals mainly with Pillar I of the Basel II Capital Accord. Notably, it deals with different types of operational risk measurement approaches: the basic indicator approach (BIA), the standardised approach (SA), the alternative standardised approach (ASA) and the advanced measurement approach (AMA). The AMA is then looked at much more deeply, as it is the most sophisticated and risk-sensitive approach. Different approaches for estimating minimum capital requirements for the advanced measurements are described. Furthermore, qualifying criteria for operational risk capital estimation are identified. Then the different aspects of the three approaches are presented to give guidance on how to select an appropriate approach.

In the second section, operational risk identification and loss profiling are discussed. This section also outlines the identification of operational key risk indicators (KRIs). Furthermore, it attempts to define the significance values for the operational risks and affected operations and the operational risk loss profile.

The last section examines operational value-at-risk (VAR) as a method for calculating minimum capital requirements. This section discusses the VAR method and its usefulness in the measurement of different types of risk and, more importantly, in integrated risk measurement, as will be discussed in Chapter 6. The section delves into estimating the minimum capital requirements for operational risks. Operational VAR using Monte Carlo dynamic simulation is estimated based on stochastic random values or random values that are driven by the operational risk losses. Eventually, top-down and bottom-up approaches are considered to aid in the estimation of operational VAR.

OPERATIONAL RISK CAPITAL REQUIREMENTS
Minimum capital requirements for operational risks
Pillar I (see Basel Committee on Banking Supervision, 2005) of the Basel II Capital Accord is used as a basis for estimating the

minimum capital requirements for different types of financial risk: market, credit and operational. According to this Pillar, credit institutions must apply measurement approaches defined by the Basel Committee as discussed extensively in the following subsections. Credit institutions will be permitted to use different approaches for different parts of their business lines. The Committee acknowledges the relationship that exists between the amount of capital held by the credit institution against its risks and the strength and the effectiveness of the bank's risk management and internal control processes.

However, increased capital should not be viewed as the only option for addressing increased operational risks confronting credit institutions. Other means of addressing risk, such as strengthening risk management, applying internal thresholds, strengthening the level of reserves and improving internal controls, must also be considered. Furthermore, capital should not be regarded as a substitute for addressing fundamentally inadequate control of risk management processes. Basel II requires banks to hold total capital equivalent to at least 8% of their risk weighted assets (see Basel Committee on Banking Supervision, 2005)

When estimating the minimum capital requirements for operational risks, there are two types of capital that can be calculated by credit institutions: *economic capital* and *regulatory capital*.

Economic capital is the amount of capital estimated by the bank's management that is required to cover and protect the shareholder from potential economic losses (unexpected negative changes in economic value). Economic capital differs from regulatory capital, which is the amount of capital that the regulators require from the institution to hold against risks. The primary purpose of economic capital is to support transaction level decision-making, whereas the main intention of regulatory capital is to assess banks' financial capability to manage their inherent risks. In contrast to regulatory capital, which is set by the regulators, economic capital is the internal estimate of capital required. It is the required capital for an unregulated institution, which may or may not be the same as the regulatory capital required for that same institution if the institution was to be regulated.

If a bank is constrained by regulatory capital, it should use the regulatory capital for its assessment; and, if the bank is constrained by economic capital, it should use the economic capital. Basel II is attempting to align economic and regulatory capital more closely to reduce the scope for regulatory arbitrage.

In order to calculate the minimum regulatory requirements for operational risk, Basel II has proposed different approaches. These approaches are discussed below.

Measurement approaches for operational risks
The framework issued by the committee presents three methods for calculating minimum capital charge for operational risk under Pillar I.

1. *The basic indicator approach*: According to this approach, the estimation of the capital charge should be derived as a fixed multiple α (alpha) of some aggregate activity measure such as gross income.
2. *The standardised approach*: Using this approach the institution has to break down its operations into eight business lines that are assigned to individual gross-activity measures (see Table 1). These measures are multiplied by a fixed factor β (beta) to calculate the regulatory capital requirement.
3. *The advanced measurement approach*: With AMA, credit institutions may use their own method for assessing their exposure to operational risk, as long as it is sufficiently comprehensive and systematic.

The basic indicator approach
Based on the BIA for estimating the capital reserve requirement, the credit institution uses two single factors:

❑ the average annual gross income (net interest income + net non-interest income); and
❑ a fixed multiplier percentage α.

Equation (1) defines the mathematical function of estimating the capital reserved under the BIA:

$$K_{BIA} = \sum_{i=1}^{n} (GI_i \times \alpha) \bigg/ n \qquad (1)$$

where, K_{BIA} is the capital charge under the BIA, GI_i is the annual gross income for the whole institution over the year i, n is the

Table 1 The eight banking business lines and β factors defined by Basel II

Business line	Indicator	β factors %
Corporate finance	Gross income	$\beta_1 = 18$
Trading and sales	Gross income	$\beta_2 = 18$
Retail banking	Gross income	$\beta_3 = 12$
Commercial banking	Gross income	$\beta_4 = 15$
Payment and settlement	Gross income	$\beta_5 = 18$
Agency services and custody	Gross income	$\beta_6 = 15$
Asset management	Gross income	$\beta_7 = 12$
Retail brokerage	Gross income	$\beta_8 = 12$

Source: Basel Committee on Banking Supervision (2001a)

number of the previous three years for which gross income was positive, α is a fixed percentage, set by the Committee (current level is set to 15%).

As a result, using the BIA, the estimation of the capital charge is 15% of the average gross income for the last three years. Note that, if negative gross income distorts a bank's Pillar I capital charge, supervisors will consider appropriate supervisory actions under Pillar II (see Basel Committee on Banking Supervision, 2004).

The standardised approach

The SA approach is a more complex variant of the BIA approach, and uses a combination of financial indicators and institutional business lines to determine the capital charge. Again, gross income is a proxy measure, but in this case it is broken down into eight standard business lines, each with a different β factor to calculate the minimum capital (see Table 1). For information on how the β factor is calculated, see Annex 3 of Basel Committee on Banking Supervision (2001a).

The Risk Management Group (RMG) of the Basel Committee has provided eight standardised business lines and several loss event types as a general means of classifying operational events. The eight business lines consist of corporate finance; trading and sales; retail banking; payment and settlement; agency services; commercial banking; asset management; and retail brokerage. The loss event types are internal fraud; external fraud; employment practices and workplace safety; clients, products, and business practices; damage to physical assets; business disruption and system failure; and execution, delivery, and process management. See Basel Committee on Banking Supervision (2004) for further explanation of the loss-event-type classification. The eight business lines are more explicitly described in Annex 2 of Basel (2001a). The principles for the business line mapping can be found in Annex 6 of Basel (2004).

The SA calls for an institution to break down its operations into the eight business lines. Each business line is assigned an exposure indicator (EI) or annual gross income (GI) in reference to the magnitude of the bank's operation in that particular area. Hence, each of the EIs is multiplied by a percentage, which reflects a business line's operational risk and thus determines the overall capital requirement of the institution. Within each business line, the capital charge is calculated by multiplying the indicator by a factor (denoted β) assigned to that business line. β is set by the Basel Committee. It should be noted that the indicator relates to the data reported for that business line, not the whole institution; that is, in retail banking, the indicator is the GI generated in the retail banking business line.

An insurance business line may also be included in both the SA and AMA, where insurance is included in a consolidated group for capital purposes. The choice of business lines and indicators is discussed further in Section VI of the Basel Committee on Banking Supervision, 2001a. If a bank is unable to allocate an activity to a particular business line, it is proposed that income relating to that activity should be subject to the highest β factor for which the bank reports activity (see Basel Committee on Banking Supervision, 2001b) or to the activity for the business line it supports. The primary incentive for the standardised approach is that most credit institutions are in the early stages of developing firm wide data on internal loss by business lines and risk types.

For the standardised approach, the capital reserve is thus calculated using:

❑ the annual GI per business line; and
❑ several indicators – related to sizes and volumes of credit institutions' activities in a business line.

The calculation for the capital reserve for standardised approach is shown in Equation (2).

$$K_{SDA} = \sum_{i=1}^{n} \max \left[\sum_{j=1}^{m} (GI_{ij} \times \beta_j), 0 \right] \bigg/ n \text{ or,} \qquad (2)$$

where, K_{SDA} is the total capital charge under the SA, n is the number of years over which the data has been collected, normally this is set to three, m is the number of the business lines, set as eight GI_{ij} is the annual GI for each of the eight business lines j in the given year i, β_j is a fixed percentage, set by the Basel Committee, related to the business line.

Note that the total capital charge K_{SDA} is calculated as the three-year average of the simple summation of the regulatory capital charges across each business line in each year.

The alternative standardised approach
Credit institutions, at the national supervisor's discretion, may be permitted to substitute an alternative measure known as the ASA in the case of retail and commercial banking. The operational risk capital charge and methodology for the ASA (see Basel Committee on Banking Supervision, 2004) is the same as that for the SA, except for two business lines: retail banking and commercial banking. The ASA for operational risk bases the operational risk charge for the retail and commercial banking business line on the portfolio volume rather than on the gross income, which is used in the SA. For these business lines, loans and advances, multiplied by a fixed factor m, replace GI. The β for retail and commercial banking are unchanged from the standardised approach. For example, the capital charge for retail banking would take the form of:

$$K_{RB} = \beta_3 \times m \times LA \qquad (3)$$

where, K_{RB} is the total capital charge under ASA for retail banking, β_3 is a fixed percentage as defined in Table 1, set by the Basel Committee, for retail banking business line, LA is the total outstanding retail loans and advances averaged over the past three years, m is the EI where its value is defined as 0.035 (3.5%).

A supervisor can choose to allow a bank to use the ASA provided the bank is able to satisfy its supervisor that this alternative approach provides an improved basis by, for example, avoiding double counting of risks (see Basel Committee on Banking Supervision, 2004). Note that, once a bank has been allowed to use the ASA, it will not be allowed to revert to using the SA without the permission of its supervisor.

The advanced measurement approach

To encourage credit institutions to improve their operational risk management frameworks, Basel II has set criteria for implementing more advanced approaches to operational risk. Of the three approaches available for calculating operational risk, the AMA is likely to have the most appeal because of its flexibility and the amount of self-discipline it provides. Moving beyond the averaging of the other methods, the bank is allowed to collect the history of its losses, analyse that history and use multiple risk factors to derive a probability of loss. The capital they will set aside under the AMA will be in accordance with certain guidelines proposed in Basel II. Under the AMA, if credit institutions invest in improved contingency procedures and systems, the investment will be reflected in a reduction in the need for operational risk capital, which is inevitably higher in the less advanced approaches. The use of these approaches will reduce the operational risk capital requirement, as is currently done for market risk capital requirements and is proposed for credit risk capital requirements. Apart from a reduction in capital requirements, more importantly, credit institutions will achieve operational risk management that will guarantee better business operational stability and performance. As a result, there is an incentive for credit institutions to use the more advanced and sophisticated approaches.

Under the AMA, credit institutions need to demonstrate that their operational risk measurement systems are closely integrated into the day-to-day management processes. For credit institutions to qualify for AMA, validation of the operational risk management system by external auditors or supervisory authorities is necessary to confirm that internal validation processes are suitable.

Estimating capital requirements for AMA. The Basel Committee does not impose exact capital required under the AMA. Credit institutions are expected to develop their own approach, provided they can calculate capital that takes into account both expected and unexpected losses. Capital charges will not be mandatory against unexpected operational losses in the AMA if credit institutions show that they have sufficiently budgeted for such losses.

The Basel Committee has affirmed that the level of capital required under the AMA will be lower than under the simpler approaches to encourage credit institutions to make the improvements in risk management and measurement needed to move towards the AMA (see Basel Committee on Banking Supervision, 2001b).

AMA measuring system. The AMA operational risk measurement system must take into account the following elements:

❑ internal data;
❑ external data;
❑ scenario analysis; and
❑ internal control and business environment factors (institutions will be expected to at least meet the minimum standards relating to internal controls as a criterion for AMA qualification).

The measurement system should also consider the following elements:

❑ risk mitigation (such as insurance); and
❑ correlations between types of risk.

There is a range of AMA internal approaches proposed by the committee which are broadly categorised as follows (see Basel Committee on Banking Supervision, 2001a).

❑ *Internal measurement approach (IMA)*: Using this approach the business lines are overlaid with a series of operational risk types. For each business line/risk type combination, regulators define an EI. Credit institutions then use internal data to define the probability of a loss event (PE) per unit of the EI, and the expected loss given such an event (LGE). Expected losses (EL) by business line and risk type are the product of these three components. Regulators supply a fixed multiplier γ (gamma) to translate these expected losses into a capital charge: the VAR figure for unexpected losses.

❑ *Loss distribution approach (LDA)*: This approach involves the esti-mation of two types of distribution based on internal loss data. One distribution is the loss associated with a single event and the other is the frequency of loss events over a given time horizon.

❑ *Scorecard approaches*: Using forward-looking risk indicators, built into "scorecards", to measure relative levels of risks. In order to qualify for the AMA, the approach must have a sound quantitative basis.

Internal measurement approaches. To calculate the capital charge under the IMAs, credit institutions will apply to the data they have collected a fixed percentage ("gamma factor") for each business line. The capital charge is calculated as the summation of expected loss multiplied by γ across particular business lines. This can be expressed as in Equation (4):

$$\text{Required capital} = \sum_i \sum_j [\gamma_{(i,j)} * EI_{(i,j)} * PE_{(i,j)} * LGE_{(i,j)}]$$
$$= \gamma_{(i,j)} * EL_{(i,j)} \tag{4}$$

where, i is the business line and j is the risk type. EI is the opera-tional risk exposure indicator, PE is the probability of a loss event, LGE is the losses given such events and EL is the expected loss.

Loss distribution approaches. Under LDAs, credit institutions esti-mate, for each business line and risk type combination, the likely distribution of operational risk losses over some time in the future. It models the distribution tails, as shown in Figure 1. The capital charge resulting from these calculations is based on a high per-centile of the loss distribution.

Such distribution estimates the likely distribution (fat tail) of the operational risk losses within a determined time horizon. According to Basel II, seven different types of distribution may be considered in reference to business lines and loss events. These includes internal and external fraud; workplace safety and employ-ment practices; products and business practices; execution, deliv-ery and process management; clients; damage to physical assets; systems failures and business distributions.

Note that most losses are distributed within the space of low impact and low probability as well as low impact and high

Figure 1 Loss distribution for operasionl risks under the LDA

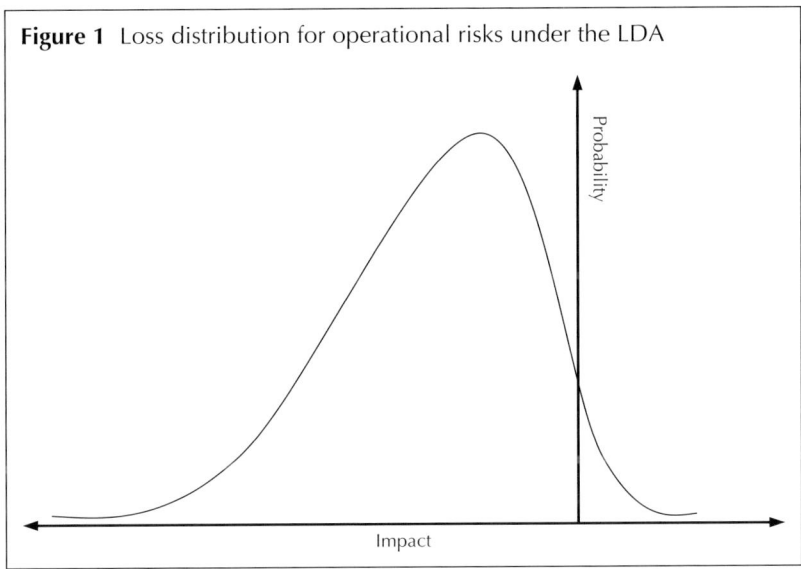

Impact

probability. On the other hand losses within the space of high impact and low probability are likely to happen at any time and are at the highest interest in risk management. However, losses within the space of high impact and high probability are out of the operational risk pragmatic state of existence simply because it is impossible for any credit institution to stand alone in the market in such case. Finally note that it could be a case of a low probability and positive impact. This is due to the fact that some causes of operational risk could result in consequences of gaining instead of loosing or even avoiding further losses.

This approach evaluates unexpected losses directly rather than via an assumption about the relationship between EL and unexpected loss. Thus, there is no need for the determination of a multiplication (γ) factor under this approach. More details about the LDA are given in Annex 6 of Basel Committee on Banking Supervision (2001a) and Georges *et al* (2000).

Scorecard approaches. In these approaches, credit institutions determine an initial level of operational risk capital at the institution or business-line level, and then modify these amounts over time on the basis of risk indicators. The scorecard approach combines loss data

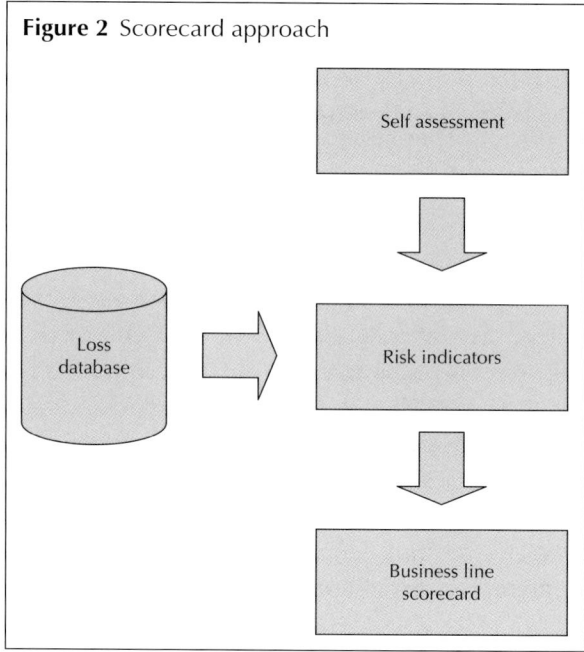

Figure 2 Scorecard approach

with risk indicators and performs a self-assessment of the potential operational risks on the business lines, as shown in Figure 2.

It does not imply that these are the final form of these approaches, or that these will necessarily be approved under the AMA. Furthermore, there is explicit recognition by the committee that alternative approaches may emerge. In developing their methodologies, institutions may combine different elements of the three approaches. A combination of such approaches would be most beneficial. Many leading credit institutions are contemplating the combination of the LDA and the scorecard approach to build methodologies with the bottom-up, objective benefits of LDA and the forward-looking responsiveness of scorecards.

AMA framework

There are some significant classifications that credit institutions must adopt within their AMA framework which include the following (see Federal Deposit Insurance Corporation, 2003).

❏ *The appropriate definition of operational risk*: The Basel II definition is the risk of loss resulting from inadequate or failed internal

Table 2 The seven loss event types

1. Internal fraud
2. External fraud
3. Employment practices and workplace safety
4. Clients, products and business practices
5. Damage to physical assets
6. Business disruption and system failures
7. Execution, delivery and process management

processes, people and systems, or from external events. An institution's definition of operational risk may include other operational risk elements as long as the supervisory definition is met.

❑ *Operational risk loss*: This is the financial impact linked with an operational event that is recorded in the institution's financial statements. Operational risk losses are differentiated by seven event types as listed in Table 2.

❑ *Operational risk exposure*: This is an approximation of the possible operational risk exposure (losses) that the institution faces at an accuracy of 99.99% confidence level over a one-year period. The institution then multiplies the exposure by 12.5% to obtain risk weighted assets for operational risk. This is added to the risk weighted assets for credit and market risk to arrive at the denominator of the regulatory capital ratio.

❑ *Business environment and internal control factor assessments*: These are the range of tools that provide a meaningful assessment of the level and trends in operational risk across the institution. Although the institution may use multiple tools in an AMA framework, they must all have the same objective of identifying key risks. A number of existing tools, such as audit scores and performance indicators, may be acceptable under this definition.

A significant point of any AMA framework is the treatment of correlations between operations, operational risks and operational risk events, which is a major point of discussion in this book.

Loss event data

For the basic and standardised approaches, it is not necessary to collect loss event data, whereas collecting loss data is at the core of the AMA. Institutions will be expected to develop an AMA framework that measures and quantifies operational risk for regulatory capital purposes. To do this, institutions will need a methodical way of collecting operational risk loss data, assessing the risks within the institution and implementing an analytical framework that translates the data and risk assessments into an operational risk exposure. Apart from information on the gross loss amount, the institution should collect information about the date of the event and any recoveries, and descriptive information about the causes and consequences of the loss event.

It is important for institutions that capture loss events, which are used differently for regulatory capital and management purposes, to show that:

❑ loss events are being captured reliably across the institution;
❑ the data systems are suitably advanced to allow for this differential handling of loss events; and
❑ credit, market and operational risk losses are being allocated in the correct manner for regulatory capital purposes.

The main loss event data to be collected should be from internal risk events inside the institution. If these data are not sufficient, they can be supplemented by external loss event data, provided that the used data are relevant to the institution. Furthermore, where internal and external data do not provide a suitably vigorous estimate of the institution's exposure to operational risk, scenario analysis could be used as a vital tool.

Internal operational risk loss event data
The institution must have several years of internal operational risk loss data obtained across all relevant business lines, events, product types and geographic locations. A widespread idea in the AMA is that the approaches are ingrained in loss data collection and verification in a way that is coherent with the frameworks set out in Basel (2001b).

Management must ensure that the operational risk loss event information acquired is uniform across the business lines. The institution must have a policy that identifies when an operational risk loss becomes a loss event and it must be added to the loss event database. Furthermore, the institution must set up appropriate operational risk data thresholds. Policies and procedures should be addressed to the relevant staffs to make certain that there is satisfactory understanding of operational risk and the data-capture requirements under the AMA operational risk management framework.

External operational risk loss event data. Where internal loss data are limited, external data may be practical in defining the institution's level of operational risk exposure as long as the data are relevant (ie, from similar institutions, with similar types of operational risks faced). Even where external loss data are not a definite input to an institution's dataset, such data give a way for the institution to comprehend industry experience and, in turn, present a way for assessing the adequacy of its internal data. The institution should have policies and procedures that provide for the use of external loss data in the operational risk framework.

Institutions may obtain external loss data in any reasonable manner. Some institutions use data gained through membership of industry groups and others use data obtained from vendor databases or public sources. In any case, management will need to assess the data source carefully to ensure that they feel comfortable that the information being reported is relevant and relatively accurate. Institutions using the AMA must use sophisticated data-management practices to produce realistic and dependable operational risk estimates for calculating their capital requirements. External data may also prove useful to undertake scenario analysis or benchmark the overall operational risk exposure results.

Scenario analysis. Scenario analysis is a methodical way of getting professional opinions from business managers and risk management experts to gain rational evaluation of the probability and impact of probable operational losses. Scenario analysis is especially useful when used to evaluate high-severity events. In some cases, an institution's internal loss history may not be enough to give a realistic estimate of exposure to future operational losses. In other cases, the use of adequate, scaled external data may itself be a form of scenario analysis. Because credit institutions are moving at such a fast technological rate, operational risks and losses that were pertinent in the past may not be applicable in the present or future. Therefore, basing the analysis only on past data may give a false warning of the present and future operational risks.

The institution must have policies and procedures that describe scenario analysis and identify its role in the operational risk framework. The policies should cover fundamentals of scenario analysis, such as the way in which the scenarios are created, the frequency with which they are updated and the extent and coverage of operational loss events they indicate.

Use of insurance under the AMA

Although there are different ways to transfer operational risk, this subsection's focal point will be on insurance coverage. Insurance is not the only form of operational risk transfer, but, since it is so extensively used and an accepted way of mitigating operational risk in Basel II, it deserves to be mentioned here. Insurance can be bought to transfer some of the institution's operational risk to an insurance company. Under the AMA, credit institutions will be allowed to recognise the risk-mitigating impact of insurance in the measures of operational risk used for regulatory minimum capital requirements. The recognition of insurance mitigation will be limited to 20% of the total operational risk capital charge calculated under the AMA (see Basel Committee on Banking Supervision, 2004).

For an institution that wishes to adjust its regulatory capital requirement as a result of the risk-mitigating impact of insurance, management must demonstrate that the insurance policy is sufficiently capital-like to provide the necessary protection.

Supervisory standards of the AMA

Institutions will be required to meet, and remain in compliance with, all supervisory standards to use an AMA framework. However, evaluating an institution's qualification with each of the individual supervisory standards will not be sufficient to determine that institution's overall readiness for the AMA. Instead, supervisors and institutions must also evaluate how well the various components of an institution's AMA framework complement and reinforce one another to achieve the overall objectives of an accurate measure and effective management of operational risk. In performing their evaluation, supervisors will exercise considerable supervisory judgement, in both evaluating the individual components and the overall operational risk framework. Furthermore, supervisors view the introduction of the AMA as an important tool to promote additional improvements in operational risk controls and management in credit institutions. Supervisors and institutions must also determine how well the various components of an institution's AMA framework complement and strengthen one another to achieve the overall objectives of an accurate measure and effective management of operational risk.

Qualifying criteria for operational risk capital estimation

An institution's ability to meet specific criteria will determine the framework adopted for its regulatory operational risk capital calculation. An initial set of guidelines for using the approaches is given below. More detailed guidelines are given in Section 560 of Basel Committee on Banking Supervision (2001c), Section 41 of Basel (2001a) and Annex 1 of Basel (2001b).

Qualifying criteria for basic indicator approach

The BIA is the easiest approach to adopt. The criteria to use it:

❑ are applicable to any bank regardless of complexity and sophistication; and

❑ need to comply with the "Sound Practices" guidance document (see Basel Committee on Banking Supervision, 2003).

Qualifying criteria for standardised approach

To qualify for the use of the SA, a bank must convince its supervisor that, at a minimum, it can:

❑ comply with the "Sound Practices" guidance document (see Basel, 2003);

❑ demonstrate the existence of an independent risk control and audit function;

❑ demonstrate effective use of risk reporting systems;

❑ demonstrate clear responsibilities assigned to operational risk management functions;

❑ demonstrate that its board of directors and senior management are actively involved in the oversight of the operational risk management framework;

❑ have an operational risk management system that is conceptually robust and is implemented with integrity; and

❏ have sufficient resources for using the approach in the major business lines as well as in the control and audit areas.

Supervisors will have the right to insist on a period of initial monitoring of a bank's SA before it is used for regulatory capital purposes.

Qualifying criteria for advanced measurement approach
More precise quantitative and qualitative entry standards are necessary before institutions are permitted to qualify for the AMA. An institution's capability of meeting explicit criteria will influence the framework to be adopted for its regulatory operational risk capital calculation. An initial set of guidelines for using the AMA is described below. More detailed guidelines are given in Section 560 of Basel (2001c) and in Section 41 of Basel (2001a).

A bank's AMA will be subjected to a phase of preliminary monitoring by its supervisor before it can be used for regulatory purposes. This time will allow the supervisor to conclude whether the approach is plausible and suitable. Four broad areas will be monitored and assessed:

1. operational risk corporate governance;
2. operational risk loss data;
3. risk quantification; and
4. risk mitigation.

Credit institutions must meet certain qualitative and quantitative standards before they are permitted to use an AMA for operational risk capital. In the AMA, business lines, risk types and exposure, indicators are set by the Committee, and institutions are able to use internal and external loss data. Supplementary to the standards required for credit institutions using the BIA, to comply with the guidance in Basel Committee on Banking Supervision (2003) – the criteria for the SA as described previously – institutions should also meet certain qualitative and quantitative qualifying criteria in order to use the AMA. A complete description of these criteria can be found in Basel (2004).

Selecting an approach
Selection of an appropriate measurement approach requires careful consideration to balance cost with accuracy, transparency and potential benefits.

The BIA might be suitable for credit institutions with a simple range of business activities and relatively small average annual GI. It is simple and transparent in computation, and it uses readily available data. It is universally applicable across credit institutions to arrive at a charge for operational risk. Its simplicity, however, comes at the price of only limited responsiveness to institution-specific needs and characteristics and implies the least risk sensitivity and risk management. Such approaches fail to distinguish between well-run and poorly run institutions. It is important to note that the estimation of the capital charges for the BIA will continue to be set by external supervisors.

The SA is still simple but better reflects varying risks across business lines. It can be used only if the credit institutions demonstrate effective management and control of operational risk.

Credit institutions that are willing to be involved with very limited or partly limited actions in risk management could choose to employ the basic or SA respectively. Furthermore, these two approaches are not out of line with the practice in many internal efforts to allocate economic, as opposed to regulatory, capital.

The Basel Committee expects internationally active credit institutions and financial institutions with significant operational risks to use a more sophisticated approach within the overall operational risk management framework. This is simply because large institutions have a high degree of complexity within their different business lines that are correlated to each other with different values and types of significance. Moreover, their involvement in supporting different financial products increases exponentially. Such credit institutions must also consider the correlation with other risk types such as market and credit risks for ensuring an integrated risk management framework as discussed in Chapter 6.

The AMA permits credit institutions to develop their own methodologies in measuring operational risks and the capital they need to set aside in accordance with certain guidelines proposed by Basel II. The Basel Committee believes that a standard definition of business lines, risk indicators and loss events should apply in the stages of developing the AMA. This approach is anticipated to be the most risk-sensitive and to relate to the experiences of each institution. Supervisors forecast that the AMA will provide the motivation to invest in new systems and practices that will reduce the likelihood of serious losses from operational risks.

Assuming satisfaction with the relevant criteria, the approach that an institution selects to calculate operational risk capital charges should be a free choice of management, appropriate to the nature and complexities of the business. Here are some key considerations:

❑ *Data availability*: Advanced models are data-intensive. The loss distribution approach, for instance, requires an institutional commitment for thorough, ongoing data collection.
❑ *Commitment to implement an operational risk framework*: All AMAs require a comprehensive risk management framework with assessments, indicators, data collection and reporting.
❑ *The framework and capital methodology*: These require technology, primarily to support the data collection efforts, the risk analytics and reporting. An appropriate budget needs to be planned.
❑ *Size of institution*: Larger institutions tend to be able to justify the investment. Smaller institutions may have fewer benefits for using advanced approaches.
❑ *Degree of sophistication in relation to economic capital*: Institutions committed to economic capital and its use as a management tool will be driven to accurate models that are risk-sensitive. Such institutions should consider the more advanced approaches.
❑ *Level of complexity*: Institutions with complex products, services and operations will have exposure to more extreme events (tail risks). Advanced models will provide more insight into the true risk profile for such institutions.

OPERATIONAL RISK IDENTIFICATION AND LOSS PROFILING
Operational risk identification
Operational risk identification, as part of the risk-assessment process, allows credit institutions to define and measure the risks within the business and better understand its operational risk loss profile. Thus, operational risk identification can be based on the operational KRIs as well as the actual losses resulting from the operational risks.

Identifying operational key risk indicators

Operational KRIs are becoming increasingly important tools in the framework of operational risk management systems. Credit institutions incorporating risk indicators into their measurement approach are using them to clearly identify, measure, and alert the business lines when higher degrees of operational risks prevails. Using KRIs is one of the most common ways of measuring the actual values of risk causes, the risk events and their risk consequences. KRIs are mathematical functions that include all those parameters that describe the operational variation of specific operations within specific business lines. Thus the main challenge for defining the KRIs is to quantify the qualified risks by identifying their mathematical functions.

In the identification of the quantifying parameters of the risk indicators, the following aspects should be considered:

❑ the actual degree of severity, size or intensity that describes the observed extent of the presence of operational risk;
❑ the frequency of risk existence and measuring their parameters – the frequency describes the number of times a risk of a given size occurs within a given time period or a given organisational unit; the frequency of existence and the time for measuring the risks need to be synchronised;
❑ the context-dependency relations, which may be different in different situations; and
❑ the possible correlation and its sign (positive or negative) with other indicators based on the common parameters among all indicators.

KRIs should be chosen so that they are measured on an ongoing basis such that data can easily be gathered. Moreover, the main guidance for identifying and designing KRI functions is to keep them simple by including a large number of parameters. It is preferable to have a larger number of simple and easy-to-understand KRIs than a smaller number of complex functions. Moreover, it is inefficient in the KRI design process to repeat the same measurement of operational risk using slightly different functions, but this could be a case if it is not clearly defined. Finally, an index for explaining all parameters could be very useful for future users and operational risk analysts.

Constructing the matrix of operational KRIs. Each credit institution is subject to its own types of operational risk. Thus, its risk appetite is different from those of other credit institutions. Therefore, KRIs that refer to its particular operational risk parameters must be defined in light of the operational risks in the particular institution. The matrix referring to the definition of the operational KRIs is a fundamental step in the design process of operational risk management systems.

Using the definition and measurement parameters **P** of the KRIs for the operational risks under study, a matrix **X** of the returns of risks *versus* operations is constructed as illustrated in Figure 3. The columns of this matrix refer to the KRIs, whereas the affected operations define the matrix's rows. Thus, there are two main ways of viewing the returns of operational risk factors:

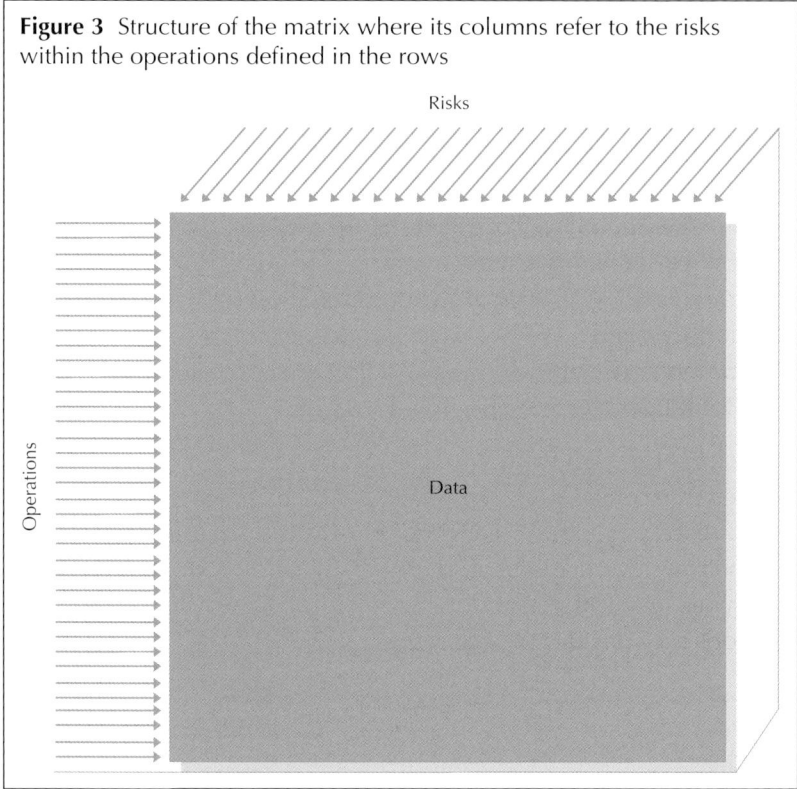

Figure 3 Structure of the matrix where its columns refer to the risks within the operations defined in the rows

❑ by looking at the columns of the matrix **X**, the values of each "operational risk" are defined within their affected common operations; and
❑ by looking at the rows of the matrix **X**, the values for each "affected operations" **X**^{T} are illustrated and defined based on the common indicators that measure their risk values.

Note that there is a third dimension in the matrix that refers to the time series, where the values denoting the risks are measured.

The matrix of the KRIs is used to identify the significance values for each operational risk and affected operations based on correlation analysis. Moreover, the actual values defined by the matrix together with their degree of significance are used in operational VAR analysis discussed in the next section.

Defining the significance values for the operational risks and affected operations

The significance values for operational risks are defined by estimating the correlations between the risks in regard to the operations that they affect, that is, considering the columns of the KRI matrix. In this analysis proposed by Akkizidis and Bouchereau (2006), the degree (in defined scale) and type (general, positive and negative) of relations and correlations are defined between:

❑ each operational risk with itself (self-volatility);
❑ each operational risk with another operational risk (co-volatility);
❑ each operational risk with all other operational risks (inter-volatility); and
❑ each operational risk with a set (or "beta") operational risk (internal or external), (β-volatility).

Moreover, the significance values for the affected operations are defined by considering the correlations between the operations with regard to common risks that affect them, that is, by considering the rows of the KRI matrix. Thus, the degrees (in defined scale) and types (general, positive and/or negative) of relations and correlations are considered between:

❑ each affected operation with internal or external business operational activities;
❑ each affected operation with another operation;

❑ each affected operation with all operations; and
❑ each affected operation with a particular set (or "beta") referring to internal or external business operational activities.

The degree and type of the above correlations are determined by considering all those uniform and non-uniform parameters that characterise the risks and the effect of the operations by the risks. The significance values SV_{cor} are defined according to the level of correlations *cor* described above. More detailed information on how to construct KRIs for operational risks and how to estimate the significance values SV_{cor} can be found in Akkizidis and Bouchereau (2006).

The definition of the operations, their risks and their corresponding significance values are the bases for estimating the operational VAR as explained in the next sections.

Defining the operational risk loss profile

Credit institutions need to record or define the losses that are or may result from operational risks. Operational VAR analysis can also be based on the distribution of the losses from the operational risks within the axes of the probability that may occur and the impact that may result. This distribution constructs the profile of the operational losses.

The methodology called *clustering operational risk profile* (ClORiP) proposed by Akkizidis and Bouchereau (2006) is used to identify the clusters within the loss distribution. In the space axes of the operational risk profiling, the coordinates defined by the probability, impact and significance degrees create position dots. These dots are grouped in terms of having similar probability, impact and significance values and are called *clusters*. These clusters are defined and analysed based on a methodology called *operational risk mountain surface* (see *ibid*). The result of such an analysis illustrates graphically the risk exposure as mountains on three-dimensional plots. The function that defines the mountain surface is constructed by combining the density of clusters and the significance value of its elements. Illustrations based on these approaches, figured in Chapter 4 refer to the extreme value theory.

There are three main steps for defining the mountains. The first is to form a two-dimensional grid on the probability and impact data space. Then, estimate the height of the mountain by calculating the distance between the intersections (nodes) of the defined grid and the coordinate values of the distributed loss data. Moreover, the actual value of the losses' probability and impact is also considered. Thus, the *height h* of the operational *risk loss mountain function* at a node $v \in V$ is as in Equation (5).

$$h(v) = \sum_{k=1}^{2} \left[\sum_{i=1}^{l} \exp\left(-\frac{\|v_k - L_{ki}\|^2}{2\sigma^2} \right) \cdot \frac{L_{ki}}{\mu_k^2} \right] \qquad (5)$$

where, l is the number of the distributed losses, L_{ki} is the ith loss data point in kth dimensional data space, σ is a constant value that determines the smoothness and height of the mountain function, μ_k is a constant value referring to the degree of strength for considering the actual value of the losses in the kth probability and impact data space.

The third step is to plot the mountain surface and define their contours at different heights.

The resulting mountains are used to identify the centres and boundaries of the clusters. The boundaries defined as contours are illustrated in different zones according to the significance level of the losses that are included within its boundary. The contours show the zone areas for the losses together with their significance degree. The different levels of the contour zones are defined by the mountains. Note that the contour areas do not always include losses with low values of probability and impact due to the parameter μ.

The degree of the operational loss exposure, within the probability and impact axis, and their cluster distribution, which defines their contour zones and significance level, are used for estimating the operational VAR based on actual operational loss returns. Operational VAR is the subject of the next section.

OPERATIONAL VALUE-AT-RISK

Credit institutions use VAR methods for quantifying the degree of their risk values. VAR has become a standard for measuring and assessing risk in credit institutions and is broadly defined as a quantile of the distribution of returns (or losses) of the portfolio in question. The measurement of VAR is used to forecast the maximum loss that could occur over a given time period with a specified confidence level. The revolution of VAR methodologies has been brought about by a convergence of several factors. These include the pressure from regulators to understand the risk value and define the capital requirements needed and the deregulation and globalisation of financial markets, which has led to the exposure of more sources of risk. Moreover, outsourcing, mergers and acquisitions as well as e-commerce, and technological innovations have made enterprise-wide risk management a not-so-distant reality.

VAR methods are well established and acceptable by financial institutions and their regulators. Approaches based on VAR methodologies are broadly used in all types of financial risk – market, credit and operational. Advantages of market and credit VAR were discussed in Chapters 1 and 2. These methods are based on the principles that are relatively easy to understand by all those who are associated with risk and performance management (from risk analysts and managers to the auditors and regulators). They are forward-looking risk measures that provide a single number that summarises the risk value and thus gives them the ability to decide whether they feel comfortable with this level of risk.

The main disadvantage of VAR methods is the natural dependence on historical trends, which may fail as a guide to specify future events. Moreover, VAR methods are difficult to implement, which results in significant cost, and even more difficult to evaluate in terms of their quality and accuracy. This is due to the high complexity of the models on which the VAR estimates are based. Note that these models are used in defining the exposure of the financial products to market and credit risks. They can also be used to define the exposure on the organisation's operational risks within different business lines.

Inaccurate and misstated models of the actual risk exposures, using VAR models, will result in the wrong estimation of the economic as well as regulatory capital reserves against financial risks. Moreover, defective information about the actual model could seriously affect the efficiency of the institution's risk management and may damage its reputation. Credit institutions must be able to demonstrate that they have conceptually sound risk measurement and management systems that have integrity. The transparency and accuracy of the VAR models, which provide an accurate account of risk exposure, is of key concern, as well as a challenge, to the risk analyst/managers and risk regulators and supervisors.

Operational VAR analysis

The estimation of the operational VAR is based on evaluating the operational risk performance. There are three main approaches that could be used as a basis for estimating operational VAR: the historical method, the variance–covariance method and the Monte Carlo simulation.

The historical method simply reorganises actual historical values – returns or performances – putting them in order from worst to best. It then assumes that history will repeat itself, from a risk perspective.

The variance–covariance method assumes that market and credit returns or operational performances are normally distributed. In other words, the method requires the estimation of only two factors – an expected (or average) return and a standard deviation – which allows for plotting a normal distribution curve. The idea behind the variance–covariance method is similar to that behind the historical method, except that it uses the normal distribution curve instead of actual data. The advantage of this curve is that it shows automatically where the worst percentage value, set according to the desired confidence, lies on the curve.

The Monte Carlo simulation involves developing a model for future returns and running multiple hypothetical trials through the model. "Monte Carlo simulation" refers to any method that randomly generates trials, but by itself does not tell us anything about the underlying methodology. This method has been established and used extensively in the analysis of VAR estimation. Table 3 illustrates the main advantages and disadvantages of the historical, Monte Carlo and variance–covariance methods.

In the Monte Carlo simulation, the estimation of the operational VAR is based on "shocking" the values of the operational risks or the affected operations. These "shocks" can be based on either a set of random values or on a set of values that are driven by the actual recorded resulting losses. Thus, the first challenge on such operational VAR analysis is to define what types of "shocks" need to be applied on the abovementioned operational values. More importantly, there is a need to define how to shock these values in terms of what types of data should be used and what are the value, strength, bandwidth and size of these data. The strength and bandwidth are defined by the significance and clustering analysis described earlier.

Table 3 Advantages and disadvantages of historic, Monte Carlo and variance–covariance methods

Methodology	Advantages	Disadvantages
Historic	Easy to calculate Based on actual results Non-parametric Can account for non-linearities	Requires large database Historical results may not be appropriate Lack of drill down ability
Monte Carlo	Can account for complex non-linear risk structure	Computationally complex Requires variance–covariance matrix Limited dependence on historical data
Variance– covariance	Easy to calculate Has drill down capability	Requires variance–covariance matrix Dependent on historical data Cannot account for non-linear behaviour

Top-down and bottom-up approaches in operational VAR

Operational VAR analysis is based on the disturbances of the actual operational performances that indicate operational risks. In this case, the allocation of the operational risks within the different business lines is used. Such operational risks are defined and measured by parametric KRIs referring to the actual disturbed operations. Moreover, operational VAR analysis can also be based on the resulting operational losses. In this case, the distribution of these losses is used. Thus, in designing the methodologies for operational VAR analysis the following aspects should be considered:

❑ the disturbances within the affected operations, initiated by operational risks, that are defined and measured by KRIs;
❑ the distribution of the operational risk losses within the probability and impact axes;
❑ the degree of significance for both operational risks; and
❑ the exposure of risk losses.

These aspects are used as the main elements in top-down and bottom-up approaches for estimating the operational VAR as presented in the following subsections.

Top-down versus bottom-up approach

In the estimation of operational VAR (mainly by applying Monte Carlo simulation method), there is a choice between a top-down and a bottom-up approach, or their integration.

Top-down approaches are applied when all *recorded* and *possible* measurements of losses, resulting from the operational risks, are considered. The term "recorded" refers to any past losses that occurred and have been measured in terms of financial impact, whereas the term "possible" indicates any expected and unexpected losses usually defined based on scenario analysis. On the other hand, with bottom-up approaches, the measurements of actual operational risks, within the different business lines, are considered. Operational KRIs, as discussed earlier, are mainly used to measure such risks; they are metrics that can provide insight into a financial institution's risk position.

The primary advantage of a top-down approach is its simplicity in terms of data considerations. Moreover, by using such approaches, there is a need for relatively low input data. Top-down approaches in operational risk measurement frameworks are appropriate for the determination of overall economic capital levels for financial institutions. However, it is a rather straightforward way to determine a capital amount for increasing operational losses that may not be covered by insurance. Additionally, top-down operational risk solutions are not appropriate for drilling down in operational procedures to discover the operational risks in any particularly exposed area of the institution. That is, neither do they exhibit fine-tuning capabilities for the implementation of operational risk controls, nor do they inform management about particular weakness in the operational processes. They combine the institution's processes and procedures and they are not satisfactory analytical tools. Furthermore, top-down solutions use information from the past or based on certain scenarios that are used to generate probabilities of the loss events' occurrences. Moreover, external industry data may also be used to calculate loss events. However, the above losses are difficult to incorporate and characterise dynamic changes in the operational risk environment that might affect the operational loss distribution over time.

In contrast to top-down operational risk solutions, more analytical and sophisticated approaches utilise bottom-up approaches. Bottom-up approaches engage the mapping of workflows in which failure may take place. In calculating operational risks, they make use of actual causal relationships between failures and resulting losses. They are sensitive to process improvement, but they are rather difficult to implement. The bottom-up approach analyses operational risks from the point of view of individual business activities in the business lines. That is, operational risks are modelled based on risk parameters that construct the KRIs used in the risk-quantification process. Thus, individual processes and procedures are mapped and monitored based on matrices that include the measurements of the risk indicators.

Bottom-up models are more transparent and forward looking, and allow drilling down into the business processes, systems and people's actions to explore their performances and risk status. Moreover, they allow shocking or stressing them to any required limits and thus evaluating their VAR up to its extreme points. Bottom-up solutions are useful to many parties within the institution, from the risk analysts and business-line managers to the internal risk auditors and regulators. Risk analysis that utilise bottom-up approaches are used to construct the framework of risk management, from the risk identification to risk policies and thus to correct weaknesses in the institution's operational elements.

The primary drawbacks of bottom-up models is their difficulty and their requirement for a vast number of data. Thorough data about precise measurements of the risk indicators and losses initiated by or resulting from risks in all areas of the institution must be collected in order to perform the analysis.

Furthermore, by going into too much detail about the institution's operational structures, bottom-up solutions should take into account the interdependencies/correlations across business lines and within operations. Overlooking correlations may lead to incorrect results. Conclusively, bottom-up models are more accurate and targeted to the measurement of specific operational risk problems, but at the same time are more complicated and difficult to characterise and analyse than top-down models.

Figure 4 compares the top-down and bottom-up approaches. Alternatively, to ensure a higher degree of confidence in terms of estimating the operational risk value, both types of approach may be employed. Thus, bottom-up approaches try to detect sources of operational risk using the process approach and identify

Figure 4 Top-down *versus* bottom-up approach

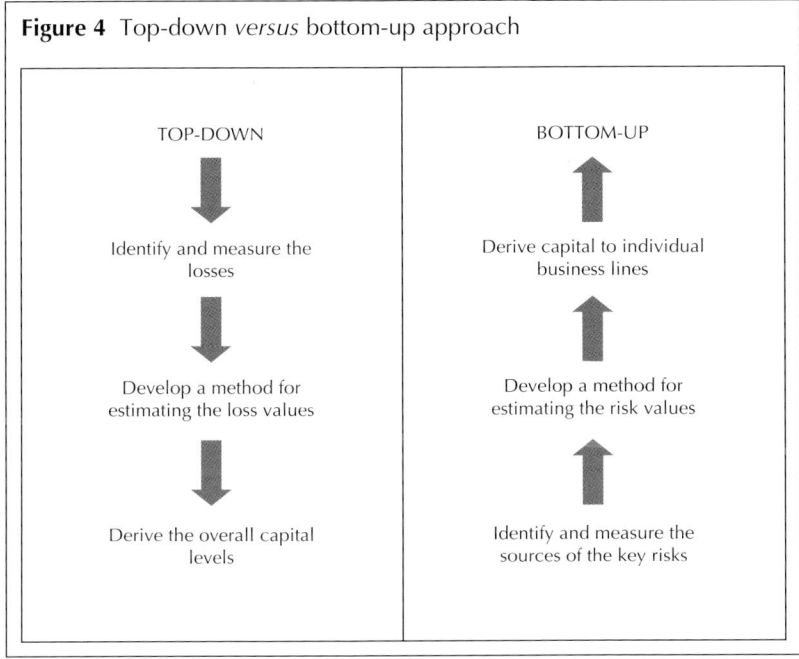

the exposure to operational risks at vital processes within the business lines. On the other hand, the top-down approaches make use of fundamental relationships between current or possible future failures with the resulting losses and their resulting consequences. The capital requirements defined for both approaches should converge to the same estimation values.

VAR analysis for operational risks

There are two different ways to estimate the operational VAR based on operational risks:

❑ by considering the actual operations that are at risk; and
❑ by considering the operational risks that affect the operations.

In both cases the affected operations are defined and measured by the risk indicators. Moreover, credit institutions need to record or define the losses that are or may result from operational risks. In the estimation of operational VAR analysis the significance value resulting from the distributions of both operational risks and affected operations plays an important role. Moreover, the distribution of the losses from the operational risks within the axes of the probability and the resulting impact can also be considered. This distribution constructs the profile of the operational losses. Thus, the analysis of both distributions referring to operational risks and the resulting losses are used to define the "force" magnitude and the amount of the random values used in the Monte Carlo simulation method as described in the next sections.

Operational VAR analysis by shocking the operational risks and affected operations (Monte Carlo dynamic simulation)
By using the Monte Carlo dynamic simulation method, the operational VAR can be estimated by shocking the decomposed matrix $\mathbf{A}^T$ of operational risks and affected operations, with vectors of:

❏ stochastic random values λ;
❏ random values η that are driven by the operational losses that have been recorded or defined using scenario analysis.

The decomposed matrix $\mathbf{A}^T$ is based on:

❏ *The correlation matrix $\mathbf{C}_R$ as defined by the matrix of returns $\mathbf{X}$ referring to operational risks*: Note that, as mentioned earlier, the returns of the operational risks are defined by the indicators that measure the risk occurrence within different operations. Thus, their values refer to the columns of the matrix $\mathbf{X}$.
❏ *The correlation matrix $\mathbf{C}_O$ as defined by the matrix of returns $\mathbf{X}^T$ referring to the actual affected operations within the different business lines.* Thus, the values that are used are the ones that are identified within the rows of the matrix $\mathbf{X}$, reflecting the affected operations.

Note that the time framework for the returns is defined by the matrix $\mathbf{X}$.

The random values λ are driven mainly by stochastic numbers that are usually normally distributed whereas the values η are driven by the distribution that construct the profile of the operational losses. Such values receive their rates accordingly:

❏ within the same bandwidth (value zones of "force" magnitude), whereas the amount of these values always has the same quantity of random numbers n; or
❏ from a bandwidth ("force" magnitude) of values that varies its boundaries – moreover, the quantity of the random numbers n,

also varies: both the boundaries and the quantity of the random numbers are set according to the degree of significance referring to risks and operations.

Thus, in the first case, there is a similar degree for both the defined bandwidth and the defined number of the values λ and η that are used to shock each affected operation and/or operational risk under study. In the second case, the λ values have different bandwidth and volume size. Their degree is defined according to the significance values as defined by:

$$\lambda_v = \exp(SV_{cor})^2 \cdot \lambda \qquad (6)$$

where, SV_{cor} is the significance value of the operational risks or their affected operations. Thus, for each affected operation or operational risk under study, the new sets of values λ_v are defined by multiplying the initial set of values λ with the exponential function of the significance levels referring to operational risks or affected operations. Note that the scale of the significance values is normalised into the scale of random values.

Moreover, in the second case and in reference to the random values η the magnitude of the "force" varies according to the degree of the exposure and distribution of the losses. This is based on the cluster blocks of losses defined by the clustering operational risk profile. The degree of force of random values η can thus be derived. As explained earlier, the boundaries of the cluster blocks of losses are defined as contours illustrated in different zones. These zones define the significance level of the losses that are included within their limits. Thus, the losses define the force η according to the level of exposure h_v as defined in Equation (5). The new set of shocking values η are defined as in:

$$\eta_v = \exp(h_v)^2 \cdot \eta \qquad (7)$$

Note that the scale of the exposure values h_v of the operational risk losses is normalised into the scale of random values.

Monte Carlo simulation in the estimation of the operational VAR

When selecting the methodology to be applied for the operational VAR, financial institutions should consider the availability of operational data referring to their risks. Among the three main methodologies that can be used to estimate operational VAR, the Monte Carlo simulation is the main one recommended to be implemented in the financial industry. This is due to the fact that the randomisations of the values used to shock the underlying operations gives more realistic results on potential values for the unexpected operational risks or losses that may occur. The main steps used in the Monte Carlo simulation method for market or credit risks can also be applied in the estimation of operational VAR. Thus, in the estimation of the operational VAR, by applying the Monte Carlo simulation the main steps to be pursued are:

❑ Synchronisation of original data series for the operational performances R_i.
❑ Calculate the corresponding operational risks and/or affected operations variance–covariance matrix from R_i.
❑ Calculate the correlation matrix used as input in the VAR estimation of the:
    ❑ C_R as defined by the matrix of returns X referring to operational risks, or
    ❑ C_O as defined by the matrix of returns referring to the actual affected operations within the different business lines.
❑ Create the matrix P_t $(1 \times n)$ for n operational assets for time t.
❑ The Correlation matrices C_R, C_O should be decomposed into A and A^T.
❑ Shock matrix A^T with the column vector $\lambda(n \times 1)$ or $\eta(n \times 1)$ random values, where n is the dimension of matrix A^T $(n \times n)$ and n is the number of operations. The column vector has one random number for each operation. Repeat the step for s times.
❑ Generate the matrix $Z = A^T\lambda(n \times 1)$, $Z = A^T\eta(n \times 1)$, for s times.
❑ Create for s times a matrix $eZ(n \times 1)$ of which every element of exponential number e is in the power of z $z_i(e^{Z_i})$.
❑ Create for s times the element matrix P_{t+1} (element) $=$ $P_t(1 \times n) \times eZ(n \times 1)$.
❑ The 99.99th percentile is the VAR for the next day (period), that is one-day (one-period) VAR.
❑ Repeat the steps for every $R_{i,t}$, where i stands for the operational performance, under risk type and t is the number of times the return of this operational performance type has appeared.
❑ Store and report the VAR for every t.

It is therefore concluded that well established approaches for the other types of risks (market and credit) can also be applicable in the estimation of operational VAR in operational risk analysis. Operational risk analysts should therefore identify where and how approaches from other types of risk can be implemented in their operational risk area. On the other hand market and credit analysts can easily participate in operational risk aspects, considering instead the underlying values of the operational performance and their risk.

SUMMARY

The Basel Committee on Banking Supervision has proposed a New Basel Capital Accord (Basel II), which seeks to implement a more risk-sensitive, flexible and sophisticated approach to financial risk management. The Accord consists of three mutually reinforcing pillars, which together contribute to increasing the safety and soundness of the financial system. This chapter has introduced the concept of the three pillars of the Accord, but has concentrated mainly on the concepts of Pillar I: estimating the minimum capital requirements. Although only Pillar I is discussed in the section "Operational risk capital requirements", it is to be noted that the Basel II Accord cannot be deemed fully realised if all three pillars are not in place.

The section "Operational risk capital requirements" focused mainly, as its title suggests, on estimating capital requirements for operational risk. The different types of approach proposed by Basel II for estimating minimum capital requirements for operational risk were highlighted, with particular emphasis on the more complex AMA approach. Criteria that need to be surpassed and factors in selecting a particular approach were also emphasised. Overall, the regulators' intention is to encourage each credit institution to implement an approach that indicates the institution's complexity, risk profile and market standing.

Operational risk identification and loss profiling were discussed in the next section, "Operational risk identification and loss profiling". The basis of this identification rests on defining and measuring operational KRIs. Furthermore, it attempted to define the significance values for the operational risks and affected operations and the operational risk loss profile by using a methodology called *clustering operational risk profile*, or ClORiP. This method identifies the clusters of the loss distribution.

The next section, "Operational value-at-risk", examined ways to estimate the minimum capital requirements for operational risks by using VAR analysis to determine the operational risk value. Furthermore, advantages and drawbacks of applying VAR approaches were highlighted. Ultimately, top-down and bottom-up approaches were considered in the estimation of operational VAR. The Monte Carlo dynamic simulation method is mainly used for estimating operational VAR. This method is based on stochastic random values or random values that are driven by the operational risk losses. The main steps for implementing the algorithm of Monte Carlo is also presented in this chapter.

REFERENCES

Akkizidis, I. S. and V. Bouchereau, 2006, *Guide to Optimal Operational Risk and Basel II* (New York: Auerbach Publications).

Basel Committee on Banking Supervision, 2001a, "Operational Risk: Supporting Document to the New Basel Capital Accord", Consultative Document, January.

Basel Committee on Banking Supervision, 2001b, "The Regulatory Treatment of Operational Risk", working paper, September.

Basel Committee on Banking Supervision, 2001c, "The New Basel Capital Accord: An explanatory note", January.

Basel Committee on Banking Supervision, 2003, "Sound Practices for the Management and Supervision of Operational Risk", February.

Basel Committee on Banking Supervision, 2004, "International Convergence of Capital Measurement and Capital Standards: A Revised Framework", June.

Basel Committee on Banking Supervision, 2005, "International Convergence of Capital Measurement and Capital Standards: A Revised Framework", November.

Federal Deposit Insurance Corporation, 2003, "Supervisory Guidance on Operational Risk: Advanced Measurement Approaches for Regulatory Capital", July.

Georges, P., *et al,* 2000, "The Loss Distribution Approach for Operational Risk", working paper, Credit Lyonnais.

4

Extreme Value Theory in Risk Management

You cannot get burnt if you are not exposed to the sun, just like you have no possibility of losing money if you make no investment

— Lampros Kalyvas

INTRODUCTION

Extreme event risk is present in all areas of risk management. Whether market, credit or operational risk – or their integration – is of interest, one of the challenges to the risk manager is to implement risk management models that allow for rare but destructive events, and allow the measurement of their consequences. In market risk, there is a concern about the day-to-day determination of the value-at-risk (VAR) for the losses incurred on a trading book due to adverse market movements. In credit or operational risk management, the goal might be the determination of the risk capital required as a protection against irregular losses from credit relegation and defaults or unpredicted operational problems.

In this chapter an overview of the role of extreme value theory (EVT) in risk management, as a method for modelling and measuring extreme risks, is discussed. EVT is separated into two approximations: the *block maxima* (BM) approach and the *peaks-over-threshold* (POT) approach, which in turn divide into several approaches. Both of these approximations are reviewed in this chapter and their advantages and disadvantages are duly presented. The expected shortfall (ES) extends beyond the level of conditional or unconditional EVT VAR in the sense that it quantifies the average value of the risk factor once the risk factor exceeds the threshold value, a coherent complement to the VAR. How the fundamental principles of EVT are applied to financial risk management it is the subject of the first section of this chapter.

Losses resulted from risks such as operational can be very heavy-tailed. Cluster analysis is introduced as a technique for partitioning the collected data into groups of natural clusters. It is combined with extreme value theory, to help determine and show graphically the actual size of the tail and the time periods referring to the observations, two elements that are of great importance in the concept of extreme value theory.

EXTREME VALUE THEORY
Extreme value theory approaches

The quantification of risks consists of random variables, recording expected and unexpected future conditions of the world into values representing profits and losses. These risks may be considered individually, or seen as part of a stochastic system where present risks depend, implicitly or explicitly, on previous quantifications of risk. The potential values of a risk follow a probability distribution that cannot be observed accurately, although past losses due to similar risks (if available) may provide partial information about the risk distribution.

In risk management analysis, unusual or rare events that cause a high value of losses are defined as extremes. Extreme events arise when a risk takes values from the tail of its distribution. In classical data analysis, the extreme events and losses are often labelled *outliers* and sometimes even ignored. In risk analysis, if the aim is only to seek estimations about everyday events, it might not matter if the extreme data are omitted. However, if the question is about events that do not happen very often, then EVT should be applied – especially as these are the situations where you have the most to lose or to win: stock market crash, war, natural disasters, etc.

EVT, as implemented by the Fisher–Tippett Theorem (see Fisher and Tippett, 1928), has only recently been methodically applied to explain extreme behaviours in the fields of insurance and finance (see McNeil, 1999; Kellezi and Gilli, 2000). In contrast to traditional approaches that presume a prespecified distribution, the EVT approach identifies extreme losses of low density and high magnitude based on the actual distribution of losses and covers a large set of distributions (for instance, normal, log-normal, χ^2, Student-t, F, gamma, exponential beta, uniform).

EVT is explicitly or implicitly based on the distribution of business losses within the probability and impact axes. Moreover, it may alternatively use the distribution of residuals (errors). In EVT, the probability is defined in terms of frequency, whereas the impact is described in terms of financial losses.

In recent years, EVT has been receiving more acceptance in the literature of time series and risk analysis. The main difference between EVT and all other methods of estimating VAR is that it uses only the values of the tail instead of using the whole dataset. EVT refers to two alternative approximations:

❏ block maxima approach; and
❏ peaks-over-threshold approach.

The first approximation refers to the collection of a set of local maxima from a huge dataset that has identically and independently distributed observations. The prerequisite for this action is to separate the whole dataset into small fractions of data before collecting the local maxima. Alternatively, the construction of the aforementioned set could refer to the selection of local minima. Whatever the nature of the extremes, EVT assists the analyst to estimate the maximum probabilistic value that may appear conditional to the use of extreme values. The second approach emphasises the full dataset without separating the sample into fractions of data. After identifying the reference pool of data, the tail is defined by finding a cut-off point.

Unconditional approaches
Block maxima
In order for the BM approach to be justified, it is essential to affirm that the data used are of high density (daily or higher) and independently and identically distributed according to an unknown distribution F. A visual representation of the block maxima approach is given in Figure 1.

In turn, the dataset is separated into m identical, consecutive and non-overlapping periods (blocks) with n length (the number of observations within the block). The length of the block should be

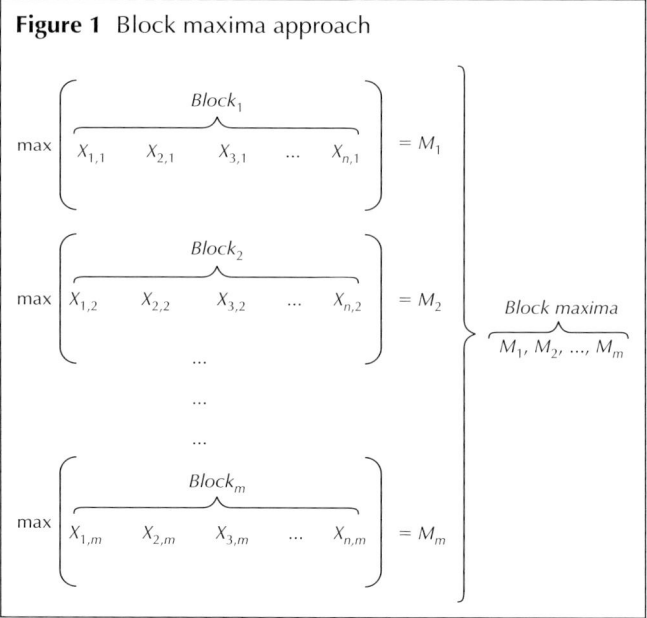

Figure 1 Block maxima approach

higher than the density of the observed data in order for the approach to be meaningful (say one week, two weeks, one month). The set of extremes is formulated from the maxima values M_j that are collected from each block j, a total number of m block maxima. When describing the BM method, X_{ij} ($i = 1\ldots n$, $j = 1\ldots m$) is the individual observation i of the block j and M_j ($j = 1\ldots m$) is the maximum (minimum) value of block j. The BM methodology is presented in Figure 1.

First theorem (Fisher and Tippett, Gnedenko)
Using the Central Limit Theorem, M_j's are normalised and they create the variable Y as follows:

$$Y_j = \frac{M_j - \mu}{\sigma} \tag{1}$$

where μ and σ represent the location and scale parameters of the distribution of M_j's, respectively, that keep up a correspondence with the mean and standard deviation of the normal distribution. When $n \to \infty$, the variable Y follows the distribution H, which in turn belongs to one of the following distributions of extremes:

Gumbel distribution (Type I)

$$\Lambda(y) = \exp(-\exp^{-y}) \quad y \in R \tag{2}$$

Fréchet distribution (Type II)

$$\Phi_\alpha(y) = \begin{cases} 0 & y \leq 0 \\ \exp(-y^{-\alpha}) & y > 0, \quad \alpha > 0 \end{cases} \tag{3}$$

Weibull distribution (Type III)

$$\Psi_\alpha(y) = \begin{cases} \exp(-(-y^{-\alpha})) & y \leq 0 \quad \alpha < 0 \\ 1 & y > 0 \end{cases} \tag{4}$$

Jenkinson (see Embrechts, 2000) suggested in 1955 a parameterisation of all above-mentioned three equations by representing them in a unique distribution H as:

$$H_\xi(y) = \begin{cases} \exp\left(-(1+\xi y)^{-\frac{1}{\xi}}\right) & \xi \neq 0 \\ \exp(-e^{-y}) & \xi = 0 \end{cases} \tag{5}$$

where y fulfils the condition $1 + \xi y > 0$.

The random variable Y, is said to belong to the *maximum domain of attraction* of an extreme value distribution ($Y \in MDA(H_\xi)$) if $\mu \in \mathbf{R}$ and $\sigma > 0$. This distribution is named *generalised extreme value distribution*. The ξ parameter is equal to zero (0) for Gumbel distribution, is equal to α^{-1} for the Fréchet distribution and is equal to $-\alpha^{-1}$ for the Weibull distribution.

If $\xi < 0$, the generalised extreme value distribution corresponds to Type II distribution, if $\xi > 0$, the distribution belongs to Type III distribution, while if $\xi = 0$ the distribution represents a Type I distribution. Alternatively, Gumbel distribution could be assumed as the distribution that bridges Fréchet and Weibull distributions because, as $\xi \to 0$, both distributions are gradually transformed into Gumbel distribution. The parameter ξ is the tail index and represents the fatness of tails and the decay index according to which the tails, for a given distribution, asymptotically approach zero. In other words, the fatter the tail, the lower the tail index and the lower the speed according to which the tail asymptotically approaches zero.

The above generalisation is very important in cases in which maximum-likelihood estimators are used for the determination of parameters, without knowing *ex ante* the BM distribution.

Nevertheless, the BM approach is not useful for time series that exhibit adequate extremes. Adequate extreme values are more likely to appear as the volume of data increases. In such circumstances the POT approach is considered to be the most appropriate.

Peaks-over-threshold
Semi-parametric approach. The POT approach consists of two subcategories, *semi-parametric* and *parametric* approaches:

❑ the semi-parametric models, which are constructed around the Hill estimator; and
❑ the parametric models, which are based on the generalised Pareto distribution.

Until recently, risk managers were supposing that risk factors tend to follow the normal distribution. However, the latest advances proved that, in some cases, risk factors follow entirely different distributions. These distributions generally exhibit fat tails, and thus belong to the domain of attraction of extreme value distributions. Bearing in mind the above assumption (fatness of tails), these distributions show a $\xi > 0$. According to this case it implies that:

$$1 - F(x) = x^{-a}L(x) \qquad (6)$$

where, $F(x)$ is the cumulative distribution function of the Fréchet distribution and $L(x)$ is a distribution that, except for the analysis of statistical properties of the distribution can be eliminated (see Embrechts, Kluppelberg and Mikosch, 1997, for more details). This elimination makes the tail estimation easier, without providing any significant estimation error.

The Hill estimator is considered the most appropriate procedure in order to provide the simplest solution for the above class of problem ($\xi > 0$ – Fréchet distributions). Hill estimators are calculated using the following steps:

1. the independency and identity of risk factors' distribution is assured;
2. the time series are sorted according to descending (ascending) order $(X_{(1)} \geq X_{(2)} \geq \cdots \geq X_{(n)})$;
3. the following equation is applied in order to estimate the tail index:

$$\xi^{H}_{n,m} = \frac{1}{m-1} \sum_{i=1}^{m-1} \ln X_{(i)} - \ln X_{(m)} \tag{7}$$

where, $\alpha = (1/\xi^{H}_{n,m})$, index m denotes the mth element that acts as the cut-off point between mean and extreme values; the determination of m is a rather vague subject, but in order to simplify its estimation two alternatives are proposed:

❏ m as a result of the square root of the number of observations; or
❏ m as a result of the 10th percentile of the number of observations.

The estimation of m index is a trapping point that may bias the estimation of the tail index. A very high cut-off point provides little information about the behaviour of extremes, while a very low cut-off point contains information that is relevant to the average values and, thus, mixes the information of extremes with the total information.

The following information is applied in order to estimate the quantile of extremes Q_q, or otherwise the VAR, that corresponds to a certain level of significance q, a number of total observations n and a number of tail observations m:

$$Q_q = X_{(m)} \left(\frac{m}{nq} \right)^{\frac{1}{a}} \tag{8}$$

Parametric approach. The cornerstone theorem that governs the distribution of peaks (Y) over a threshold (u) is the one expressed by Picklands, Balkema and de Hann (see Embrechts, 2000). This theorem is as follows:

$$F_u(y) = P\{X - u \le y \mid X > u\} \tag{9}$$

or

$$F_u(y) = \frac{F(y+u) - F(u)}{1 - F(u)} \tag{10}$$

where, $y > 0$.

The above equations represent the probability that X exceeds a certain threshold u by at most the quantity y, given that X exceeds the threshold u. For all common continuous distributions that are met in statistics (normal, log-normal, χ^2, student-t, γ, exponential, uniform, beta and so on) there is a function $\beta(u)$ for which it holds that:

$$\lim_{u \to x_0} \sup_{0 \le y < x_0 - u} \left| F_u(y) - G_{\xi, \beta(u)}(y) \right| = 0 \tag{11}$$

The model assumes that for the risk factor X_i that follows the distribution F and for some u's the distribution of peaks over threshold is a generalised Pareto distribution for some values of ξ and β. This distribution is shown by:

$$F_u(y) = G_{\xi, \beta}(y) \tag{12}$$

where

$$G_{\xi, \beta}(y) = \begin{cases} 1 - \left(1 + \xi \frac{y}{\beta}\right)^{-\frac{1}{\xi}} & \xi \ne 0 \\ 1 - e^{-\frac{y}{\beta}} & \xi = 0 \end{cases} \tag{13}$$

with the restrictions:

$$\beta > 0 \quad \text{and} \quad y \ge 0 \,\forall\, \xi \ge 0 \quad \text{and} \quad -\beta/\xi \ge y \ge 0 \,\forall\, \xi < 0$$

Combining the above equations:

$$F(y+u) = G_{\xi,\beta}(y)[1-F(u)] + F(u) \qquad (14)$$

or, given that $x = y + u$,

$$F(x) = G_{\xi,\beta}(y)[1-F(u)] + F(u) \qquad (15)$$

Once, the unknown parameters presented in the equations above have been estimated, the above distribution becomes as follows:

$$F(x) = 1 - \frac{N_u}{n}\left(1 + \hat{\xi}\frac{y}{\hat{\beta}}\right)^{-\frac{1}{\hat{\xi}}} \qquad (16)$$

where $y = x - u$, N_u represents the number of observations that exceeds the cut-off point u and n is the total number of observations. The VAR figure is defined as the inverse function of the aforementioned function, for a given probability $q \geq (n - N_u)/n$:

$$VAR_q = u + \frac{\hat{\beta}}{\hat{\xi}}\left\{\left[(1-q)\frac{n}{N_u}\right]^{-\hat{\xi}} - 1\right\} \qquad (17)$$

where VAR_q is the inverse distribution of distribution F. The parameters capped with "^" should be estimated.

Conditional approach
The parametric version of POT approach is applied to the pure, sorted, available data after small modifications. However, the data may evolve according to some kind of trend that appears in the markets where the risk factors are found. Moreover, a specific class of data may be influenced by other kinds of data or by the realisations of the same class of data that appears in previous periods. The latter case is more apparent when financial data have to be modelled.

Although the econometric modelling of financial data seems to be reasonable, it provides estimation only for the mean values of risk factors. By following this approximation, the estimation errors arising from the deviations between actual values of the risk factors and predicted values provided by an econometric model remain apparent. Thus, this source of risk has to be modelled.

The implementation of conditional POT EVT approach is a procedure of two consecutive steps:

1. estimation of a Garch-type regression for log returns using the maximum-likelihood estimation procedure; and
2. estimation of the EVT extreme quantile, depicted above, using the normalised residuals instead of using the pure sorted data.

The procedure assumes that residual data produced by the estimated regression should also be sorted in a descending (ascending) order. Then, the regression for estimation is represented by the following formula:

$$r_t = \alpha_0 + \alpha_1 r_{t-1} + \varepsilon_t \tag{18}$$

where, $\varepsilon_t = \sigma_t e_t$, α_0 and α_1 are parameters for estimation, r_{t-1} stands for the logarithmic change that happened the day before and e_t are the independently and identically distributed residuals with 0 for mean and 1 for standard deviation.

If it is supposed that the conditional volatility σ_t^2 of ε_t realisations follows a Garch(1,1) procedure, then this is generated as:

$$\sigma_t^2 = \beta_0 + \beta_1 \varepsilon_{t-1}^2 + \beta_2 \sigma_{t-1}^2 \tag{19}$$

where, $\beta_0, \beta_1, \beta_2 > 0$.

In order for the above procedure to be statistically stationary, the condition of $\beta_1 + \beta_2 < 1$ should be held.

The function of the maximum logarithmic likelihood, for standardised residuals e_t, is given by:

$$L(\theta) = -\frac{n}{2}\log(2\pi) - \frac{1}{2}\sum_{t=2}^{n}\log(\sigma_t) - \frac{1}{2}\sum_{t=2}^{n}\frac{(r_t - \alpha_0 - \alpha_1 r_{t-1})^2}{\sigma_t} \tag{20}$$

The estimation of the set of unknown parameters results in the formulation of the following equations for the prediction of the next day's mean and volatility values, that is:

$$\mu_{t+1} = \alpha_0 + \alpha_1 r_t \tag{21}$$

$$\sigma_{t+1}^2 = \beta_0 + \beta_1 \varepsilon_t^2 + \beta_2 \sigma_t^2 \tag{22}$$

where,

$$\varepsilon_t = r_t - \mu_t \tag{23}$$

The standardised residuals are calculated by standardising the difference between the standardised values resulting from the estimated parameters α_0, α_1, β_0, β_1 and β_2, and the standardised actual values, as follows:

$$\left(e_{t-n+1}, \ldots, e_t\right) = \left(\frac{r_{t-n+1} - \alpha_0 - \alpha_1 r_{t-n}}{\sigma_{t-n+1}}, \ldots, \frac{r_t - \alpha_0 - \alpha_1 r_{t-1}}{\sigma_t}\right) \tag{24}$$

The estimated standardised residuals should be sorted in a descending (ascending) order to create new time series that will act as inputs in the mechanism of VAR estimation according to the POT approach. The estimation of the VAR value for the standardised residuals $[VAR(e)_q]$ represents the quantile of the distribution that corresponds to the level of confidence q. Finally, the daily VAR value for pure risk factor changes (VAR_q) is given by:

$$VAR_q \equiv \mu_t + \sigma_{t+1} VAR(e)_q = \alpha_0 + \alpha_1 r_{t-1} + \sigma_{t+1} VAR(e)_q \tag{25}$$

Table 1 summarises the main functions used in estimating operational VAR for BM and POT approaches together with their advantages and disadvantages.

Expected shortfall
Expected shortfall (ES) consists of an additional informative risk measure. ES extends beyond the level of conditional or unconditional EVT VAR in the sense that it quantifies the average value of the risk factor once the risk factor exceeds the threshold value. Given than the EVT VAR is already a conservative measure compared with traditional risk measures (such as variance–covariance, historical simulation and Monte Carlo simulation), ES is by definition a natural indicator that measures the impact of highly unlikely events on the value of the banking portfolio. The ES is expressed as:

$$ES_q = E(X \mid X > VAR_q) \tag{26}$$

which can be rewritten as:

$$ES_q = VAR_q + E(X - VAR_q \mid X > VAR_q) \tag{27}$$

Table 1 Main functions used in estimation of VAR for block maxima and peaks-over-threshold approaches together with their advantages and disadvantages (see Akkizidis and Bouchereau, 2006)

Approach	Function	Advantages	Disadvantages
Block maxima (BM)	$VAR = H^{-1}\left(1 - \dfrac{1}{k}\right)$	Used when there are adequate available extreme losses for each block. The method is applicable for every source of risk	The maximum value in a block could be insignificant in the entire dataset
Peaks-over-threshold (POT)			
Semi-parametric	$VAR_q = X_{(m)}\left(\dfrac{m}{nq}\right)^{\xi}$	Used when there are large samples of observed data referring to the extreme losses. The method is easy to implement, as it is relatively simple for a naïve determination of the tail characteristics. There is a need for one parameter estimation	Do not use information concerning extreme value distribution
Parametric			
Conditional	$VAR_q = F(VaR(e)_q)$	Describes the behaviour of losses in a dynamic manner	Significantly, in a better position than the aforementioned approaches. However, assumes that distribution remains stable over time
		Is not based on any behavioural assumptions related to losses	
Unconditional	$VAR_q = u + \dfrac{\hat{\beta}}{\hat{\xi}}\left\{\left[(1-q)\dfrac{n}{N_u}\right]^{-\xi} - 1\right\}$	Used when there are available and reliable information data that describe the losses for credit institutions	Subject to model error risk
		It describes the unexpected extreme event that cannot be captured by the model applied	

where the second part of the right-hand side of the above equation represents the mean value of the distribution of VAR overshootings. In other words, it represents the mean value of reality-exceeded VAR estimations. The function of ES for the generalised Pareto distribution, with $\xi < 1$, takes the following form:

$$e(z) = E(X - z \mid X > z) = \frac{\beta + \xi z}{1 - \xi}, \quad \sigma + \xi z > 0 \tag{28}$$

The above equation provides the analyst with the expected shortfall of X in relation to the values of z. Having in mind the above equations, where $z = VAR_q - u$ and X represents the values that exceed the threshold u, the following equation is derived:

$$ES_q = VAR_q + \frac{\beta + \xi(VAR_q - u)}{1 - \xi} = \frac{VAR_q}{1 - \xi} + \frac{\beta - \xi u}{1 - \xi} \tag{29}$$

It is apparent that the value produced lies beyond the VAR estimation and consists of a better approximation of extreme events. This fact provides both credit institutions and supervisors with an additional tool for the establishment of stress testing scenarios.

CLUSTERING ANALYSIS IN EVT
Clustering analysis applied to extreme value theory
Extreme values are constructed by past extreme events and/or by using scenario analysis. In the distribution analysis extreme losses appear in the zone of the tail of low probability and high impact. Alternatively, EVT can be efficiently used for the estimation of VAR values. By applying EVT, two main issues must be considered carefully:

❏ the tail size; and
❏ the time dependency.

Both issues are discussed below.

The tail size
The choice for the tail size of the return distribution could significantly affect the estimation of VAR value. However, it is difficult to define how large the tail should be – that is, the size of tail index ξ. This is because the choice of tail size is based on the trade-off between variance and bias. If the tail's size increases and thus the

number of observations also increases, the threshold moves towards the centre of the chosen distribution. This results in an increased precision, whereas it reduces the variance of the tail estimator. Moreover, this increases its bias by placing relatively more weight on central observations that they do not deserve. On the other hand, if the size of the tail decreases, the number of the observations is reduced with the result of increasing the variance and decreasing the bias.

In reality, the data observations are distributed and grouped as inhomogeneous clusters. The boundary and size of these clusters are defined according to their significance levels based on the mountain methods as referenced and described in Chapters 3 and 6. The extreme values of the return observations are grouped as clusters with relatively long-boundary contour shapes. All these groups construct the tail of the extreme values. The degree of significance that defines the zone of the groups is the main characteristic that is used to define the size of the tail in terms of length and height, that is, defining how long and fat should the tail be.

Figure 2 illustrates a distribution of losses in probability and impact axes. Figure 3 illustrates the contours that define the zone of

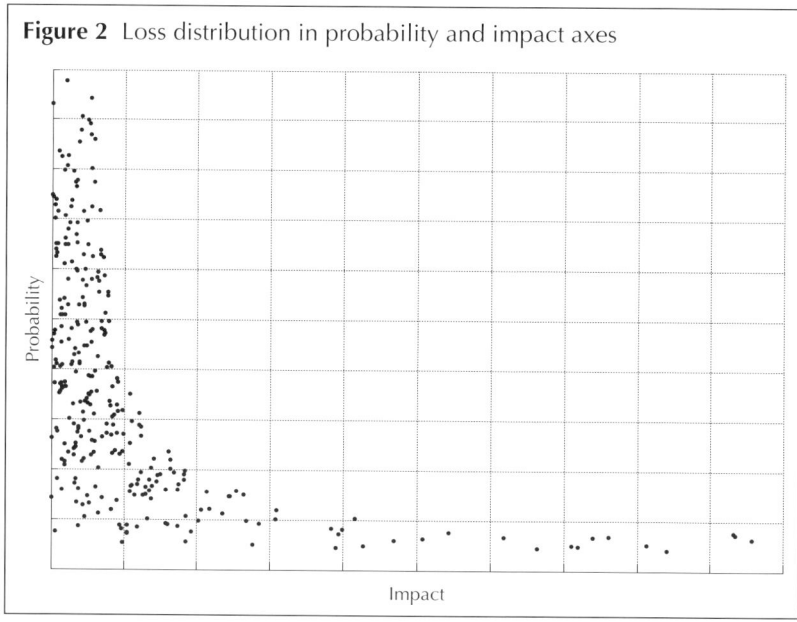

Figure 2 Loss distribution in probability and impact axes

Probability

Impact

Figure 3 The extreme values of the return values are grouped and defined as clusters. The length and size of the tails of these returns are defined by the contours within the axes of low probability and medium to high impact. The size of the blocks for the observed time period is defined by the clusters' weight referring to the frequency (probability) dimension

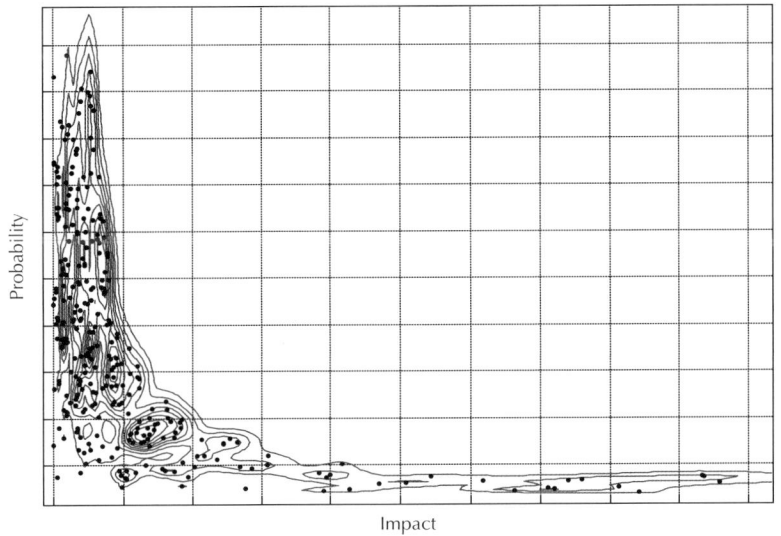

the tail in terms of its length and height characteristics. Each observation within the tail is a member of a group with a level of significance illustrated in the contour level graph of Figure 4. These levels are defined by the mountains illustrated in Figure 5. Figures 6 and 7 represent a different case, which also illustrates contours that define the zone of the tail in terms of its length and height characteristics.

Time dependency
The choice of the time periods (blocks) referring to the observations is the second element that needs careful consideration. The theory of the extreme value assumes that observations are identically and independently distributed over time. However, most financial and operational returns exhibit some form of *clustering*, with periods of alternating high and low volatility. The appearances of data clusters within the tail violate the above key assumption and force the

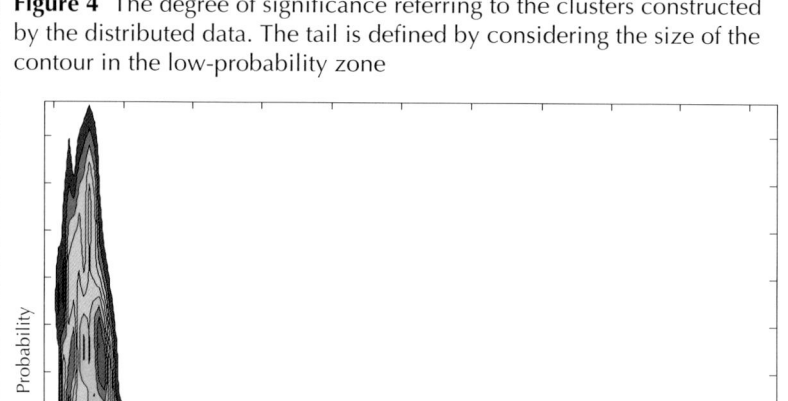

Figure 4 The degree of significance referring to the clusters constructed by the distributed data. The tail is defined by considering the size of the contour in the low-probability zone

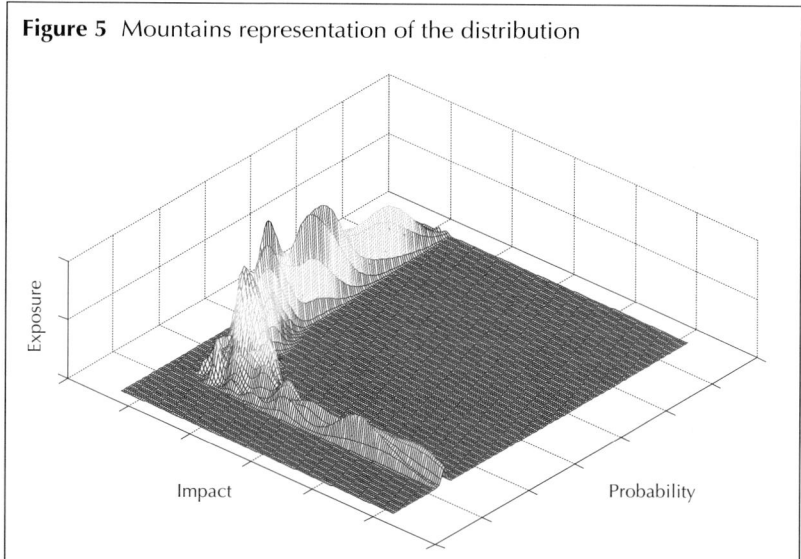

Figure 5 Mountains representation of the distribution

Figure 6 The extreme values of the return observations are grouped as clusters with relatively long-boundary contour shapes in the tail. The degree of significance is illustrated by the boundary zones of the groups and is used to define the size of the tail in terms of length and height. Moreover, it defines the time zone in the probability dimension

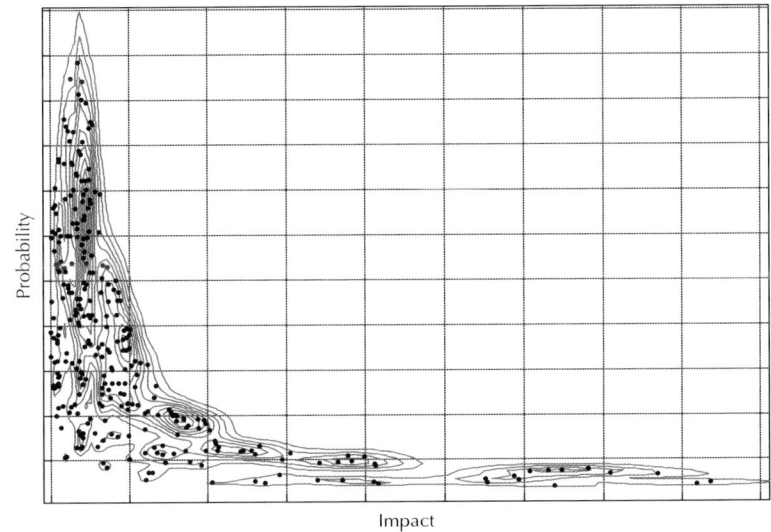

Figure 7 The contours of the groups defined by their degree of significance

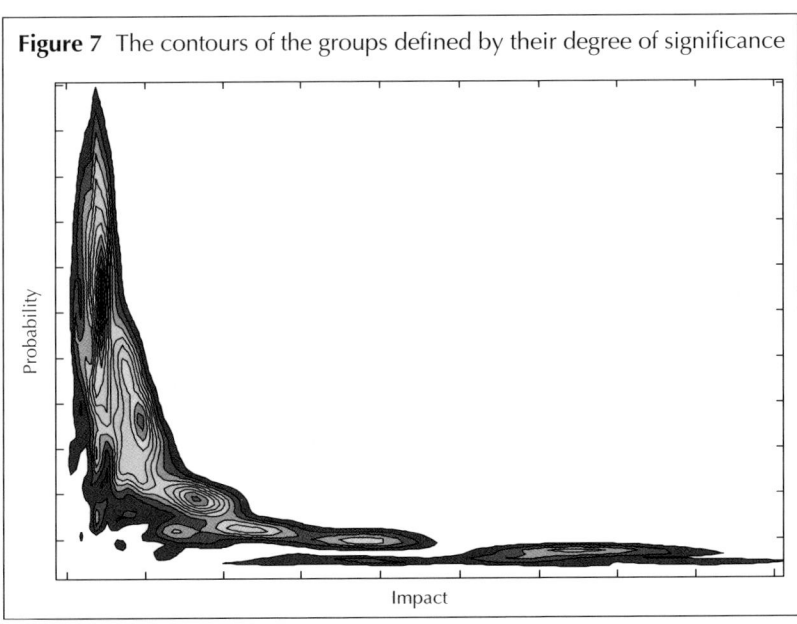

application of approaches based on clustering analysis. Based on this analysis in the distribution of the returns, the groups that are constructed define the blocks of the observed time period. Thus, in Figures 3 and 6, the size of the blocks is defined by the cluster weight, referring to their frequency (probability) axis. In case there is an overlap between the boundaries of the groups, the fusion between the time blocks is based on the significance degree (from high to low) of the clusters.

SUMMARY

The conventional approaches for estimating VAR do not always account for fat tails of the distribution of returns. On the other hand, they assume that the distribution of returns follow a unique distribution for the entire range of values. EVT acts complementarily and separates the distribution of the values around the mean and the distribution of returns that belongs to the tails. Thus, EVT attempts to find the optimal point beyond which all values belong to the tail. After finding the cut-off point that separates the body distribution from the tail distribution, the latter has to be modelled.

In order to model the tail distribution, two approaches have been discussed, namely, BM and POT. The latter approach is further differentiated into two sub-approaches: the semi-parametric approach, structured around the Hill estimator, and the parametric approach, which is applied by defining the exact parameters of the distribution of returns. The mathematical equations together with their advantages and disadvantages for these approaches were also discussed (see Table 1).

Apart from the use of EVT methods in estimating VAR measures, they are valuable in constructing stress-testing scenarios for all sources of risk. The measure that efficiently constructs the stress-testing scenarios is the ES. ES describes the expected loss once the VAR measure is exceeded and can potentially stand for an alternative, historically based stress-testing scenario for all sources of risk (market, credit and operational). An explanation on the use of ES was also given.

Clustering analysis was proposed to define the size of the tail as well as for the time dependency. Both are very critical issues in the analysis of the extreme values. The proposed approaches are based on how the observed values are distributed in common clusters.

Examples were illustrated to show visually the applicability of these approaches in the aspects of EVT.

REFERENCES

Akkizidis, I. S. and V. Bouchereau, 2006, *Guide to Optimal Operational Risk and Basel II* (New York: Auerbach Publications).

Embrechts, P. (ed), 2000, *Extremes and Integrated Risk Management* (London: Risk Books).

Embrechts, P., C. Kluppelberg, and T. Mikosch, 1997, "Modelling Extremal Events for Insurance and Finance", *Applications of Mathematics* **33**.

Fisher, R. A. and L. H. C. Tippett, 1928, "Limiting Forms of the Frequency Distribution of the Largest and Smallest Member of a Sample", *Proc Cambridge Phil Soc* **24**, pp 180–190.

Kellezi, E. and M. Gilli, 2000, "Extreme Value Theory for Tail-Related Risk Measures", Working Paper, Department of Econometrics and FAME, University of Geneva.

McNeil, A. J., 1999, *Internal Modelling and CAD II* (London: Risk Books), pp 93–113.

5

Characteristics, Strengths and Weaknesses of the Basel II Framework

In the middle of difficulty lies opportunity
– Albert Einstein

INTRODUCTION

The constitution of the Basel Committee and the resulting documents that follow this constitution were the first attempt by an international body to standardise and unify the world credit and financial system. For the first time, credit institutions have the impression and simultaneously the hope that they will compete on a level playing field. The rules and regulations were supposed to be unified across, at least, all countries that are represented in the Committee. However, the proposals of the Committee are not free of biases and inconsistencies. These disadvantages are scattered throughout the documents of Basel II and most of them are implied rather than explicitly shown. Because the advantages of the Basel Committee are explicitly stated by the Committee itself in the various documents published, this book concentrates on the disadvantages and proposes alternatives wherever they are applicable. For this reason, the weaknesses are distinguished according to the source of risk they belong to, namely market risk, credit risk and operational risk.

Moreover, this chapter focuses on the regulatory methodologies that have not previously been mentioned in the book and aims to explore the characteristics, strengths and weaknesses of the Basel II framework for market, credit and operational risk in order for them

to be efficiently introduced in the calculation of capital requirements on an aggregated basis in Chapter 6.

The New Basel Capital Accord (Basel II) versus Basel I

Handling credit risk as well as other risks, like market and operational risks, is an important but difficult task. These risks must not
lead to instabilities in the financial sector. For this reason special
supervisory rules, which go beyond the credit institutions' risk
provisioning, have been created. The Basel Committee on Banking
Supervision published the Capital Adequacy Accord in 1988 (it is
also known as the Basel Capital Accord or simply Basel I),[1] which
set the regulatory capital requirement framework. The New Basel
Capital Accord (Basel II) was proposed, as a revised version of the
initial Accord. So, Basel II is an "improvement" on the initial Basel
Accord.

The new proposal aims to make the capital requirements for
banks more strongly dependent than before on the economic risk
and to take into consideration, by the institutions' risk management, the recent developments in financial markets. Although the
Basel II Accord was initially directed only towards internationally
operating banks, it has now become the globally recognised capital
standard for banks and is applied in more than 100 countries. Also,
the relative directives at EU level have been substantially influenced by the Basel II Accord.

Basel I was strongly criticised for inflexibility, mostly because it
could not capture new financial instruments and methods of risk
management (credit derivatives, collaterals and guarantees, securitisation of assets and credit risk models, operational risks). However,
what is important for a bank is its risk and profit profile, which
is determined by management, as well as the bank's ability to
manage risks and sustain them over the long term. The Basel
Committee encourages further development of the banks' internal
risk management systems and the monitoring of these systems by the
responsible supervisory bodies.

The fundamental objective of the Committee's work to revise
the 1988 Accord (Basel I) has been to develop a framework that
would further strengthen the soundness and stability of the international banking system. The Committee believes that the revised
Framework (Basel II) will promote the implementation of stronger

risk management practices by the banking industry, and views this implementation as one of its major benefits.

The Basel II Capital Accord consists of three Pillars (see Basel Committee on Banking Supervision, 2005), aiming to protect in a better way the stability of the national and international banking system.

Pillar I: Minimum capital requirements
Pillar I defines what capital is and sets out the minimum regulatory capital requirements, letting banks develop their strategies so as to deal with credit, market and operational risk. It should be stressed while calculating the capital ratio under Pillar I that it must be no lower than 8% as shown in Equation (1):

$$\frac{Capital}{total\ risk-weighted\ assets\ for\ credit\ risk\ +\ (capital\ charges\ for\ market\ risk\ and\ operational\ risk) \times 12.5} \geq 8\%$$

(1)

While the minimum capital ratio of 8% has remained unchanged (from Basel I to Basel II), the operational risk has now been added to the existing two types of risk; credit and market risk.

Pillar II: Supervisory review process
Pillar II defines the structure of reporting to regulators that has to be adopted by banks. The supervisory review process of the framework is intended not only to ensure that credit institutions have adequate capital to support all the risks in their business, but also to encourage them to develop and use better risk management techniques in monitoring and managing their risks. Under this pillar, the supervisors will review the risk management frameworks of the credit institution.

Pillar III: Enhanced disclosure
The third pillar sets out the requirement for disclosure to markets, leading to greater transparency and accountability from bank managements. Diagrammatically, the three pillars are depicted in Figure 1.

Building appropriate risk management capabilities requires substantial investment in processes and technology. Basel II has now

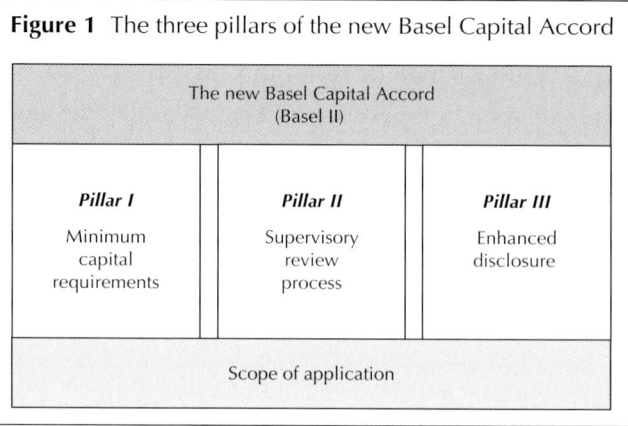

Figure 1 The three pillars of the new Basel Capital Accord

given an opportunity to have a framework that can be used for both compliance and risk management. Its main purpose is to encourage strong risk management practices and procedures. Since Basel I, many large international banks have been arguing that the Accord's "simplistic" method of capital charges has overstated their portfolio risks, requiring them to carry more capital than it is actually needed. Subject to their supervisor's permission, they will now have the opportunity to prove their point. Basel II puts the responsibility for the measurement and management of risks, and the better relating of them to capital, on the shoulders of the board of directors and top management. It is very important that they integrate this approach into their governance system and actively manage their institutions with this risk focus in mind.

Objectives of Basel II

Some main objectives of Basel II are:

❏ to encourage best-practice, sophisticated, analytically-driven risk management policies based on each credit institution's experience;
❏ to establish a more comprehensive approach for addressing the different types of risk;
❏ to promote safety and soundness in the financial system; the new framework should at least maintain the current overall level of capital in the system;

❑ to increase the effectiveness of operational risk quantification;
❑ to increase informative integration across the whole business to manage market, credit and operational risks;
❑ to increase the need to focus on loss data collection and ensure information data reliability and timeliness of measurements;
❑ to define more effective ways to track, calculate, monitor, analyse and report risk measures;
❑ to ensure appropriate documentation of risk management systems;
❑ to effectively integrate different risk types; and
❑ to promote a national supervisory and regulatory process to ensure the maintenance of adequate capital.

Further information on the objectives of Basel II can be found in Overview of the New Basel Capital Accord (see Basel Committee on Banking Supervision, 2001).

THE FRAMEWORK FOR MARKET RISK
The framework for market risk in Basel II
The regulatory framework proposed by the Basel Committee relies heavily on the realisation of failures to predict the reality (see Chapter 1). The number of failures realised over a year is assigned to a multiplication factor, given the condition that these failures are not more than 10 over the year. Consequently, the multiplication factor is multiplied by the 60-days average value-at-risk (VAR) value in order to produce the relevant capital requirements. Thus, the level of capital requirements relies on both:

❑ the multiplication factor; and
❑ the inter-temporal level of VAR measures.

In order for efficient models to be truly rewarded, the lower multiplication factor assigned to them should eliminate the effect of the higher VAR estimation in the calculation of capital requirements (see Kalyvas and Sfetsos, 2006). However, this is not the case in the calculation of capital requirements under the Basel II regulatory framework. This can be easily shown in the following case study.

Empirical comparison using the Basel regulatory framework
In this case study, a combined portfolio of two financial products, stocks as they are represented by the S&P 500 index and open

exchange rate position in US dollars (the US$/€ exchange rate), were examined. The data concern daily values from 2 January, 1997 to 14 March, 2004. In order to avoid asynchronous sampling, only dates that disseminate data for both products were considered.

The combined portfolio, that was supposed to stand for an imaginary portfolio, was formed using random positions, which change on a daily basis, since investment choices could be influenced by a number of factors not previously known (such as different hedging techniques and different investment strategies). The position of the exchange rate was selected from a range of US$0–1,000,000, whereas the number of stock pieces ranged from 0 to 2,000 contracts of the S&P 500 index. This was based on the assumption that positions in the aforementioned ranges follow uniform distribution and change every day. The above procedure was performed 1,000 times resulting in 1,000 different paths for the "trading portfolio" value composition. However, for the sake of simplicity, we analysed the path that resulted from the average portfolio composition for each day.

The stocks that form the portfolio were assumed to be those that composed the S&P 500 index, thus ignoring any specific risk. In order to ensure comparability between the examined methods, VAR was estimated on the same portfolio composition for all methods used.

Impact on the credit institution

In literature, there are two main approaches that evaluate the VAR estimates of any method: statistical, such as root mean square error (RMSE), mean error (ME), mean absolute error (MAE); and economic, such as the number of exceedances of predictions from real values and the success of a trading rule. However, the former are often biased and noisy estimators (see Christodoulakis and Satchell, 2004). Thus, in the present case study, the financial measures included in the Basel Committee Amendment were selected. This approach shows the most efficient model to be the one with the smallest number of overshootings using backtesting.

Using the previously described approach, the combined portfolios contain, on average, 965 contracts of stock index and US$495,364 in open exchange rate position. The highest (lowest) position of stocks was 1997 (0) contracts, whereas the respective position in exchange rates was US$999,766 (US$138).

Table 1 Capital requirements for VAR estimates

	EVT	CHS	HS	VC
Daily VAR	40,651	35,343	35,467	34,828
10-days VAR	128,550	111,764	112,157	110,136
Mean multiplier	3.00	3.17	3.15	3.23
Capital requirements	487,526	449,937	447,127	447,814

The specification that proved to be suitable for the application of the conditional methods (HS and EVT) was the AR(1) – GARCH(1,1) model. For the majority of the runs for consecutive moving windows, the model parameters were statistically significant, except for some estimates of the constant term that are (were) included in both equations, which do not significantly influence the VAR estimation.

The highest VAR estimate during the entire seven-year period was produced by the EVT with a value of €200,497, whereas the lowest one from the conditional HS was €829. The biggest percentage difference between the VAR estimates of the four models for the same day was found between EVT and VC, equal to 307% in favour of the first. The respective difference between the estimates of EVT to the other models was about 15% on average. The rest of the three models (VC, HS and CHS) exhibited, on average, similar estimates (see Table 1).

First, the conservatism exhibited by EVT, in terms of higher VAR estimates, seems to deter financial institutions from adopting it in the daily estimate of market risks. However, one has to thoroughly examine the effectiveness of the EVT approach to determine whether this conservatism is counterbalanced by lower multiplier values against other methods.

The utilised data for the daily "back-testing" to measure the effectiveness of each method spanned from 2 January, 1998 to 14 March, 2004. This is because under the Basel Committee at least 250 "effective" observations are required to evaluate a model. Under this prism, EVT produces the smallest number of overshootings (9) whereas the rest of the methods produce higher numbers (VC 22, HS 20 and CHS 21). The number of annual overshootings is shown in Figure 2. The larger the area below the black line, the higher the efficiency of the model used.

EVT appears to produce the smallest number of overshootings on backtesting when these are estimated using a moving window of the

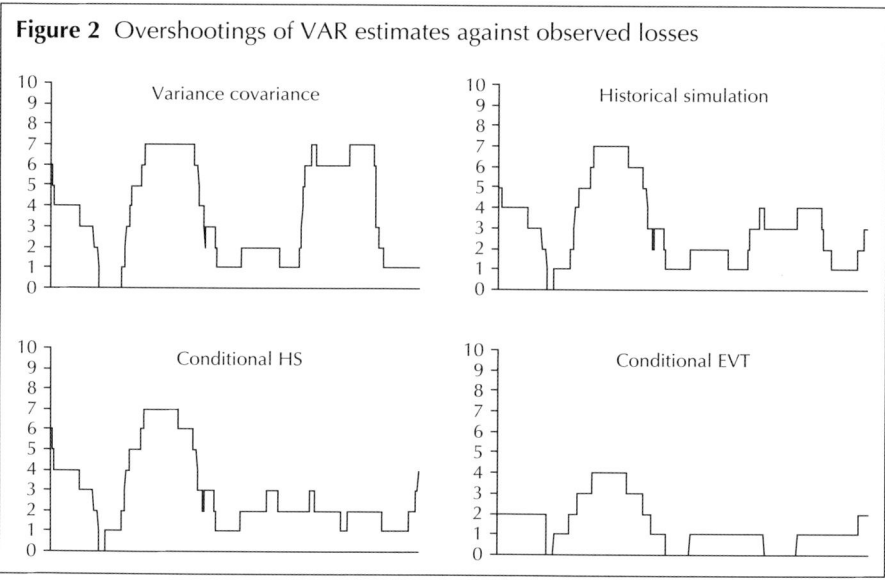

Figure 2 Overshootings of VAR estimates against observed losses

last 250 observations. The maximum number produced by EVT was found equal to 4, whereas the other models produce a maximum of 7. These results, taking into consideration the Basel Committee framework, show that EVT is located in the "green zone" for the entire period, thus being an acceptable method, whereas the other approaches are placed during certain periods in the "yellow zone", thus being under probation. The mean multiplier for the EVT equalled 3, whereas for CHS, HS and VC they equalled 3.17, 3.15 and 3.23, respectively. Despite the lower multiplication factors, the higher VAR estimates of EVT are not sufficiently counterbalanced by them. Thus, the resulting capital requirements according to the EVT are higher compared with the other models on a percentage basis that ranges between 8.4%, for the CHS and 9.0% for the HS.

The findings of this case study are in accordance with those found in literature such as those of Danielsson and de Vries (2000) and Gencay and Selcuk (2004), who showed that semi-parametric EVT is the optimal estimator of VAR against other methodologies. Adding to the conclusions of other studies, the empirical findings showed that novel methodologies in the estimation of VAR appear to be effective for every risk factor they have been applied to. But for the moment, they do not seem to be the optimal solution, in terms of capital requirements for financial institutions, when their portfolios comprise the examined products.

However, since EVT includes the element of extreme events, the benefits to other portfolios with highly risky products (such as options and swaps) should be thoroughly examined. Furthermore, the fact that EVT is also used to model crisis situations should also be accounted for, which may significantly reduce operational risk.

THE FRAMEWORK FOR CREDIT RISK
The framework for credit risk in Basel II
The Basel Committee proposes two approaches for measuring the capital requirements for credit risk:

❑ the standardised approach (SA); and
❑ the internal ratings-based approach (IRB).

Standardised approach
In the SA, the bank allocates a risk weight to different types of claim. The risk weights are 0%, 20%, 50%, 100% and 150% and the main risk groups are banks, non-banks (such as corporate) and sovereigns. Then, the bank allocates a sum of risk weighted asset values. For example, a risk weight of 50% indicates that the exposure will be included in the calculation of assets at half the value. The capital charge is therefore 8% of the asset value (see Nayak, 2003).

In the SA, the risk weighting for the individual risk groups (banks, non-banks and sovereigns) will substantially depend on assessments by external credit-assessment institutions (the recognition of external credit-assessment institutions as suitable for assigning regulatory risk weights is done by national supervisors. So, in order to be recognised, the rating agencies – which are responsible for the external credit assessment – must satisfy several criteria set out by the Basel Committee. Then the rating given by a recognised rating agency is mapped onto a six-grade rating scale and to the relevant risk weights, which respond to each grade.

Internal ratings-based approach
Under the IRB approach, banks use their own methods of management and credit risk measurement in order to calculate the regulatory capital. The internal rating methods are subject to

supervisory recognition, so the banks have to fulfil a number of minimum requirements if they want to qualify for the IRB approach. This is similar to the AMA for operational risk.

Banks that receive supervisory approval to use the IRB approach may rely on their own internal estimates of risk components in determining the capital requirement for a given exposure. The risk components include measures of the probability of default (PD), loss given default (LGD), exposure at default (EAD) and effective maturity (M). The IRB approach is based on measures of unexpected losses (UL) and expected losses (EL). The risk weighted functions produce capital requirements for the UL portion. Expected losses are treated separately (EL = PD x LGD x EAD).

The risk components serve as inputs to the risk weighted functions that have been developed for separate asset classes. For example there is a different risk weight function for the corporate exposures and another one for qualifying revolving retail exposures.

Categorisation of exposures and key elements
for each asset class category
Under the IRB approach, banks must categorise their banking book exposures into five broad classes of assets with different risk characteristics:

1. banks;
2. sovereigns;
3. corporates;
4. retail; and
5. equity.

Under Basel II, for each of the five asset classes there are three key elements:

1. *Risk components – estimates of the risk parameters*: The risk components of exposures to "corporates", banks and sovereigns: the borrower is first of all assigned to an internal rating grade of the bank's rating scale. Then, the PD is estimated (for a one-year time horizon) for each rating grade. If the borrower defaults, then the potential loss depends on the recovery of the borrower. This measure is captured through the LGD parameter (LGD = 1-Recovery Rate). The variable is usually expressed as a percentage

of the expected exposure to the borrower at the time of default, which is the EAD. Moreover, the residual maturity of a loan, called *effective maturity* (M) is also a risk component, which plays an important role in this approach.

2. *Risk weighted functions*: The risk weighted functions conclude to the calculation of the risk weighted assets and therefore capital requirements (see Basel Committee on Banking Supervision, 2004).

3. *Minimum requirements*: IRB banks that aim to calculate the supervisory capital with their own methodologies must, first of all, satisfy several minimum requirements for the authorisation of the internal rating procedures. Among the minimum requirements, particular emphasis should be placed upon internal validation. The validation criteria intend to ensure that the internal rating systems are appropriate not only for regulation purposes, but also for the banks' internal risk management.

Alternative IRB methodologies

Basel II provides two alternative IRB methodologies:

1. *Foundation IRB (FIRB)*: Under the FIRB approach, banks must make their own estimates on the PD, while the remaining three components (LGD, EAD and M) are specified by the supervisory authorities.

2. *Advanced IRB (AIRB)*: Under the AIRB approach, banks are allowed to use their internal estimations, not only for the PD, but also for the LGD and EAD (except the maturity).

Banks have the incentive to continue developing and upgrading their internal management methods, because by moving to more advanced methodologies they are rewarded by a more precise capital allocation. Furthermore, good-quality portfolios are rewarded by a moderate relaxation of the capital requirements (benefits of advanced approaches over the standardised approach).

Capital requirements

Equations (2), (3) and (4) describe a sample set of formulas for calculating capital rqeuirements (K). In Equation (2) the pair-wise correlation between different assets, which is a function of PD, is calculated. The weakness of the methodology for calculating capital requirements is that it assumes a unique correlation factor (ρ_{unique}). In other words, it assumes that there is a theoretical asset that exhibits the same correlation in relation to every single asset included in the credit portfolio. This means that all assets would have the same pairwise correlation, which is not true in reality. In Equation (2), the correlation coefficient that applies for the exposure to corporates, institutions, central governments and central banks, is shown. In reality, the correlation coefficient for the aforementioned class of assets ranges between 0.12 and 0.24 and arises by interpolating according to the value of PD. Similarly, but with different parameters, the correlation coefficient arises for all other classes (see Basel Committee on Banking Supervision, 2004) of exposures.

$$\rho_{unique} = 0.12 \times \frac{1-e^{-50 \times PD}}{1-e^{-50}} + 0.24 \times \frac{1-(1-e^{-50 \times PD})}{1-e^{-50}} \tag{2}$$

$$b = (0.11852 - 0.05478 \times \ln(PD))^2 \tag{3}$$

$$K = \left\{ \left[LGD \times N \left(\frac{G(PD)}{\sqrt{1-\rho_{unique}}} + \sqrt{\frac{\rho_{unique}}{1-\rho_{unique}}} \times G(0.999) \right) \right] \right.$$
$$\left. - PD \times LGD \right\} \times \frac{1+(M-2.5) \times b}{1-1.5 \times b} \tag{4}$$

$$RWA(CR) = K \times 12.5 \times EAD \tag{5}$$

where, b is the maturity adjustment factor, $RWA(CR)$ stands for risk weighted assets for credit risk, $N(x)$ denotes the cumulative distribution function for a standard normal random variable (mean = zero, variance = unit), that is the probability the variable is less than or equal to x), $G(x)$ denotes the inverse cumulative distribution function for a standard nomal random variable.

Furthermore, it should be noted that, in Equation (4), the second part of the product of the equation becomes one when the maturity of the asset extends to one year. In this case, only the first part of the product of the equation remains.

Criticism on Basel II for credit risk

A serious criticism is that the operation of Basel II will lead to a more important business cycle. This criticism appears because the credit models used for Pillar I compliance typically use a one-year time horizon. This would mean that, during a downturn in the business cycle, banks would need to reduce lending as their models forecast increased losses, increasing the magnitude of the downturn. Regulators should be aware of this risk and can be expected to include it in their assessment of the bank models used.

Further criticisms are that more complicated risk measures unjustly advantage the larger banks that are able to use them and, from the same viewpoint, that developing countries generally also do not have these banks and that Basel II will disadvantage the economically marginalised by limiting their access to credit or by making it more expensive. The first criticism is a legitimate point, but it is difficult to see how this can be overcome. More risk-sensitive risk measures are required for the larger, more sophisticated banks and, while the less complicated measures are easier to calculate, due to their lower risk-sensitivity they need to be more conservative. The second criticism is partly true: the better credit risks will be advantaged as banks move towards true pricing for risk. Experience with these systems in the United States and the United Kingdom, however, shows that the improved risk sensitivity means that banks are more willing to lend to higher risk borrowers, simply with higher prices. Borrowers previously not allowed to borrow have now a chance to establish a good credit history.

THE FRAMEWORK FOR OPERATIONAL RISK
Characteristics of operational risk from a Basel II viewpoint
The current definition of operational risk proposed by Basel II is "the risk of loss resulting from inadequate or failed internal processes, people and systems or from external events" (see Basel Committee on Banking Supervision, 2004) and is clearly based upon the causes of operational risk. The above definition includes legal risks which are exposure to fines, penalties and damages resulting from private settlements.

Operational risk is not equivalent to operational loss experience. If the losses suffered by retail banks were steady from one year to another, the banks would simply feature these expected "operational losses" into their business plans factor and pricing schemes. Instead, operational risk is the risk of huge and unexpected inconsistency in operational losses over time.

Operational risk in the past was controlled based on qualitative risk management practices involving checklists and operations manuals. It has become evident that operational risks that financial institutions face today have become more complex than ever before as a result of the faster pace of change in the complexity of their operations, and also due to increased risk awareness. Financial institutions, therefore, have found limits to this traditional, qualitative, operational risk management. The problem of economic capital explains why some institutions were experimenting with ways to put a number against their operational risks well before the regulators began to take an interest in such calculations in the late 1990s. At that time, however, many institutions that calculated economic capital used a rather unsophisticated indicator of operational risk such as the non-interest expenses for each business line. In contrast to market and credit risk, financial institutions may try to limit market disclosure giving any evidence of operational risks and their resulting losses. This is due to the fact that more operational risks (such as fraud) are caused by internal factors and thus may affect more negatively their reputation. On the other hand credit and market risks are results of external factors such as market volatility (eg, variation of interest rate).

Over the course of time, financial institutions have developed, and have capitalised on, new business opportunities given advances made in IT, deregulation and severe international competition. These methods were received well by their customers seeking more advanced financial services but opened doors to more operational risks. On the other hand, the sophistication of operational processes aided by information technology, increase the applicability of business intelligence in financial institutes that can effectively be used in the framework of operational risk management.

Operational risk measurement will stay at the top of the agenda (see Jameson, 2002) in risk management because of:

❑ regulatory concern and the operational risk capital charge in the new Basel II Accord;
❑ increased use of economic-capital models that require the factoring in of operational risk;

- automation, outsourcing, large-volume service provision and fee-based businesses, meaning that financial institutions are increasingly exposed to operational risk;
- the ease for financial institutions to substitute measured risk (such as credit risk) for unmeasured operational risk (such as legal risk in credit derivatives); and
- shareholders penalising banks that have not identified and communicated their operational risk profile.

Strengths of Basel II in the operational risk framework

One of the foremost benefits of the new Basel II Accord in terms of operational risk management is the fact that it has acknowledged that operational risk is an area that needs attention in the financial industry. It has thus enforced that regulatory capital be reserved for it. Furthermore, it has given a definition of operational risk. There did not exist a universal definition of operational risk that the financial industry has agreed upon over the years. Initial definitions of operational risks were mostly based on an exclusion rule such as "every type of non-quantifiable risk" or "all risks that are not market and credit risk". While Basel I implicitly assumed that operational risk was being captured in the calculations of credit and market risk, Basel II seeks to measure this risk separately.

The flexibility of the Basel II Accord, allowing regulators and banks to choose among different approaches for calculating capital requirements, is one of the Accord's primary benefits. It is more so for operational risk, as the management of operational risk is in its infancy, and standard methodologies are not well known. For the AMA, for instance, it gives financial institutions the ability for invention and to develop systems that are more representative of their inherent operational risk and the way they approach operational risk management in their own institution. The Basel II Accord permits regulators to allow "sophisticated" banks to use their own internal ratings to establish risk levels rather than those assigned by private credit-rating agencies.

Having the choice of basic and standardised approaches also helps smaller institutions grasp the concept of operational risk management. The fact that they can move from one approach to another and even use different approaches for different business lines will encourage them to develop more sophisticated approaches in the future as business lines need to be given incentives that motivate them to reduce operational risk. This evolutionary approach will reduce the implementation risk for the bank as a whole and allow smaller business units, which are likely to use less sophisticated risk management techniques to evolve more naturally towards the advanced stage.

Additionally, since its introduction in Basel II, operational risk management has become a driver for shareholder value because banks view it as a tool to reduce volatility in earnings.

Weaknesses of Basel II in the operational risk framework

In spite of its many benefits, there are numerous criticisms that are made of Basel II in the context of operational risk management. There are concerns over the complexity of the requirements and the continuing lack of transparency around operational risk practices. There have also been concerns about how difficult the requirements will be to implement and how challenging it will be for supervisors to monitor compliance. Some of the most prominent concerns are highlighted in the following subsections.

Operational risk transfer

Financial institutions are exposed to a range of operational risks. In general, an institution has several ways of addressing these risks:

❑ decline to accept the risk (for instance, by avoiding certain business strategies or customers);
❑ accept and retain the risk, but introduce mitigating internal controls and introduce risk financing through pricing, reserving and capital; and/or
❑ accept the risk and then transfer it in part or in whole to others, either within or outside the institution.

The transfer of operational risk between financial sectors gives rise to the possibility for regulatory capital arbitrage. Where it is a consideration for capital adequacy, supervisors should seek to determine the extent to which operational risk transfer is done to mitigate risk, or whether it is done with the sole or primary purpose of advantageously changing capital ratios. Operational risk transfer has been raised in part because, as currently proposed, the Basel II Accord permits banks to reduce their regulatory capital requirement under the AMA for operational risk through the use of insurance. Banks already transfer operational risk through insurance and other means, but the Basel II Accord could create incentives for greater operational risk transfer. Uncertainties about the effectiveness of such transfers have led the Basel Committee to restrict the maximum discount amount to 20% of total operational risk capital charge. Operational risk transfer is not an area for which disclosure practices are well developed. Both supervisors and financial institutions need to understand better how effective particular methods are in transferring risk and what new risks (such as legal) can arise from the transfers.

Even if the definition of operational risk established in Basel II were to be generally adopted across the financial sector, it is very broad and encompasses a wide range of loss-event types. Each of these event types, in turn, is not efficiently defined. In the absence of consistent definitions and precision about transferable risks, legal uncertainty and disagreements about the scope of coverage will continue to create major challenges for the development of operational risk transfer systems. Furthermore, in today's market, there is little desire in the insurance industry to develop inventive new products to more broadly cover operational risks, and any such products would probably be very expensive.

Assessment of operational risks
It is difficult to assess an institution's operational risk profile, which depends in part on its loss history, internal control environment and various other factors. Financial institutions have recently been developing systematic internal loss-event data, and it is difficult for the supervisors to assess the quality of an institution's internal controls. In assessing and measuring operational risk, challenging problems exist such as defining the period of risk measurement, establishing the confidence interval such as 99%, 99.9% or 99.975%, and recognising the assumptions made for the distribution functions (see Hiwatashi, 2002). Another challenge posed by the Basel II framework is the need for banks to validate, and for the supervisors to review banks' validation of, the systems used to produce the parameters that are used as inputs. A bank must validate its own rating system to demonstrate how it arrived at its operational risk estimates and confirm that its processes for assigning

risk estimates are going to work as proposed and continue to perform as expected. The role of supervisors is then to review the bank's validation processes and outcomes. This will not prove an easy task for the supervisors, considering that every bank opting for the advanced approaches will have developed their own methodology and be using their internal developed systems for assigning operational risk estimates.

Data availability

For most institutions trying to implement a system for dealing with operational risk, data and systems are proving to be the biggest challenge of Basel II. Temporary partial use has given institutions the opportunity to review the design and implementation of their technical architecture. Data quality, data availability and data consistency are among the greatest challenges that banks face for Basel II, notably in the framework of operational risk, as the data are scattered around the whole institution, since operational risk is not concentrated in any particular area of the business.

Financial institutions will have to overcome a number of challenges with regard to data. A significant amount of data will need to be collected from a number of different sources. The data must be collected at regular intervals and larger or more complex institutions will probably need to use extract-transform-load (ETL) tools to do this. The data will also need to be checked for consistency and to ensure that they are in the right format before being stored in a data warehouse at group or business unit level, ready for processing. This is particularly difficult as the required operational risk data could come from a number of different business units, different countries (including different time zones and languages) or even from sources external to the institution. Institutions can address these challenges by developing common data standards and definitions, processes for measuring data quality and integrated policies for data collection, and ensuring that sound data-verification processes are in place for all relevant systems.

Data collected through the Operational Risk Loss Data Collection Exercise (LDCE) launched by the Risk Management Group (RMG) of the Basel Committee on Banking Supervision in June 2002 (see Basel Committee on Banking Supervision, 2002) suggest that the banking industry has made progress in its operational risk data-collection efforts. However, even this very large database failed to provide a fully comprehensive sense of the range of potential operational risk loss events experienced by banks, because of gaps in data collection. These factors suggest that it is necessary to be careful in using the data to draw firm conclusions about the amount of operational risk exposures. Regardless of these problems, discussions with banks suggest that the quality and quantity of operational risk data collected by many institutions are improving quickly, and that future data collections task could produce correspondingly better results.

Operational risk modelling

The accuracy of operational risk measurement methods strongly depends on the accuracy of operational risk models and the availability of data. Proper operational risk modelling requires a good understanding of repetitive patterns that cause the operational risk under consideration. The appropriateness of those operational risk models is fundamentally linked to data availability (see Muermann and Oktem, 2002). Many banks do not yet have an internal database of historical operational loss events. Those databases that exist are occupied mostly by high-frequency, low-severity events, and by a few large losses. As a result, relatively little modelling of operational risk has occurred, and banks have been prone to allocate operational risk capital via a top-down approach (see De Fontnouvelle, DeJesus-Rueff and Rosengren, 2003).

According to Basel II, as one of the quantitative qualifying criteria for the AMA (see Deutsche Bundesbank, 2001), internal data can be supplemented with external loss data to improve significantly the banks' models of operational risk. While it is beneficial to pool data from external sources to supplement the internal data, publicly available operational loss data create unique modelling challenges, the most substantial being that not all losses are publicly reported. If the probability that an operational loss is reported increases as the loss amount increases, there will be an uneven number of very large losses relative to smaller losses appearing in external databases. External databases may be available to banks, but, in the course of using them, banks may face the challenge of mapping that external data into an internal database with incompatible transaction volumes. Moreover, banks should use external data only if the losses refer to common business lines. This gives more accurate operational risk models based on external loss data.

Expected losses and unexpected losses

The Basel II Accord sets capital requirements to cover both EL and UL without differentiating between the two. However, the definition of capital is not changed to reflect the capital that supports EL and the pricing margins that act as additional protection against losses. In the context of operational risk, EL are routinely built into pricing.

Beta values

Another challenge posed by the Basel II Accord is whether the different beta values across business lines (See Table 1 in Chapter 3) can really be distinguished and whether the distribution in beta estimates reflects differences across banks in the quality and calibration of their internal economic measures.

SUMMARY

Basel II defines requirements for financial organisations and their processes; it provides guidelines for risk management and for risk models as well as the requirements for data. Initially, it is targeted at internationally active financial institutions. However, based on the individual decisions of national regulators, Basel II can be incorporated into national regulation, potentially targeting all financial institutions at a national level.

In the quantification of market risk there are several alternative models that can be used. Some of them produce higher VAR values, making doing business safer. Also, the Basel Committee rewards these models with a multiplication factor that depends on the failures these models exhibited to predict actual portfolio changes. Apparently, VAR models that consistently produce higher values are assigned an equal or lower multiplication factor. In order for the efficient models to be truly rewarded, the lower multiplication factor assigned to them should eliminate the effect the higher VAR estimation would have in the calculation of capital requirements. However, this is not the case in the calculation of capital requirements under the Basel II regulatory framework. This issue has been highlighted in this chapter as one of the major weaknesses of Basel II in the framework of market risk.

As discussed in this chapter, the Basel Committee proposes two approaches for measuring the capital requirements for credit risk: the standardised approach (SA) and the internal ratings-based approach (IRB). In the SA, risk weights are specified for certain types of claim. Under the IRB, banks use their internal estimations to assess credit risk. The estimates are translated into potential future loss, defining the basis of minimum capital requirements. In order to encourage a larger number of banks to move to the IRB approach, the new Basel Accord provides two alternative methodologies: the simpler "foundation IRB approach" and the "advanced IRB approach", the latter being based on a broader use of banks' own internal assessments of risk components.

While one of the main strengths of the Basel II is the introduction of regulatory capital allocation for operational risk, there are various weaknesses still surrounding its application in the operational risk management framework. Some of the issues – such as operational risk transfer, assessment of operational risks, data availability, difficulties in operational risk modelling due to data availability, the differentiation between EL and UL and distinction between the beta values set for the business lines – were highlighted in this chapter. Since the measurement and management of operational risk in the context of Basel II is still in its infancy, many of the weaknesses that occupy risk managers today will eventually be resolved and new challenges will be on the horizon.

---

1   The central bank governors of the Group of Ten (G10) countries established this accord in 1975. It consists of senior representatives of central banks and bank supervisory authorities from Belgium, Canada, France, Germany, Italy, Japan, Luxembourg, the Netherlands, Sweden, Switzerland, the UK and the US.

REFERENCES

Basel Committee on Banking Supervision, 2001, "Overview of the New Basel Capital Accord", consultative document, January.

Basel Committee on Banking Supervision, 2002, "The 2002 Loss Data Collection Exercise for Operational Risk: Summary of the Data Collected", March.

Basel Committee on Banking Supervision, 2004, "International Convergence of Capital Measurement and Capital Standards: A Revised Framework", June.

Basel Committee on Banking Supervision, 2005, "International Convergence of Capital Measurement and Capital Standards: A Revised Framework", November.

Christodoulakis, G. A. and S. E. Satchell, 2004, "Forecast Evaluation in the Presence of Unobserved Volatility", *Econometric Reviews* **23**(3), pp 175–198.

Danielsson, J. and C. G. de Vries, 2000, "Value-at-Risk and Extreme Returns", *Annales d'Economie et de Statistique* **60**, special issue, pp 236–269.

De Fontnouvelle, P., V. DeJesus-Rueff, and J.-J. Rosengren, 2003, "Capital and Risk: New Evidence on Implications of Large Operational Losses", Federal Reserve Bank of Boston, September.

Deutsche Bundesbank, 2001, "The New Basel Capital Accord (Basel II)", Monthly Report, April.

Gencay, R. and F. Selcuk, 2004, "Extreme Value Theory and Value-at-Risk: Relative Performance in Emerging Markets", *International Journal of Forecasting* **20**(2), pp 287–303.

Hiwatashi J., 2002, "Capital Markets News", *Solutions on Measuring Operational Risk*, September.

Jameson, R., 2002, "The True Cost of Operational Risk", Integrated Risk and Capital Management Solutions, URL: http://www.ERisk.com, accessed February 2006.

Kalyvas, L. and A. Sfetsos, 2006, "Does the Application of Innovative Internal Models Diminish Regulatory Capital?", *International Journal of Theoretical and Applied Finance* **9**(2), pp 217–226.

Muermann, A. and U. Oktem, 2002, The Near-Miss Management of Operational Risk, *Journal of Risk Finance* **4**(1), pp 25–36.

Nayak, S., 2003, "Basel II: Implications for Financial Service Providers", white paper, Patni Computer System Ltd.

6

Integrated Risk Management
Framework

Before learning from and instead of regretting your mistakes, strive to limit their consequences

– Lampros Kalyvas

INTRODUCTION

It is well known that market, credit and operational risks, faced by credit institutions, are integrated to a certain extent (see Figure 1). This is due to the fact that many financial portfolios or even single financial products (or contracts) and operations are exposed to more than one types of risk. The fundamental steps of the assessment phase in the integrated risk management framework involve identifying, modelling, monitoring and evaluating the different types of risk. In this chapter, a framework for assessing integrated (market, credit, operational) risks and losses, arising from them, is discussed.

During the identification phase, the detection of the qualitative and quantitative parameters of integrated risks is highlighted. Guidance on when and how to define the integrated key risk indicators (IKRIs) is also presented. The measurement of these indicators, for the information data extraction process, is presented. Based on the above information, the design of modelling, mapping and monitoring strategies for integrated risks is discussed. Correlation analysis is used as one of the main techniques for executing the modelling, mapping and monitoring framework.

The chapter presents advanced ways of efficiently monitoring the integrated risks. Furthermore, integrated risk modelling based on

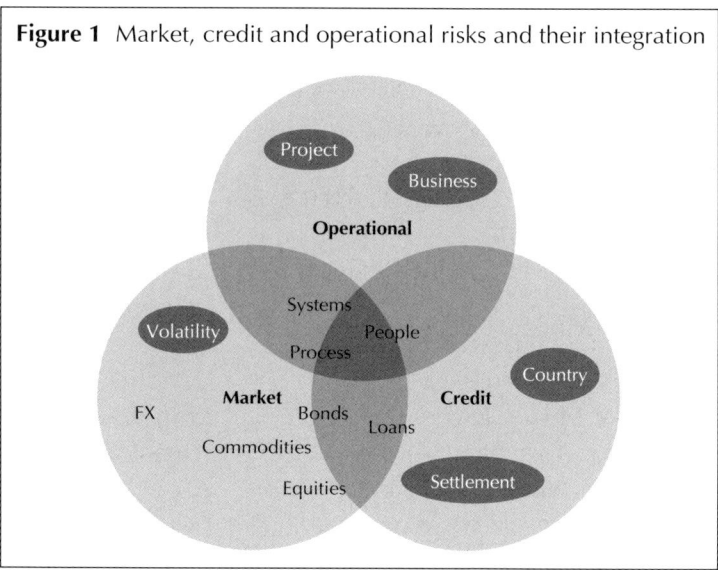

Figure 1 Market, credit and operational risks and their integration

distribution of credit, market and operational losses is discussed as well as mapping and monitoring of the integrated risk model based on loss distribution. Graphical outputs are presented throughout to show the results. The combination of the phases of identification, modelling, mapping and monitoring are employed for integrated risk assessment analysis.

Moreover, the concept of economic capital integration has become one of the most attractive academic and applied fields in financial risk management. The integration of economic capital takes two forms: *intra-risk integration* and *inter-risk integration*. The former has to do with the diversification effect that is utilised within each risk category, namely, market risk, credit risk and operational risk, separately. The techniques for intra-risk integration are extensively discussed in Chapter 1. On the other hand, the latter type of integration involves the diversification effect that appears among the three broad risk categories. Banking professionals have not been involved with the inter-risk integration in order to come up with a bank-wide measure of economic capital. Then again, the Basel Committee has made an effort to evaluate each risk category and to force banks towards regulatory aggregation. However, the calculation of the aggregated regulatory capital does not currently take fully into account possible diversification effects that may exist in a bank. For that reason, this book proposes a method to incorporate, to some extent, possible diversification effects of economic capital into the regulatory capital.

INTEGRATING MARKET, CREDIT AND OPERATIONAL RISK
The integration of risks

Probably the most infamous financial case study of recent years is that of Barings Bank. Although the senior trader in the Singapore office (Nick Leeson) was entitled to exploit low-risk arbitrage opportunities between similar equity derivatives traded on both the Singapore Money Exchange (Simex) and the Osaka Exchange, he took an initiative: he was taking much riskier positions by buying and selling different amounts of contracts on the two exchanges or buying and selling contracts of different types. These actions exposed the portfolio of the bank to an additional market risk in relation to the one that its headquarters permitted.

In reality, this exposure resulted from undertaking improper operations despite the fact that the bank, consequently, was exposed to market risk. Moreover, thanks to the negligent attitude of senior management, Leeson was given control over both the trading and back-office functions. It was not only his strategy but also his inappropriate operations that were breaching the prevailing rules set by the bank. Moreover, the event of the earthquake in Kobe, Japan, caused the Nikkei index to drop sharply and the losses faced by the bank increased rapidly, to approximately US$1 billion.

The case of Barings Bank is an obvious paradigm for the interrelations that may appear between market and operational risks. If Leeson was not taking improper or extreme positions (operational risk), he would not have faced the extreme losses he faced (market risk).

Another possible interrelation between the above-mentioned risks is the Kobe earthquake. If it had not happened, the losses would not have been too high. Thus, the market losses were caused by an unexpected event (earthquake), but they were reflected in the marketplace as a decrease in market prices. Thus, the losses were caused by two operational events (inappropriate operations and physical disaster), but they were reflected by a market event (fall of market values).

Table 1 Interrelationship among different sources of risk

Response impulse	Market	Credit	Operational
Market	Intra-risk influence	Inter-risk influence	Inter-risk influence
Credit	Inter-risk influence	Intra-risk influence	Inter-risk influence
Operational	Inter-risk influence	Inter-risk influence	Intra-risk influence

An additional example of interrelations between different sources of risk is the case of Enron. The top management of Enron systematically concealed the actual credit standing of the company. However, the fact that the company had financial problems, not revealed, did not protect investors from taking positions on the stock of the company. Instead, they took positions in the absence of an accurate view of the company and, eventually, they increased their losses. The case of Enron is an explicit one of an interrelation between credit and operational risk. The credit losses of investors were magnified by the conduct of illegal operations from the top management.

In that sense, there is potential interrelationship among all sources of risk (see Table 1 and also Table 1, Introduction).

Table 1 shows all possible interrelations between market, credit and operational risks. As shown, market risk can cause a change in another type of market risk, in credit risk and in operational risk. On the other hand, credit risk may be reflected in the market and may change the operational risk in an adverse direction. For instance, if the credit risk in a credit institution is increasing, it will impose tight rules on the operations for approving the grant of loans and, thus, the overall operational risk will decrease. Adversely, if the credit risk in a credit institution is decreasing, management will feel free to relax the rules on the operations for approving the grant of loans and, thus, the overall operational risk will increase.

Finally, due to changes in the operational risk level, changes may be observed in the market and credit risk, the direction of which depends on the nature of the financial product and on the nature of the operations under discussion.

Qualitative and quantitative risk identification

In a portfolio management that includes bonds, equities and commodities, there is a different degree of market, credit and operational

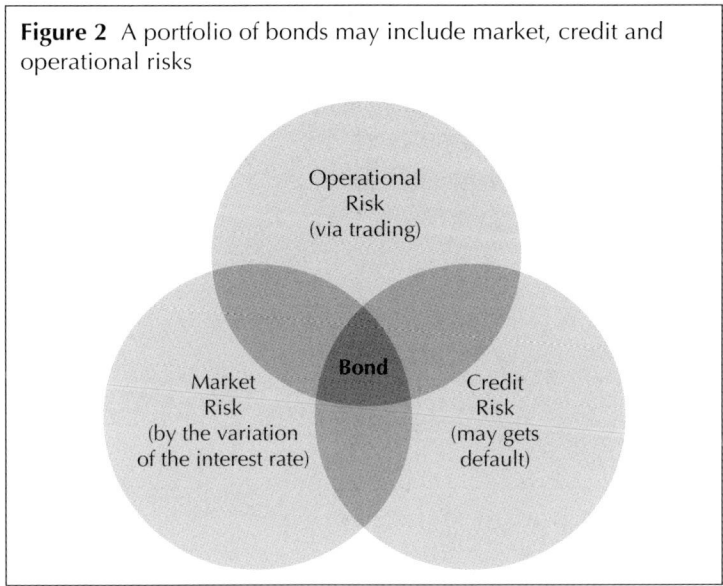

Figure 2 A portfolio of bonds may include market, credit and operational risks

risk that may interact with each other. The term *interaction* means that market risks may initiate credit and operational risk and/or *vice versa*. For example, an increase in coupon rates due to interest rates increase may cause credit inability to loans and, thus, a cause for defaults. Moreover, inappropriate operational activities may cause some credit defaults or other credit events. Another case could be an inappropriate/unauthorised trading that may increase the probability and impact of portfolios' losses and thus their exposures to operational, credit and even market risks (according to the portfolios' type and size). A portfolio of bonds includes credit risk as it may be defaulted; moreover it includes market risk as it is directly influenced by the change of interest rates; finally, via its trading processes it may have some operational risks (see Figure 2).

Most financial products are managed via their associated (underlined) operations and therefore the identification of these operations together with their risk can be the basis for risk integration. Thus, in the integrated risk identification process, all operations that refer to financial products, and thus define and/or measure the disturbances that may appear within the performance of these products, are considered. The integrated risk identification process needs to define all these underlying parameters that describe qualitatively and measure quantitatively the market, credit and operational risks that commonly exist within financial products.

Qualitative integrated risk identification

The qualitative approach of the integrated risks can be based on mapping all key activities that relate to financial operations and contracts (such as those referring to trading) that can also indicate risks. Thus, this analysis is based on defining qualitatively all the parameters that describe how and where financial operations and contracts are subjected to market, credit and/or operational risks. In addition, there is a need to identify what relations should be based on the different risks. The mapping of the financial instruments that refers to the financial operations, products (or contracts) can be used to define the key parameters that can measure and indicate market, credit and operational risks.

Integrated risk-mapping process. The mapping of the financial instruments would help banks identify key indicators and design a roadmap for combining them. The result will take the form of an "integrated map", defining inputs and outputs and linkage between the different types of risk. In the integrated risk-mapping process, all possible risks that might affect operational, market and credit capability status should be identified. The integrated risk mapping is used as the basis for the identification of the IKRIs that are used to measure, quantitatively, the integrated risks.

Quantitative integrated risk identification

The ability to measure quantitatively market, credit and operational risks, forms the basis for designing the IKRIs. These indicators include parameters that refer to different types of risk. Thus, parameters that can actually measure the risks via their common operations could be considered. For instance, an indicator that measures the volume variation of trading activities, for different equities within a portfolio, could be considered in relation to their volatility. Such an indicator includes both operational activities and market variations where both indicate operational and market risks.

Integrated key risk indicators. IKRIs are functional metrics, which can provide insight into a financial product's risk position. These indicators need to access the data and metrics referring to operations and to financial market and credit products. Listed below are the key aspects that should be considered for designing the IKRIs.

❑ *Parameters of the risk indicators*: The "bandwidth" of parameters for the IKRIs should refer to and measure at least two or more types of risk. For instance, in an integrated risk indicator, the unexpected volume and the price variation of a portfolio that includes derivatives should be considered together with their overtrading operations that indicate risks. Note that all of the parameters that are considered for the indicators should cover all integrated market and credit risks together with their associated operations. However, in order to design realistic indicators, it is important to be able to access the relevant data that refer to their parameters.

❑ *Frequency of collecting information data referring to risk parameters*: A key issue is not only to access the data and matrices, but to access them at the "right set time" to give value to the collected information. The frequency of collecting the information data could be "constant", "periodic" and "as per needed" according to the ability of accessing the information as well as their significance level. In most cases, the information data to be measured that refer to the above-mentioned parameters need to be reviewed on a periodic basis. This is mainly to give alerts of changes that may be indicative of risk concerns.

❑ *Depth of time and holding period*: The parameters of the indicators should measure the risks in a comprehensive and reasonable depth of time. The term "depth of time" should be distinguished from the term "holding period" that was introduced in Chapter 1. The depth of time is related to historical time-series information that should be extracted and considered in the risk-assessment analysis. Note that the holding period or time horizon, considered for the three types of risk is different, with the shortest in market risk and longest in operational risk. The Basel II Accord is also tied to this time horizon.

Market risk modelling lies at the short time horizon end of the spectrum for good reasons: the horizon over which market risk is measured should reflect the underlying business activities and decisions, such as the frequency at which a position can be liquidated if needed. Credit risk is typically calibrated to a one-year time horizon, as is operational risk. To measure IKRIs, the holding period that refers to the risk with the longest period should be considered. The risks with the shortest period should be considered as a subset of the longest ones. For the integration of the holding period, refer to the section "Integrating market, credit and operational losses" below.

A general function of such indicators is described as:

$$IKRI = f_t(a \cdot p_{mr}, b \cdot p_{cr}, c \cdot p_{or}) \tag{1}$$

where t refers to time series, a, b, c are the weighted factors and p_{mr}, p_{cr} and p_{or} are the parameters referring to market, credit and operational risks accordingly.

It is important to note that an IKRI must have parameters from at least two different types of risks. Moreover, for efficiently constructing IKRIs, the parallel consequence of different risks is considered. For instance a variation of interest rate indicates market risk and thus can be used as a parameter of the market risk part of a IKRI; the result from this variation defaults or partially defaults on loans, which may also be considered a parameter of the credit risk part, in this case, of the IKRI; finally any improper operations (in reference to processes, people and systems) that supports the avoidance of the loan to be defaulted such as modifying the limits of the pay duty, could be considered as a parameter of a IKRI for the operational risk part.

Note that the term partial default means that a counterparty may cover partially his/her payment duty.

Note finally that two or more IKRIs may have almost identical meaning. This will increase their significance level as the significance level depends highly on the degree of correlation between the indicators. This is avoided however by considering both correlations between the indicators as well as between their parameters. For two or more indicators if correlations are giving equivalent (or almost equivalent) results only one of the indicators is considered.

By putting together, the integrated risk indicators a multidimensional data matrix **KR** that includes the associated risk measurements can be constructed. Therefore, the matrix is filled by the values of the individual risks, considered for integration, referring to the affected financial products within a particular depth of time *and holding period*. Note that the values of the measurements should be harmonised to a common scale so they can easily be used in the risk correlation and comparative analysis.

Risk identification and measurement is vital for the subsequent development of a viable risk-monitoring system that tries to identify "what is going wrong" and "what could go wrong". Its output must be an integral part of the modelling, evaluation of the integrated risk profile and controlling their exposure.

Integrated risk modelling
The identification analysis of the integrated risks, discussed previously, is used as the basis for designing the model that defines the integration of different types of risk as well as the model that defines the "health" level of the affected portfolios. The resulting models are used in the monitoring analysis, in the integrated evaluation process, risk profiling, and, in general, in almost every process for designing the framework of the integrated risk management. The modelling steps are based on correlation analysis (as will be explained in subsequent sections) between the indicators and their parameters that define and measure the different types of risk. Moreover, the correlation between the affected financial products where the risk appears (equities, loans, commodities and so forth), together with their associated operations is also considered.

Integrated risk model based on IKRIs
Key indicators that define common functions and measure the integrated risks may be related to each other. This relational combination of measurement offers information capture, retrieval and interpretation to give a clearer picture of the financial products portfolio's performance and its risk levels. Therefore, the need to understand these relationships is very important. From the standpoint of a modelling of risks and performance, the goal is to find correlations between the integrated risk indicators. The levels of these correlations define the significance of the indicators and the risks defined by them.

Correlation analysis for identifying the significance values of integrated risk indicators. When a risk indicator has a high degree of correlation

it means that any variation of its parameters results in a significance variation to parameters of other related risks and visa versa.
Note that these variations result in proportional volatility to financial products under study. The degree of significance is defined by
considering the dependencies and interactions among risks that
could be general, positive or negative to identify:

❑ which risks appear together;
❑ which financial products and operations that are supporting
   them are affected in parallel and to a similar degree; and
❑ what is the relative degree (general, positive and/or negative)
   for both integrated risks and their affected financial products.

The three main types of correlation needed to be identified are:

❑ the "general" one, G_{cor}, which considers both positive and negative correlations and indicates the overall directional tendency;
❑ the "positive" one, P_{cor}, which considers only the correlations
   with similar directional tendency for two or more risks to have
   similar effects or the affected financial products to appear simultaneously; and
❑ the "negative" one, N_{cor}, which considers only the correlations
   with dissimilar directional tendency.

The significance level is estimated by considering the correlation
between integrated risk indicators with the following:

❑ *Itself to identify its variation in*:
   ❑ a particular point in time; and
   ❑ a time horizon;
❑ *Another integrated risk indicator*: This one-to-one correlation
   analysis defines how different indicators are related to each
   other; high significance indicates similar behaviour (positive or
   negative) between the integrated risk indicators and *vice versa*;
❑ *All other integrated risk indicators*: This is to define the overall
   relation of each indicator with all the other indicators. In this
   case, if for instance an indicator has low significance level (correlation) it means that this particular risk behaves independently
   of the others. On the other hand, if the significance level is
   high, its appearance will affect the others with a high degree of
   probability.

Moreover, the correlation between the affected financial products can be used to define the significance level. In this case the correlation is considered between the following:

❑ *Different affected financial products*: This correlation analysis defines how different financial products together with their underlying operations are related to each other, in terms of their risks. High degree of significance means that there is similar effect to the financial products caused by the risks.
❑ *All affected financial products*: The overall relationship between each affected financial product and all the others is considered in this analysis. For instance, financial products with a high degree of significance have dependent effect and *vice versa*.

The degrees and types of the above correlations define the significance level of the risks and affected financial products and underlying operation, that is, high correlations indicate a high degree of significance. As defined above, according to what type of correlation is considered, the significance levels have different meanings. It is also important to note that the identification of the non-correlation between the different risks provides valuable information for the process of integrated risk management. Non-correlation implies that the different risk parameters are behaving independently. Thus, any appearance of one of them implies the nonexistence of the other. Moreover, any corrective action taken on one of them, will not affect the other.

For the estimation of the correlations that are used to define the significance levels, all those homogeneous and inhomogeneous parameters that characterise the integrated risk indicators are considered. The mathematical functions that define these correlations can be from statistically linear to Gaussian and non-linear functions, according to the degree of complexity and non-linearity of the financial products and operations under scrutiny.

It is advisable that the same correlation function should be used for all of the above correlation of indexes so they can be evaluated on a common basis.

Illustrating the integrated risk model
The correlation analysis is used as a foundation to illustrate the integrated three-dimensional correlation model in terms of the

Figure 3 Surface illustration of the three-dimensional correlation model for the financial products based on the integrated key-risk indicators

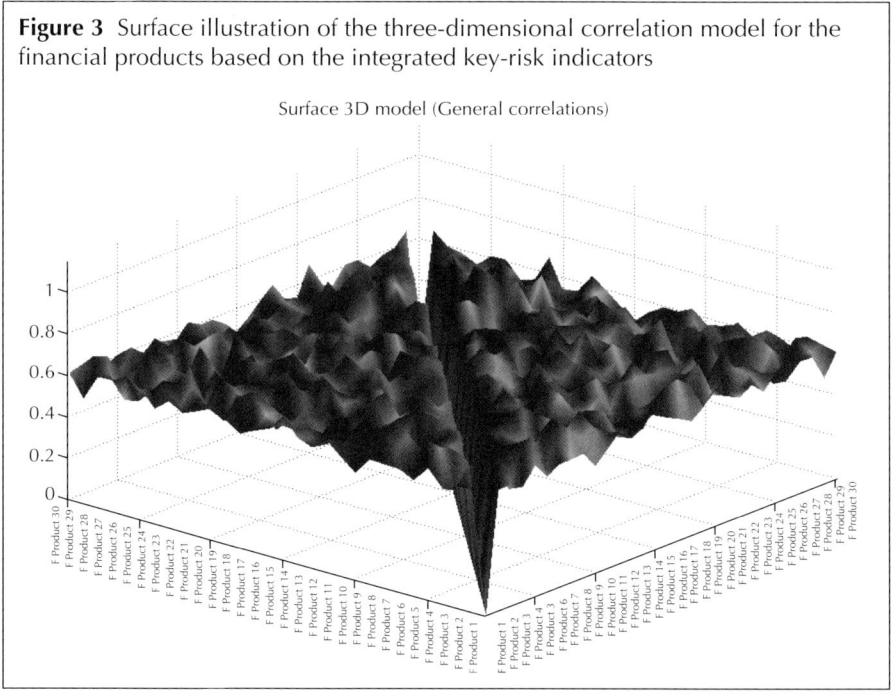

Surface 3D model (General correlations)

financial products and their integrated risks. Figure 3 illustrates the surface representation of the integrated risk model of the financial products based on the IKRIs. In Figure 4, the surface represents the model of the integrated parametric indicators defining the different financial products.

Such representations show the degree of the model's non-linearity. High peaks on the surface indicate a high degree of correlation, and *vice versa*. By analysing the value of the above correlations, any dynamic changes in integrated risks are noted as they happen. Using these correlation models, credit institutions are able to identify how different types of products' risks are linked to each other. This analysis is implemented extensively, in the integrated risk mapping, monitoring and assessment processes.

Integrated risk mapping and monitoring

One of the first steps in the process of integrated risk mapping and monitoring is to construct a "picture" of the financial products and their supported operations that are at risk and how significant

Figure 4 Surface of a three-dimensional correlation model illustrating the integrated parametric key-risk indicators for all financial products

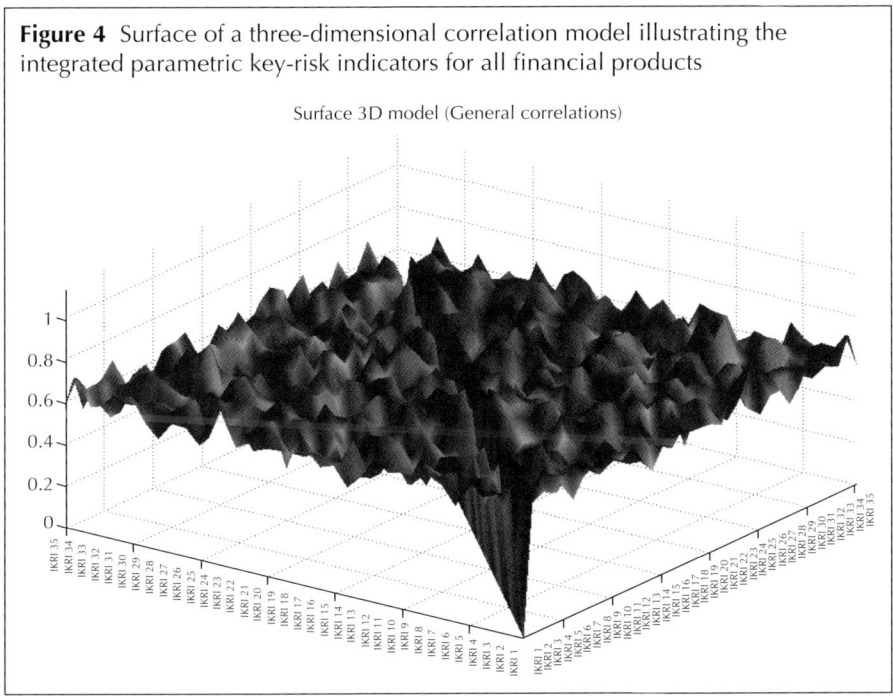

Surface 3D model (General correlations)

these risks are. Mapping and monitoring are one of the most difficult processes in an integrated risk approach because the number of the financial products and their integrated risk indicators is rather substantial, and even larger is the number of their parameters. In efficient mapping and monitoring, the integrated risks and their affected financial products should be illustrated at any requested time.

By understanding the correlations between the financial products and their integrated risks it is easier to drill down and around to discover underlying causes of problems, variances, alarms and unsatisfactory trends. The monitoring system should be employed to alert supervisors about "problematic areas" for different types of risk, before they become threatening or even catastrophic. An efficient integrated risk management system that takes into account the above-mentioned correlations as well as the use of their analysis is most appropriate to help in this matter.

The topographic pattern illustrated in Figure 5 is used to map and monitor the correlations of the financial products and their integrated

Figure 5 Pattern topographic mapping of the financial products and their integrated risks

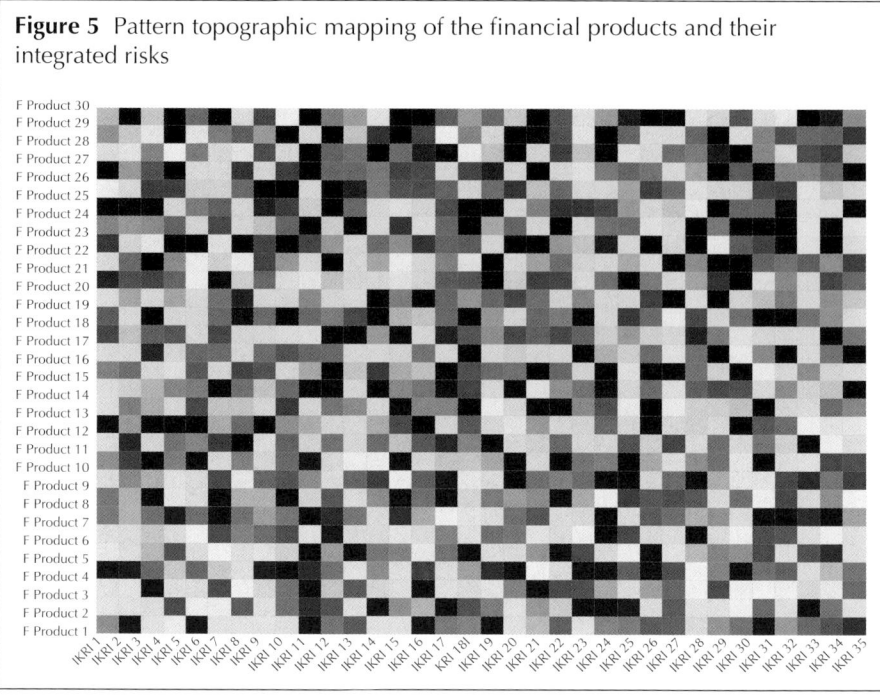

risks; that is, when a risk changes how much will it affect the financial product? Figures 6 and 7 illustrate the topographic mapping of financial products and the integrated risks accordingly. These are correlation maps that show the "areas" where different financial products together their underlying operations as well as their integrated risks have significant value in terms of their correlations. That is, when a risk appears in one product, by how much will it affect the others? Note that the pallet in the greyscale defines the correlation between them. Dark tones represent high correlations, whereas light tones indicate lower correlation values.

Both pattern and contour topographic maps are used in monitoring systems and can give a good indication of how the risks are distributed according to their significance level within the portfolio under study. With this monitoring representation, the areas or contours are at certain times changing quite frequently. The modification of these contours indicates the trend of the risks under examination. It is very effective to build such "monitoring windows" to be used by the technical staff involved in daily risk

Figure 6 Topographic mapping of the financial products

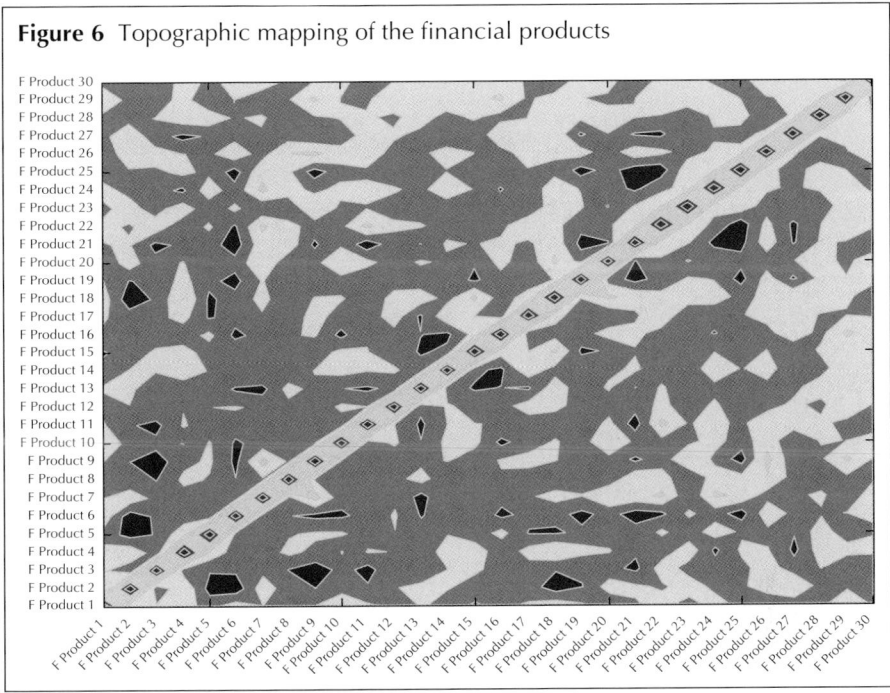

management processes. They are usually monitoring experts who should also be involved in further analysis of the design process of the risk management system. Monitoring systems are used as high-level visual radars, where an observation can be used as a basis of an alarm signalling system. Moreover, in case of presetting specific and well-defined risks, alarms may also ring when a threshold is exceeded.

INTEGRATING MARKET, CREDIT AND OPERATIONAL LOSSES
Identification and modelling of integrated losses
In order to identify and model the integration of market, credit and operational risk losses, cluster analysis is used. Analysis of the cluster values referring to losses is based on their significance values and density within the clusters and defines whether and where the different losses are grouped in terms of their exposure. The analysis of loss distribution is also used in integrated risk modelling for market, credit and operational risks. A methodology called *integrated*

Figure 7 Topographic mapping of integrated risks

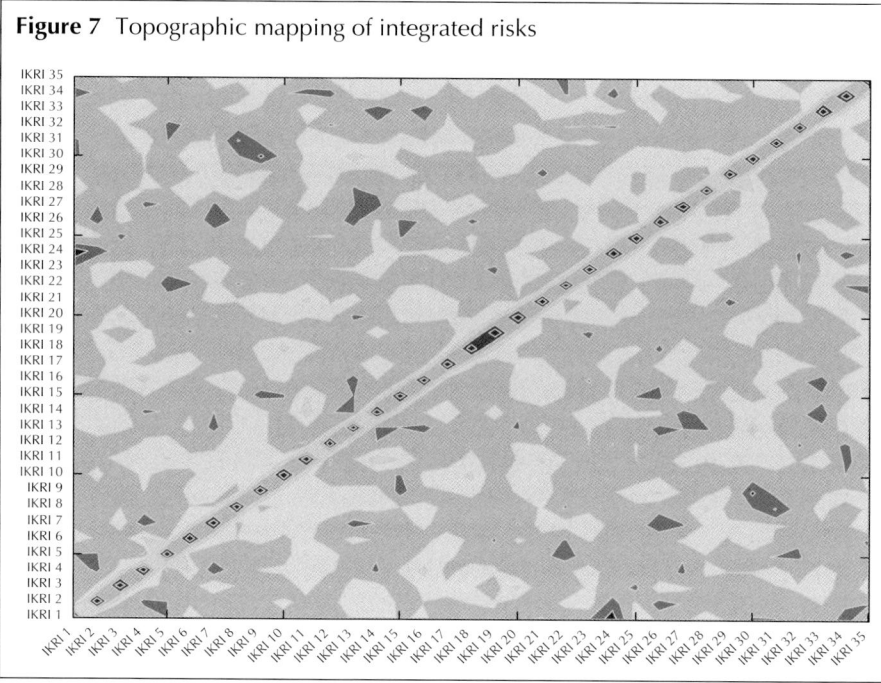

risk loss mountain surface (IRiLMoS) is used to identify, model, map and monitor the integrated losses.

Distribution of credit, market and operational integrated losses

Integrated loss modelling can also be defined based on the market, credit and operational profile of their losses. For each of the three types of risk the profile of their losses is defined within three-dimensional space axes of their probability, impact and exposure. The coordinates defined by the values of the losses within the probability and impact space constructs positional value dots as illustrated in Figure 8. These dots are distributed in the subspace areas (groups) that are called clusters.

Clusters define the group of homogeneous classes that are more similar to one another than to members of other clusters. The term *similarity* has an important effect on the clustering results since it indicates which mathematical properties of the dataset (distance, connectivity and intensity) should be used and in what way in order

Figure 8 Distribution of the loss values defined by the coordinates set from the degrees of their probability and impact. The contours show the zone areas for the losses together with their significance degree. The different levels are defined by the mountains height (see Figure 9)

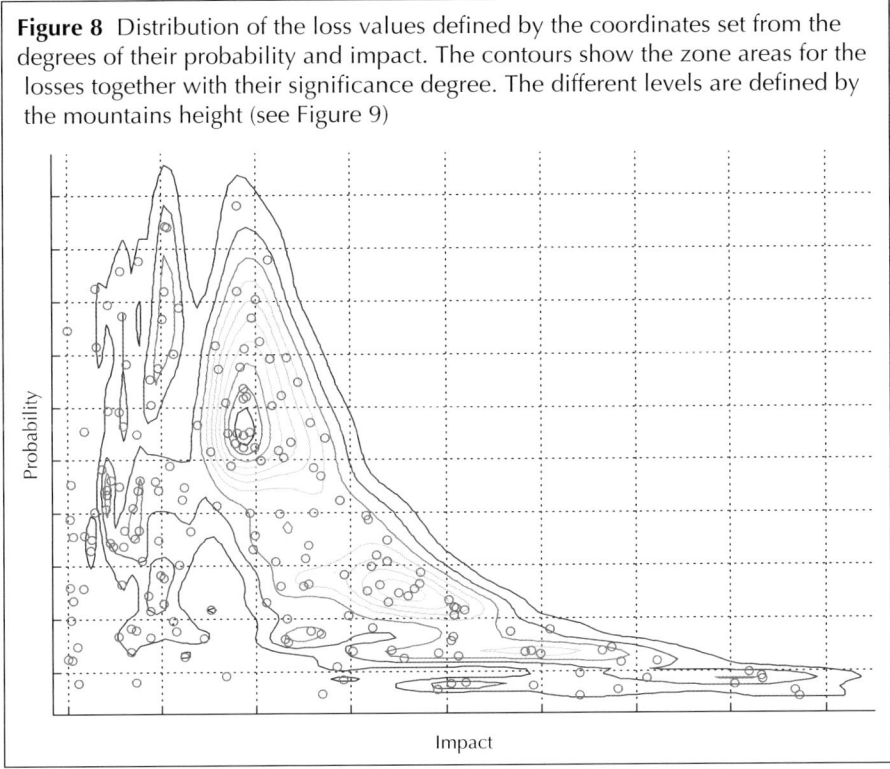

to identify the clusters. Distance can be measured among the loss-data vectors themselves, or as a distance from a loss-data vector to some prototypical object of the cluster. The prototypes (which are usually the centres of the clusters) or *centroids* are usually not known beforehand, and are sought by the clustering algorithms simultaneously with the partitioning of the loss data. The prototypes may be vectors of the same dimensions as the data objects, but they can also be defined as "high-level" geometrical objects, such as linear or non-linear subspaces or functions.

Analysis of the cluster values referring to losses is based on their significance values and density within the clusters and defines whether the different losses are grouped in terms of having similar levels of exposure. The boundaries, called *contours*, of these groups of clusters are also identified in terms of their exposure severity levels. Their centroids are also identified and used in defining the peaks and the trends of these losses within the groups. IRiLMoS is employed for these identification analyses. The IRiLMoS method is based on the operational risk mountain surface proposed by Akkizidis and Bouchereau (2006), its main elements are presented in the following subsections.

Definition of integrated losses. The analysis of loss distribution can also be used in integrated risk modelling for market, credit and operational risks. The analysis is based on the three types of sets of losses referring to credit, market and operational losses. Their values are distributed, for each set, in three-dimensional spaces constructed by the probability, impact and exposure axes. The values of the probability, impact and exposure define the risk profiling matrix as in Equation (2).

$$
RP_{mr} = \begin{vmatrix} P_1^{mr} & I_1^{mr} & E_1^{mr} \\ P_2^{mr} & I_2^{mr} & E_2^{mr} \\ \dots & \dots & \dots \\ P_n^{mr} & I_n^{mr} & E_n^{mr} \end{vmatrix} \quad RP_{cr} = \begin{vmatrix} P_1^{cr} & I_1^{cr} & E_1^{cr} \\ P_2^{cr} & I_2^{cr} & E_2^{cr} \\ \dots & \dots & \dots \\ P_n^{cr} & I_n^{cr} & E_n^{cr} \end{vmatrix} \quad RP_{or} = \begin{vmatrix} P_1^{or} & I_1^{or} & E_1^{or} \\ P_2^{or} & I_2^{or} & E_2^{or} \\ \dots & \dots & \dots \\ P_n^{or} & I_n^{or} & E_n^{or} \end{vmatrix} \quad (2)
$$

Therefore, there are three types of loss distribution within the same time period referring to market, credit and operational risks that are considered in the integrated risk model. As discussed extensively in the section "Economic and regulatory capital integration" below, based on regulatory rules, the holding period and the confidence level proposed by the Basel Committee for capital requirements for the three types or, alternatively stated, sources of risk (market, credit and operational) are different. However, in an integrated risk model, the time that is considered for the measurement of losses should be one year for all types of risk, which covers the maximum regulatory period set for the different sources of risk by the Basel Committee – the one-year period. The conversion factor CF_i, which is proposed is used in the analysis of the distribution of losses for the loss distribution referring to market risk in order to homogenise holding periods for all sources of risk.

The values of probability and impact are used as a basis in the IRiLMoS method to define the integrated risk model as discussed in the following subsection.

Integrated loss analysis based on risk loss mountain surface method

In this book, IRiLMoS is used to identify the integrated risk model. The model is based on the clusters that are defined by the groups of losses distributed within the probability and impact space. This method is based on the number of their positional values together with the validity measures (density) of the clusters. Moreover, the degrees of the actual positional values referring to losses within the space are also considered. The main principles of the method that uses the risk mountain function have been introduced by Akkizidis and Bouchereau (2006).

The method is divided into three main steps. The first step involves forming a six-dimensional grid on the three axes of probability and three axes of impact data space for the three types of risk losses. The intersections (nodes) of the gridlines constitute the exposure weight value for each point of the data clusters within the space, denoted as a set V.

The second step uses the observed distributed values of losses to construct the risk loss distribution mountain function. The *height h* of the risk mountain function at a node $v \in V$ is as in Equation (3):

$$h(v) = \sum_{i=1}^{N} \left[\sum_{k}^{n} \exp\left(-\frac{\|v_k - P_{ki}\|^2}{2\sigma^2} \cdot \frac{P_{ki}}{\delta_k^2} \right) \right] \cdot CF_i \qquad (3)$$

where N is 3 that refers to the three types of risk; P_{ki} is the ith data point in kth dimensional data space of all types of risk; σ is an application-specific constant and determines the height as well as the smoothness of the resultant integrated risk mountain function; δ_k is a constant value referring to the degree of strength for considering the actual value of the losses in the kth dimensional data space of all types of risks; CF_i is the conversion factor used to harmonise the function with the holding period. Note that, CF_i is equal to unity for credit and operational risks. For market risk, CF_i is as defined in the next section.

The third step is to plot the integration risk mountain surface based on losses in the probability and impact axes and define their contours at the different heights.

The closer a data point is to the node, and the higher is its actual value (defined in the corresponding axis), the more it contributes to the score at the node. Note that the top of the mountain defines the centre of the cluster, so the higher the mountain function value at a node, the higher is its potential to be a cluster centre. Therefore, the value of the integrated risk mountain function is related to the potential ability of a grid point to be a cluster centre.

A few remarks are appropriate here.

❑ A finer grid increases the accuracy of the clusters' definitions, but it also increases the computations required. The grid is generally evenly spaced, but it is not a requirement. If *a priori* knowledge of data distribution is available, an unevenly spaced grid can be used.

❑ It is evident from the construction of the mountain function that its values are approximations of the density and the actual value of the data points referring to losses in the vicinity of each node. The mountain function actually measures the density and degree of the losses around each intersection of the grid lines.

❑ The method is actually based on what a human does when visually forming clusters of dataset. High density in the subspace of a probability and impact together with their actual values means high significance of the distributed losses.

❑ The parameter σ is chosen on a trial-and-error basis.

❑ The parameter δ is responsible for the losses with low probability and impact not to be included within the clusters' contour areas.

❑ Different inhomogeneous parameters are considered and combined to design the dynamic mapping of loss distribution and risk exposure in terms of losses.

❑ The significance value of the area of the distributed losses is identified, not only at the points where they are, within the multidimensional axes, but, most importantly, at each point of the grid space.

The resulting mountains are used to map and monitor the integrated risk model as illustrated in the subsections below.

Mapping and monitoring the integrated loss distribution

The integrated risk model, based on loss distribution for the different sources of risk, is used to map and monitor the exposure and the groups of losses within the probability and impact axes. Therefore, this model is used to identify and illustrate:

Figure 9 Mountain surface representation that illustrates the degree of integrated risk exposures, in regards to their losses, for each point within the probability and impact axes. The height and size of the mountains indicate the significance and area of the risk and loss exposures

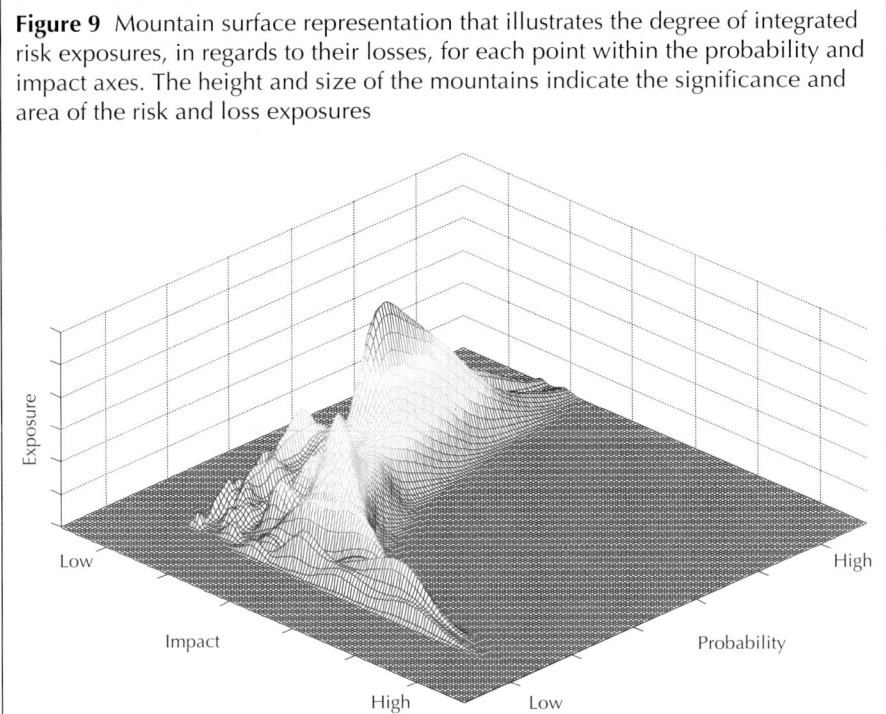

❏ the risk exposure profile in a single graph;
❏ the losses defined as groups; and
❏ the boundaries of the groups.

The mountain surface representation in Figure 9 illustrates the degree of integrated risk exposures, with regard to their losses, for each point within the probability and impact axes. The height and size of the mountains indicate the significance and area of the risk and the exposures to losses.

Based on the IRiLMoS, the clusters of the distributed losses are identified and illustrated within the contour areas. The contour (boundary) area of these clusters is defined by tracing the mountains at different height levels. Therefore, the contour shapes of the clusters vary according to the surface of the mountains and the level from where the trace is applied. Note that the difference in height between the levels is equal. When the height level of the mountain is higher, its surface size is smaller and thus the contour defined by its trace is smaller. Higher levels of mountains – or, in other words, smaller contours – indicate higher levels of exposure. They are defined by their actual values and their density in the subspace of the probability and impact axes. In Figure 8 the contours show the zone areas for the losses together with their significance degree. The different levels are defined by the mountain height. Figure 9 maps the contour zones for different degrees of the integrated exposure to risk losses within the area that is defined by their probability and impact axes.

As a result the cluster contours are used to classify:

❑ the degree of the integrated risk exposure in terms of losses;
❑ the groups of losses; and
❑ the zones (contours) of their occurrence according to their exposure significance degree.

Figure 10 Map that illustrates the contour zones for different degrees of the integrated exposure to risk losses within the area that is defined by their probability and impact axes

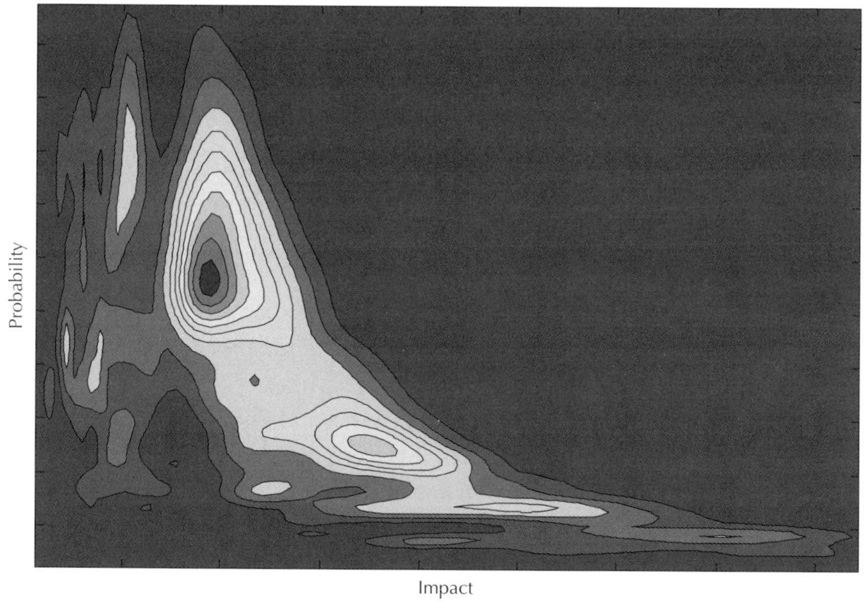

The integrated risk exposure for a particular loss distributed in the coordinates of the probability and impact axes is defined by searching for the height of the mountain $h(v)$ on these coordinates.

The mapping of losses is mainly based on the distribution of past losses for a set time period. However, for monitoring the losses their distribution needs to be updated dynamically to reflect the risk mountain surface as illustrated in Figure 10 and thus their exposure status.

ECONOMIC AND REGULATORY CAPITAL INTEGRATION
Theoretical framework on integrating market, credit and operational risks

A key objective of modern risk management is to ensure that credit institutions do not ignore any potential sources of risk. Banks have to estimate two different types of capital: economic and regulatory. Economic capital is directed to cover probable unexpected losses arising from business activities. Regulatory capital is required by regulatory and supervisory authorities to fulfil their expectations about the different sources of risk and to account for possible model error risks of the internal models used to estimate economic capital (see Kalyvas and Sfetsos, 2006). By this effort, the Basel Committee demonstrated the basic principles in order to evaluate each source of risk. Consequently, banks employ mathematical and statistical techniques in order to fulfil the quantitative and qualitative standards set by the Committee. These VAR techniques, widely known as internal models, retain an inherent disadvantage in the sense that they evaluate each risk separately. Thus, banks produce separate estimations for economic and regulatory capital needed to cover market, credit and operational risk. The bank wide regulatory capital is just the sum of all risk specific regulatory capitals. Such suggestions for calculating the overall regulatory capital explicitly support risk aggregation in the estimation of regulatory capital.

Risk aggregation does not take into consideration possible interrelations among different sources of risk. Interrelations are not taken into account either among financial sub-risks (such as interest rate risk, equity risk, foreign exchange risk within market risk) estimated within each source of risk (intra-risk aggregation), or among different sources of risk (such as market, credit, operational). Thus, any diversification effect is not accounted for. Going beyond, aggregation does not provide the bank's top management with a homogeneous measure of bank wide risk. This happens because each kind of risk is estimated according to different specifications – namely, according to different confidence levels and different holding periods.

By examining each type of risk, market risk quantification is the most short-sighted estimation of risk given that it assumes a 10-day holding period (combined with 99% confidence level). In turn, regulatory capital for operational risk is based on 1–3-year holding periods and, usually, at 99.99% confidence level. Regulatory capital for credit risk is directed to cover potential losses expected to appear the following year, usually, with a confidence level of 99.97%. The 99.97% confidence level represents the possibility that a AA-rated corporate whose bonds or loans are incorporated in a bank's credit portfolio will remain "healthy" (not defaulted) during the next year. The confidence level may vary according to the objectives of the bank and its aims on the quality of the credit portfolio. If the risk tolerance of a credit institution permits the retaining of a credit portfolio of lower-quality bonds or loans, the confidence level can be, accordingly, lowered in order to reflect the new credit rating. Instead, if the risk culture of a credit institution requires a AAA credit portfolio, the confidence level should be altered to higher than 99.97%.

The Basel Committee suggests that the average probability of default (PD) estimated by the internal ratings-based (IRB) approach should not be less than 0.03%. On the other hand, the formula for calculating capital requirements implicitly supports the view that, in the long run, the confidence level for PD tail estimation is 99.9% (see Chapter 5). The 99.9% confidence level will be used for credit risk quantification in the following analysis.

Bearing in mind the aforementioned restrictions, at a first glance it seems impossible to combine all measures to a unique value-at-risk (VAR) measure taking into account the correlations among them. Moreover, except for the different specifications used for the quantification of each source of risk, the frequency of the observed data differs. However, only if implicit or explicit measures of co-movements for all combinations of risk sources are known, the risk integration can be achieved. Due to the above-mentioned inconsistencies, none of the historically based approaches of estimating VAR is suitable for inter-risk integration. Instead, Monte Carlo simulation could be the most suitable approximation because it can create a number of different but analogous scenarios for all sources of risk. Thus, the inconsistency that has to be resolved, before applying Monte Carlo simulation, is to specify a common holding period and a common confidence level for all sources of risk. For the sake of simplicity, the common confidence level should coincide with the highest confidence level and the longest holding period.

Aggregated economic capital

The primary objective of the aggregated economic capital estimation is to estimate each source of risk, separately. Each source of risk is estimated by taking into account every diversification effect that appears within it. The estimation of co-movements within each risk source is carried out easily because it is based on common assumptions about the frequency of the data employed. Furthermore, the VAR is estimated according to individual assumptions about the holding period and the confidence level. The economic capital corresponding to market risk is based on a 10-day holding period and 99% confidence level; the economic capital of credit risk is based on one-year holding period and on a confidence level that depends on the asset quality required by the bank, usually close to 99.9%; the economic capital corresponding to operational risk is based on one-year holding period and 99.99% confidence level. The aggregated economic capital of a credit institution is calculated by adding all individual economic capitals for each source of risk and is given by Equation (4):

$$AEC = MREC + CREC + OREC \qquad (4)$$

where AEC represents aggregated economic capital, $MREC$, $CREC$ and $OREC$ stand for market risk, credit risk and operational risk economic capital, respectively.

The aggregation of the economic capital is meaningful in the sense that it reflects the individual characteristics of each source of risk. For example, the 10-days holding period in market risk reflects the ability of the bank to liquidate its positions in a fair value within 10 days. Most credit institutions use the results of the aggregated economic capital for internal purposes in order to assess the risk undertaken by different sources. Aggregated economic capital does not account for the existence of diversification effects among the different sources of risk. In order to unify the specifications for all sources of risk, all risks should be calculated according to the same holding periods and confidence levels. Although this technique seems to contradict the sensible representation of the products comprising each source of risk, it acts only as an intermediary step in order to achieve regulatory capital integration (see below).

Aggregated regulatory capital
Credit institutions are, to some extent certain about the efficiency of the model they use. For that reason, they confidently accept its results. However, regulatory and supervisory authorities are doubtful about the quality of the model because they cannot investigate its nature in depth. In order to overcome this problem, regulatory and supervisory authorities usually place an implicit or explicit multiplication factor on the results, in a way that it magnifies them. This multiplication factor stands for two main sources of risk:

❑ false input of data; and
❑ model error risk.

Equation (5) illustrates the calculation of the aggregated regulatory capital:

$$ARC = MRRC + CRRC + ORRC \tag{5}$$

where *ARC* represents aggregated regulatory capital, *MRRC*, *CRRC* and *ORRC* stand for market risk, credit risk and operational risk regulatory capital, respectively.

$MRRC =$

$$\left.\begin{array}{l} \max\left({}^{MR}VAR_t^{(10\,days,\ 99\%)} ,\ M_t\ \dfrac{1}{60}\sum_{i=1}^{60} {}^{MR}VAR_{t-i}^{(10\,days,\ 99\%)} + SR_t \right) \\[4mm] CRRC = {}^{CR}VAR_t^{(1\,year,\ 99.9\%)} - EL \\[2mm] ORRC = {}^{OR}VAR_t^{(1\,year,\ 99.99\%)} \end{array}\right\} ARC \tag{6}$$

Alternatively, credit risk capital requirements may be rewritten as if it is assumed that the original maturity of the loan portfolio is equal to one year (see Chapter 5):

$$CRRC = \left[LGD \times N\left(\dfrac{G(PD)}{\sqrt{1-\rho_{unique}}} + \sqrt{\dfrac{\rho_{unique}}{1-\rho_{unique}}} \times G(0.999) \right) \right] \\ -PD \times LGD \tag{7}$$

where ρ_{unique} is the common correlation factor applied to all pairs of credit assets and, $^{MR}VAR_t^{(10\ days,\ 99\%)}$, $^{CR}VAR_t^{(1\ year,\ 99.9\%)}$, and $^{OR}VAR_t^{(1\ year,\ 99.99\%)}$ are VAR values at time t for market risk, credit risk and operational risk, respectively, for 10 days – 1 year holding period and 99–99.99% confidence level.

Integrated economic capital

The concept of integrated economic capital has been the prevailing notion in risk management over the last decade. The notion has started to be applied in market risk by taking into account possible diversification effects arising from the heterogeneity and the different behaviour of risk factors. However, in this book the concept of integration is used to depict the integration among different sources of risk, that is inter-risk integration. For this purpose, the methodologies used for each and every source of risk should be identical and the specifications should be unified across all risk sources. One way to make the specifications compatible is to increase both confidence levels and holding periods in a way that makes them all equal to the highest confidence level and holding period used to quantify a source of risk.

The risk analyst may choose a confidence level and a holding period that corresponds to different specifications (eg 99% confidence level and 10-day holding period). This choice retains two major drawbacks. On the one hand, the data for such high frequency is not available for credit and operational risk. On the other hand, it will probably diminish the impact of operational risk on the overall integrated risk quantification, due to the lower confidence level, because operational risk factors usually follow fat tail distributions. According to this alternative, some extreme operational losses will be neglected. In general, the methodology depicted below can potentially be applied to different confidence levels. However, the participation of each source of risk to the overall risk quantification will differ slightly because their returns distributions tend to exhibit different shapes.

As mentioned above, operational risk is the source of risk with these characteristics, which is estimated according to 99.99% confidence level and a one-year holding period. Again, for market risk, it is not meaningful to estimate VAR for 99.99% confidence level and one-year holding period. However, the aforementioned estimation is made only to facilitate the estimation of an integrated value for VAR with the abovementioned specifications. In turn, the VAR corresponding to integrated economic capital is used in order to derive the appropriate inputs for the estimation of the regulatory capital.

The scaling of VAR measures may be done by applying either the scaling factor or by simulating future co-movements of all risk factors for all sources of risk. The former has the disadvantage that it does not take into account possible non-linearities in time series data. Thus, the latter is the approximation that is considered the more appropriate for risk factors that exhibit non-linear behaviour (eg, bonds, options, swaptions) in relation to the fair values of the financial products.

Except for the effort to estimate all related sources of risk according to homogenised specifications, the risk manager should independently estimate conversion factors between different confidence levels and holding periods. The VAR for market risk is estimated for three different confidence levels and two different holding periods using Monte Carlo simulation. At first, the holding period is kept unchanged and only the confidence level changes. By dividing the VAR with the higher confidence level by the VAR with the lower confidence level, the confidence level conversion factor (CLCF) is derived. In turn, the increased confidence level is kept stable and the holding period is increased. In the same way as the one depicted for the confidence level conversion factor, the holding period conversion factor (HPCF) is calculated. Equally, the conversion factor for the credit risk is calculated. In the case of credit risk only one conversion factor should be estimated (confidence level conversion factor), because the holding period of credit VAR coincides with the holding period of operational VAR. Apart from the above calculations, the conversion factor may be time-dependent and its statistical stationarity should be tested throughout time using the appropriate statistical methods.

$$\overbrace{{}^{MR}VAR_t^{(10\,days,\,99\%)} \quad {}^{MR}VAR_t^{(10\,days,\,99.99\%)}}^{{}^{MR}CLCF} \mapsto {}^{MR}CLCF = \frac{{}^{MR}VAR_t^{(10\,days,\,99.99\%)}}{{}^{MR}VAR_t^{(10\,days,\,99\%)}}$$

$$\overbrace{{}^{MR}VAR_t^{(10\,days,\,99.99\%)} \quad {}^{MR}VAR_t^{(1\,year,\,99.99\%)}}^{{}^{MR}HPCF} \mapsto {}^{MR}HPCF = \frac{{}^{MR}VAR_t^{(1\,year,\,99.99\%)}}{{}^{MR}VAR_t^{(10\,days,\,99.99\%)}}$$

$$\overbrace{{}^{CR}VAR_t^{(1\,year,\,99.9\%)} \quad {}^{CR}VAR_t^{(1\,year,\,99.99\%)}}^{{}^{CR}CLCF} \mapsto {}^{CR}CLCF = \frac{{}^{CR}VAR_t^{(1\,year,\,99.99\%)}}{{}^{CR}VAR_t^{(1\,year,\,99.9\%)}} \qquad (8)$$

where $^{MR}CLCF$ is the confidence level conversion factor for market risk, $^{MR}HPCF$ is the holding period conversion factor for market risk and $^{CR}CLCF$ is the confidence level conversion factor for credit risk.

Thus, the unitary VARs for every risk source, with the desired specifications, can be estimated. A prerequisite for the estimation of the different types of conversion factors is the existence of time series with adequate observations for VARs on a standalone basis for all different available combinations of confidence level and holding period. Ultimately, from the three sequences of VARs which exhibit the same specifications, the correlations can be estimated or implied according to one of the parametric or non-parametric VAR methods. The resulting time series for conversion factors can also be used for testing their statistical stationarity.

$$\left.\begin{array}{l} ^{MR}VAR_t^{(1\,year,\,99.99\%)} \\ ^{CR}VAR_t^{(1\,year,\,99.99\%)} \\ ^{OR}VAR_t^{(1\,year,\,99.99\%)} \end{array}\right\} IEC\left(^{TR}VAR_t^{(1\,year,\,99.99\%)}\right) \qquad (9)$$

where $IEC\,(^{TR}VAR_t^{(1\,year,\,99.99\%)})$ is the integrated economic capital that arises by employing possible co-movements between the three sources of risk. The integrated economic capital is estimated by using the VAR for all sources of risk for the one-year holding period and 99.99% confidence level.

In the case of aggregated risk management, the participation of each source of risk is clearly documented. However, their participation in the integrated risk quantification is not as easy. In order to carry out this task the marginal VAR should, first, be estimated.

Marginal VAR. Marginal VAR measures the impact on integrated VAR from an infinitesimal change in a given position of a specific source of risk. It is the partial derivative of the integrated VAR, taking into account market, credit and operational VAR, with respect to the portfolio component weight. This measure describes the linear relationship between the position in a source of risk and the integrated VAR, and it is equivalent to the measures of "delta" for options or "beta" for stocks. The marginal VAR is given by:

$$MVAR_{i,t}^{(1\,year,\,99.99\%)} = \frac{\partial\,^{TR}VAR_t^{(1\,year,\,99.99\%)}}{\partial w_i} \qquad (10)$$

where $MVAR_{i,t}^{(1\,year,\;99.99\%)}$ is the marginal integrated VAR and w_i is the participation of the position of risk source i in the total exposure given by:

$$w_i = \frac{v_i}{\displaystyle\sum_{i=1}^{3} v_i} \tag{11}$$

where v_i is the absolute level of the position related to the risk factor i. The position related to operational risk is an issue under discussion and can take many interpretations. The exploration of the optimal estimator, corresponding to the position related to operational risk, can be an issue for future investigation. The marginal VAR can be calculated by incrementing the position by a small amount. For the highest precision of the method the change in the position of the risk source should be less than 0.1%. The smaller the increment, the higher the precision of the marginal VAR. Alternatively, the marginal VAR can be expressed as:

$$MVAR_{i,t}^{(1\,year,\;99.99\%)} = \left[{}^{TR}VAR_{t}^{1\,year,\;99.99\%} \mid w_i \right] - \left[{}^{TR}VAR_{t}^{1\,year,\;99.99\%} \mid w_i + dw_i \right]$$

$$\tag{12}$$

where ${}^{TR}VAR_{t}^{(1\,year,\;99.99\%)} \mid w_i + dw_i$ is the total risk produced by increaseing or decreasing the participation of the position of the source of risk i (w_i) and dw_i and ${}^{TR}VAR_{t}^{(1\,year,\;99.99\%)} \mid w_i + dw_i$ is the total risk for a given relative position w_i.

The aforementioned method is able to resemble a real change in a position of a certain risk factor. However, this resemblance cannot be made for positions that assume huge trading units or positions that are not so liquid. In both cases, the position cannot be traded in very small increments. Nevertheless, if the purpose of the calculation of marginal VAR is solely the calculation of the component VAR, the change that is to be applied to the original position is irrelevant to the trading unit of the position. In other words, marginal VAR is the relationship between total integrated VAR and the position taken in a specific risk source (see Figure 11).

Component VAR. Component VAR is the participation of each risk factor VAR in the total integrated VAR. In the calculation of

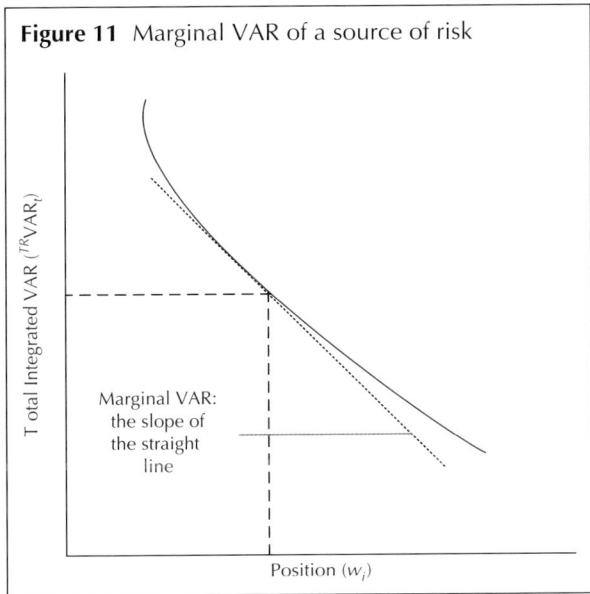

Figure 11 Marginal VAR of a source of risk

aggregated VAR (because of the absence of inter-risk diversification effects), the component VAR is simply the VAR of each source of risk. Nonetheless, in the case of integrated VAR the percentage participation of each source of risk to the total integrated VAR may differ due to different characteristics, although, in absolute terms, the participation of each risk type is usually lower. If all positions in the portfolio are long, all component VARs should exhibit positive value, while if the portfolio is well hedged, component VARs may exhibit both negative and positive values. However, if VARs examined correspond to the entire individual market, credit and operational risk, all values are positive.

Component VAR is calculated by using the marginal VAR to allocate the portfolio VAR across the various sub-components of the portfolio under consideration. Thus the component VAR is given by:

$$CVAR_{i,t}^{(1\,year,\,99.99\%)} = MVAR_{i,t}^{(1\,year,\,99.99\%)} * w_i \qquad (13)$$

Component VARs, corresponding to the three different sources of risk, are considered additive – that is, the sum of the component

VARs equals the VAR of the diversified portfolio. Thus, the above property of component VAR can be expressed as:

$$^{TR}VAR_t^{(1\,year,\,99.99\%)} = \sum_{i=1}^{3} CVAR_{i,t}^{(1\,year,\,99.99\%)} \tag{14}$$

where $i = 1, 2, 3$ corresponds to t market, credit and operational risks, respectively.

Transformation of VARs according to their original specifications. Once the component VARs have been estimated the only task that remains to be done is the transformation of these VAR measures in order to correspond to their original specifications. All component VARs correspond to a one-year holding period and a 99.99% confidence level, as we have seen above. However, only the calculation of capital requirements for operational risk corresponds to these specifications. Market risk capital requirements should have been estimated according to a 10-day holding period and 99% confidence level while credit risk capital requirements should have been calculated on a basis corresponding to a one-year holding period and 99.9% confidence level. At this stage, the conversion factors described above should be used.

In the case of market risk, two conversion factors should be utilised:

❏ the conversion factor that corresponds to the holding period; and
❏ the conversion factor that corresponds to the confidence level.

Thus, the VAR for market risk is expressed as:

$$^{MR}VAR_t^{(10\,days,\,99\%)} = \frac{CVAR_{1,t}^{(1\,year,\,99.99\%)}}{^{MR}CF_1 \times {}^{MR}CF_2} \tag{15}$$

In the case of credit risk, only one risk factor, estimated above, should be utilised. This happens because only the confidence level differs in relation to the component VAR already estimated for credit risk. Thus, the diversified VAR for credit risk is estimated as follows:

$$^{CR}VAR_t^{(1\,year,\,99.9\%)} = \frac{CVAR_{2,t}^{(1\,year,\,99.99\%)}}{^{CR}CF_1} \tag{16}$$

where $CVAR_{1,t}^{(1\,year,\,99.99\%)}$ and $CVAR_{2,t}^{(1\,year,\,99.99\%)}$ correspond to market and credit component VARs, respectively.

Integrated regulatory capital
Regulatory issues. The Basel Committee on Banking Supervision (1998) sets "a package of supervisory proposals for *applying capital charges to the market risks* incurred by banks". No other specific comment has been made in recent years in order to clarify the nature of the portion attributed to market risk. The same applies to the remaining sources of risk: credit and operational. A twofold enquiry that arises is whether "individual unitary sources of risk, as expressed by unitary VARs, should be used as inputs in the reg-ulatory formula for the calculation of capital requirements" or "component VARs, arising from the integrated total enterprise VAR, should be used instead".

The banking community, in practice, seems to have already given an answer to the aforementioned enquiry. Since the banking industry has not yet developed an integrated risk management framework, the best that a bank can do is calculate every source of risk separately. But, inevitably, some questions arise from the cur-rent state:

❑ "what will happen if the present inability of achieving inter-risk integration will be overcome in the future?"
❑ "will banks be allowed to use other measures as inputs in the regulatory formula?"; "if yes, which of them would be the nat-ural candidates?"

The current practice, to be applied by risk management depart-ments of credit institutions, is the calculation of economic capital on an enterprise-wide basis. The benefits from such a calculation could, potentially, influence the calculation of the regulatory cap-ital. As mentioned above, credit institutions benefit from the diver-sification effect when calculating economic capital, because the quantity of risk attributed to each source of risk is diminished after integrating sub-categories within each risk source. This quantity corresponding to component VAR of each source of risk can be used as an input in the regulatory formulas described in Equation (6) and Equation (7). Thus, a natural candidate for an alternative calculation of regulatory capital would be the component VAR of each source of risk, the specifications of the quantification of individual VAR have been accounted for.

Apart from the appropriate mathematical background, the Basel framework proposes a backtesting technique in order to formulate a multiplication factor for market risk. The same does not explicitly apply to credit and operational risk quantifications. Multiplication factors are related to events according to which the internally based model fails to predict the actual movement of a specific source of risk. Furthermore, the count of all failures appears on a standalone basis, without taking into account the portion of one source of risk that is observed under the umbrella of another source of risk (see Table 1).

In operational risk, all notions concerning it are relatively new and there is no unique way to test the performance of operational risk models or to suggest a unique manner of quantification. In the case of market risk, the Basel Committee imposes the use of a multiplication factor when calculating capital requirements according to VAR methodology. However, if the component VAR is used as an input, the number of model fallacies in relation to actual observations may differ because a consistently lower quantity (component VAR < unitary VAR) will be compared to the actual change that in both cases would have the same reference value. Thus, the fallacies of the integrated risk model and, consequently, the fallacies of an individual component VAR would be more – or in the best case the same – in relation to the fallacies the unitary VAR produces when making the same comparison.

The implementation of the above-mentioned approximation produces doubtful results concerning the level of capital requirements. If the multiplication factor becomes greater, capital requirements will be formulated in a level that may be lower or higher in relation to the original level of capital requirements. Instead, if the multiplication factor remains the same, capital requirements would certainly be decreased because the component VAR input is lower than the unitary VAR input.

Split of component credit VAR into expected and unexpected loss. In the regulatory formula (see Chapter 5), the inputs needed for the calculation of capital requirements are the PD and LGD. By following the approach described above, the risk manager acquires only a figure that stands for the component credit VAR transformed for the needs of the specifications required for credit risk. However, both expected loss and unexpected loss should be approached in order to come up with the two components of the regulatory formula. In order for the risk manager to define the above-mentioned parameters, the available information about the component credit VAR, the unitary credit VAR and the transformed component credit VAR should be fully utilised.

The credit risk manager should compare the transformed component credit VAR with the unitary credit VAR. The unitary credit VAR is composed of expected loss and the difference between unitary credit VAR and expected loss that stands for the unexpected loss. However, the respective information needed for the transformed component credit VAR is not available. So, in order to find out the cut-off point between expected and unexpected loss, the methodology described below should be followed. Finally, the expected loss should be further split into PD and LGD using the methodology described in Chapter 2.

Identifying the β line between expected and unexpected losses. In the loss distribution it is significantly important to identify the β (boundary) line between expected and unexpected losses. The zone of the expected losses is used in order to determine the frontier that corresponds to the highest level at which a loss can be characterised as expected. In turn, the expected loss is used in order to derive its constituents, which are PD and LGD. Moreover, the expected loss can directly substitute the part of the supervisory formula (see Chapter 5) that corresponds to expected loss for credit risk (PD $\times$ LGD) or, alternatively, to provisions. The definition of the zone for the unexpected losses, up to the set confidence level, is used in order to estimate the unexpected loss that corresponds to capital requirements, once the provisions for the expected loss have been taken into account.

The following introduces a four-step methodology for identifying the β line between expected and unexpected losses.

Step 1: Forming a candidate β line. In this step the dimension of the impact space is divided equally into p number of intervals. These points are constituents of the candidate β lines, denoted as a set of $L(v)$. Note that finer intervals increase the number of potential candidate β lines, but they also increase the computation required.

Step 2: Estimating the space distance (intervals) β_d between the candidate β lines $L(v)$ with the distributed loss impacts. Two different types of interval are constructed from the differences between the candidate β lines and the loss impact values I that have smaller or greater degree accordingly.

The summation of the square value of the absolute values for the two differentiations is estimated as defined in Equation (17) and Equation (18):

$$\beta_{d(max)} = \sum_{i=1}^{k} \left(\left\| \frac{L(v) - I_i}{\sigma} \right\|^2 \right), \quad \text{for } L(v) > I \qquad (17)$$

$$\beta_{d(min)} = \sum_{j=1}^{q} \left(\left\| \frac{L(v) - I_j}{\sigma} \right\|^2 \right), \quad \text{for } L(v) > I \qquad (18)$$

where q and k is the number of impact values I that are greater or smaller than the interval point p of the candidate β lines $L(v)$, σ is the scale parameter.

Note that the estimation of the intervals in the above Equation (17) and Equation (18) can also be defined using exponential basis functions, for the inverse values of the intervals, when the tail of the distribution is very long. This will consider less the far-distance values and shift the β value closer to the space area where most values are placed.

Step 3: Estimating the weight values β_w of the candidate β points. For each interval point p the absolute value of the differentiation between the sums of the space distances is calculated as defined in Equation (19). The matrix in Equation (20) contains all these differentiations for the p number of intervals defined in Step 1.

$$\beta_d = \left\| \beta_{d(max)} - \beta_{d(min)} \right\| \qquad (19)$$

$$\beta_w = \begin{vmatrix} \beta_{d_1} \\ \beta_{d_2} \\ \dots \\ \beta_{d_p} \end{vmatrix} \qquad (20)$$

Figure 12 β line between expected and unexpected losses

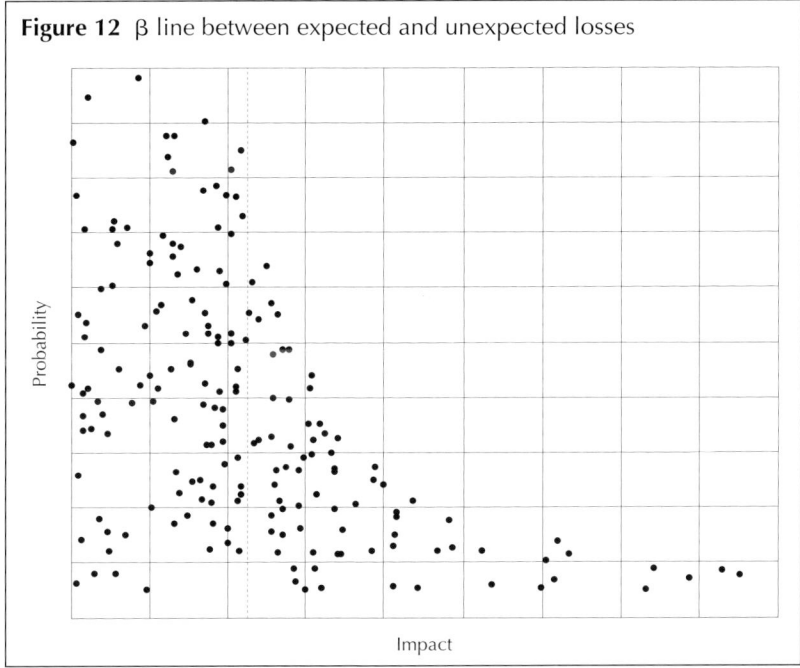

Step 4: Selecting the β line between expected and unexpected losses. The β is on the point interval that has the minimum value among the weight values of the candidate β point as defined in Equation (21):

$$\beta = \min (\beta_{eq}) \qquad\qquad (21)$$

Figure 12 gives an example of a β line between expected and unexpected losses that is estimated according to the above method.

ASPECTS OF INTEGRATED VAR
Integrated VAR analysis based on integrated risks and losses

In market risk, the estimation of VAR is based on the actual returns of the portfolio products. On the other hand, in credit risk, the credit VAR is estimated by considering the actual losses of the credit portfolio. There is more flexibility in operational VAR analysis, where both the returns of the operational risks and their resulting losses can be considered. Similarly to the operational VAR, the integrated VAR analysis can be based on:

❑ the returns of the integrated risks indicators; or
❑ the integrated losses.

In the latter case, the exposure and the distribution of the losses are the main elements needed to be considered for the integrated VAR estimation. However, in the former case the returns of the integrated risk indicators and their significance levels play an important role in integrated VAR analysis.

Different VAR approaches can be applied based on the above types of the retuned data of the IKRIs and the integrated losses. By applying a parametric VAR approach, the change of the integrated portfolio performance P for every change of the risk factors defined by the integrated key-risk indicators d($IKRI$) (use of the delta VAR approach) is evaluated.

When using the parametric VAR approach the following fundamental assumptions have to be made:

❑ the risk factors are approximately lognormally distributed;
❑ the relationship between the portfolio price and the risk factors is linear (delta VAR); and
❑ the time value of the contracts may be neglected.

The changes of VAR with the change in the risk exposure as defined by the loss distribution can also be applied using the integrated VAR approach. Historical simulation can also be used on the basis of the integrated indicators that refer to the past historical information as well as for recording integrated losses. Monte Carlo VAR uses a certain number of random values (random sets) for different holding periods. These sets can be used to shock both the integrated risk indicators and the integrated losses.

The distribution of the chosen random values can also be driven by the distribution of the returns referring to integrated risks or the distribution of the integrated losses within the probability and impact axes. This means that, if there is an idea about the actual distribution of integrated returns, it will lead the choice on which distribution is the basis of the derivation of random numbers. In the integrated risk analysis it is important to define the strength of the shocked values and the bandwidth of the random and historical values that are used.

Defining the shocking values for integrated VAR analysis
Similar to the approach described in the operational VAR in Chapter 3, integrated VAR can also be estimated by shocking, with vectors of historical or random values $\boldsymbol{\varepsilon}$, the decomposed matrix $\mathbf{A}^T$ of the correlation matrix $\mathbf{C_R}$ is defined by the matrix of returns $\mathbf{KR}$ referring to integrated risks defined and measured via the IKRIs. $\mathbf{L_R}$ is defined by the matrix of the loss returns $\mathbf{RP}$. Note that for the first set of returns the time framework for the returns is defined by the matrix $\mathbf{KR}$, whereas for the loss returns the holding period is harmonised by the conversion factor CF.

Defining the historical and random values for integrated VAR analysis
For both cases there are two types of historical or random values $\boldsymbol{\varepsilon}$ that can be used to shock the integrated risks returns or integrated losses:

❏ by getting their rates within the same distribution bandwidth (value zones), whereby the amount of these values always have the same quantity of random numbers n; or
❏ by getting their rates from a variable-distribution bandwidth – moreover, the quantity of the historical/random numbers n is also varied.

In the former case the variation of both the zone limits and the quantity of historical/random numbers are set according to the degree of significance referring to each set of the integrated risk returns or to the values of the integrated risk exposure for each of the losses.

Thus, the new set of the historical/random values that is driven by the degree of significance values and the integrated risk exposure values $h(v)$ is as defined in Equation (22) and Equation (23) respectively.

$$\epsilon_{new} = \epsilon \cdot \left(\frac{\exp(SV_{cor})^2}{\sigma} \right) \qquad (22)$$

$$\epsilon_{new} = \epsilon \cdot \left(\frac{\exp(h_v)^2}{\sigma} \right) \qquad (23)$$

Where $\boldsymbol{\varepsilon}_{new}$ are the new sets of the initial historical or random values; σ is a constant value smaller then one; SV_{cor}^2 is the degree of significance value for the integrated risks return; h_v^2 is the exposure value of the integrated losses.

SUMMARY

Integrated risk identification is based on both qualitative and quantitative risk identification. The qualitative aspect maps all key activities that relate to financial products and can also indicate risks, whereas the quantitative aspect identifies IKRIs and their parameters to define measurement functions. The identification analysis of the integrated risks is then used as the basis for designing the model. The integrated risk modelling can be based either on the IKRIs that define the significance value of the risk parameters or on the distribution of market, credit and operational losses. By the use of key risk indicators, the qualitatively defined risks are turned into quantitative measurements so that relevant data can be collected for them. The IKRIs are then used to construct the matrix of risk measurements. Based on the correlation analysis that identifies the significance values of the above information, the models are defined. The correlation analysis is used as a foundation to illustrate the integrated three-dimensional correlation model in terms of the financial product and their integrated risks.

Mapping and monitoring the integrated risks gives an overview of risk hazards. Risk managers must be able to understand how one source of risk can affect other risks and how parameters of risk indicators are intertwined. This understanding is achieved by analysing correlations between the different sources of risk and the correlations between the parameters that measure the different risks, as discussed above. This facilitates a sophisticated monitoring of the integrated risks. More importantly, it can be used as a "warning signal".

The integrated risk can also be based on distribution of market, credit and operational losses. Using the methodology called IRiLMoS, the identification of such an integrated model was defined and illustrated in this section. The model is based on the clusters defined by the groups of losses that are distributed within the probability and impact space. The surface defined by the IRiLMoS method illustrates the actual exposure for the different sources of risk. The mapping of losses is mainly based on the distribution of past losses for a set time period. However, for monitoring the losses, their distribution needs to be dynamically updated.

Three-dimensional surface graphs that result from the accompanying software show graphically the models of the loss distribution.

In this chapter, several aspects of the integration among different sources of risk – market, credit and operational – along with several paradigms were discussed, in order to illustrate the interrelation among these sources of risk. In turn, the concepts of aggregating and integrating the economic and regulatory capital were exemplified. The risk management community is keen on the idea of aggregating the regulatory capital and/or integrating economic capital, although the latter remains in its early stages. This chapter proposes a method for integrating the regulatory capital as well. The Basel Committee neither permits such treatment nor explicitly prohibits such methodology. Albeit supervisory authorities are not, currently, familiar with such treatment, in future years they will search for methodologies in order to improve the fair regulatory quantification of risks by taking into account inter-risk diversification effects. The methodologies presented in this book move in this direction.

The different approaches for the estimation of the integrated VAR, from the historical to Monte Carlo simulation, can be driven by the two different types of integrated risks return or integrated losses as well as the set of shocking values as described in this chapter. Thus, integrated VAR can be estimated based on historical or random values that obtain their rates from the fixed or variable distribution bandwidth and volume. The variation is derived from the degree of significance referring to the integrated risk returns, or it can also be defined by the exposure degree of the integrated risk losses. Accordingly, these historical or random values are used to shock the values of integrated risks or losses.

REFERENCES

Akkizidis, I. S. and V. Bouchereau, 2006, *Guide to Optimal Operational Risk and Basel II* (New York: Auerbach Publications).

Basel Committee on Banking Supervision, 1996, "Overview of the Amendment to the Capital Accord to Incorporate Market Risks," January (updated on April 1998).

Kalyvas, L. and A. Sfetsos, 2006, "Does the Application of Innovative Internal Models Diminish Regulatory Capital?", *International Journal of Theoretical and Applied Finance* **9(2)**, pp 217–226.

Conclusions

It is not the strongest species that survive, nor the most intelligent, but the ones most responsive to change

— Charles Darwin

The key objective of this book has been to present the theoretical background that corresponds to different types of risk. The ultimate objective was to integrate the methodologies for each and every source of risk (market, credit and operational). In order for this to be done, it was necessary to present, in a practical manner, a spectrum of products and risks related to them.

The first chapter dealt with market risk and consisted of four sections. The first presented major market risk factors that influence the value of the assets held by a credit or financial institution. The market risk factors were separated into three major categories, which included interest rate risk, foreign exchange risk and equity risk. The most concern was given to the interest rate risk because of the complexity of its estimation and the existence of non-linear relationships between interest rates for different cashflows and the value of the interest rate asset. It also demonstrated what data are needed to represent each of the risk factors. Moreover, this chapter in synergy with the Appendix examined the impact of each risk factor on the valuation of derivative products with non-linear characteristics, such as options.

The purpose of the next section was to introduce the reader to the widespread methods for estimating value-at-risk (VAR) and to provide evidence of the possible superiority of one method over the others. The delta-normal model uses parameters based on historical data, such as those implemented by traditional estimation procedures or by RiskMetrics, or on implied volatilities derived from heavily traded over-the-counter (OTC) or exchange-traded options. Both approximations generate a covariance matrix over which the linear or quasi-linear positions are applied in order to calculate the portfolio VAR. Among full valuation models, historical simulation (HS) is the easiest to implement, but it is criticised for the single, past-related path that it provides. This path may miss time periods during which the volatility changes may be significant. On the other hand, the Monte Carlo (MC) simulation is the most comprehensive model – because it provides simulations of numerous different paths – but it is also the most difficult to implement. For portfolios that do not contain options or embedded options in their synthesis, the delta-normal method may well be the best choice. However, for portfolios containing option positions, it is not appropriate. As an alternative, the management of financial institutions prefer to turn to historical or Monte Carlo simulations.

Apart from the generic market risk, most financial institutions face a significant amount of specific market risk. This type of risk, discussed in the next section of Chapter 1, is very important, especially for banks that do not utilise the full and exact dataset of market risk factors relevant to the nature of the portfolio. The quantification of specific risk is very difficult in terms of available data and storage costs for the data. That section focused more on the quantification of specific risk on fixed-income securities.

Corporate, or non-risk-free, fixed-income securities retain an excess level of risk that is reflected in the market price and represented by interest rate spreads. However, interest rate spreads are not fully attributed to market risk factors. Instead, other risk factors attributed to credit and operational risks and reflected in the price of fixed-income securities may also be attributed to interest rate spread. These risks may be analysed from data derived from either the marketplace or internal data provided by credit institutions. This section referred to and analysed the various risk factors that drive the level of interest rate spread. The quantification of these risk factors was extensively analysed in Chapter 2.

The soundness of the models should be proved by their statistical accuracy. On the other hand, the Basel Committee, implicitly, supports a model that is valid for internal use if its predictions are more conservative than the actual VAR. The amendment of Basel I along with the forthcoming changes in its context (rules related to market risk are expected to remain unchanged), not only allows, but also stimulates, credit and financial institutions to apply their own internal models. Furthermore, the Basel Committee proposes a test of appropriateness in economic terms. In this context, the fourth section of Chapter 1 dealt with the intention of the Basel Committee to provide credit institutions with the appropriate tools to evaluate every method within the same financial environment.

Bearing in mind the exact methodology for the determination of capital requirements, the only task that competent authorities and credit institutions have to carry out is to define the regulatory parameters for capital requirements. That section thus dealt with back- and stress-testing of market risk exposures.

In Chapter 2 the commonly used credit assessment models were examined. There are a number of models and techniques that aim to capture credit risk and provide reliable estimates of credit risk parameters. Credit institutions are upgrading their risk management systems by increasing the level of sophistication of the techniques they use in their effort to predict the creditworthiness of obligors. The existing models as well as new promising ones appear to be powerful in the estimation and prediction of credit risk. The appropriate methodology for each credit institution is based on the type of portfolio, the profile of obligors, the credit policy adopted by each institution, the business cycle and so on. That is why model developers should take into consideration the purpose of the model development, the phase of the economic cycle, the assumptions of each method and its advantages and disadvantages before concluding the appropriate model.

In the next section, the estimation of fundamental parameters was examined. Their estimation is carried out by either implying them from traded credit derivatives or using the internal data of the credit institution. Credit default swaps were proposed as the optimal products, in order to imply the parameters of credit risk. However, it is complicated, or even impossible, to estimate simultaneously probability of default (PD) and loss given default (LGD) from credit default swaps. For this reason one of the two parameters should be estimated independently.

On the other hand, fully parametric models, which use internal information about the behaviour of loans incorporated into a portfolio, should carefully evaluate the available information and incorporate the prerequisites set from top management about the notion of risk. Thus, the section proposes various quantification techniques for the independent quantification of probability of default in order for every credit institution to find its own risk attitude and articulate it into these techniques.

In the next section of Chapter 2, credit-rating systems and the issue of validation were examined. Credit ratings are summary indicators of the credit risk on a credit exposure. There are many forms of credit-rating system. Regardless of the form, meaningful credit ratings should group credits in order to discriminate between possible outcomes of the credit analysis and at the same time should rank the perceived levels of credit risk.

The integrity of a credit-rating system is checked through qualitative and quantitative validation. Greater focus should be given to the qualitative validation process. In the case of unsuccessful results in the qualitative validation, the system should be regarded as inappropriate for the assessment of credit risk. In the quantitative validation process it is important to transact all three validations: in-sample, out-of-sample and out-of-time.

Financial institutions and supervisors have been paying increasing attention to operational risk in recent years. While firms have always had in place internal controls and systems to minimise the losses from events such as fraud and transaction failures, of late a number of firms have begun to view operational risk as a distinct and substantial class of risk. As institutions' activities have grown more complex, so too have their operational risk profiles. For example, while the growing reliance on automation has generally reduced the frequency of human errors at a number of institutions (although a number of high-profile losses make clear that people risks remain substantial), system-failure risks from interconnected internal and external systems have grown concurrently. Likewise, large-scale financial-industry mergers, acquisitions, and consolidations test the viability of new, or newly integrated, systems. In light of these trends, a number of firms have devoted resources to operational risk measurement with the objective of improved risk management, including via risk transfer. Chapter 3 discussed the subject of Operational Risk.

The first section of Chapter 3 introduced the concept of the three pillars of the accord, but concentrated mainly on Pillar I – estimating the minimum capital requirements. The different types of approach proposed by Basel II for estimating minimum capital requirements for operational risk were highlighted, with particular emphasis on the more complex AMA approach. Criteria that need to be surpassed and factors in selecting a particular approach were also emphasised.

Operational risk identification and loss profiling were discussed in the second section. The basis of this identification rests on defining and measuring operational key-risk indicators (KRIs). Furthermore, it attempted to define the significance values for the operational risks and affected operations and the operational risk loss profile by using a methodology called *clustering operational risk profile*. This method identifies the clusters within the loss distribution. The results of the analysis illustrate graphically the risk exposure as mountains on three-dimensional plots.

The third section of Chapter 3 examined operational value-at-risk (VAR) as a method for calculating minimum capital requirement. This section discussed the VAR method and its usefulness in the measurement of different types of risk. The section showed ways to estimate the minimum capital requirements for operational risks by using VAR analysis to determine the operational risk value. Furthermore, advantages and drawbacks of applying VAR approaches were highlighted. Finally, top-down and bottom-up approaches were considered to help in the estimation of operational VAR.

The conventional approaches for estimating VAR do not always account for fat tails of the distribution of returns. On the other hand, they assume that returns follow a unique distribution for the entire range of their values. Extreme-value theory (EVT), examined in Chapter 4, acts complementarily and separates the distribution of the values around the mean and the distribution of returns that belongs to the tails. Thus, EVT attempts to find the optimal point beyond which all values belong to the tail. After finding the cut-off point that separates the body distribution from the tail distribution, the latter has to be modelled. In order to model the tail distribution, two approaches were discussed in this chapter, namely, *block maxima* and *peaks-over-threshold*. The latter approach is further differentiated into two sub-approaches: the *semi-parametric approach*, structured around the Hill estimator; and the *parametric approach*, which is applied by defining the exact parameters of the distribution of returns. The mathematical equations together with their advantages and disadvantages for these approaches were also highlighted.

Apart from the use of EVT methods in estimating VAR measures, they are valuable in constructing stress-testing scenarios for all sources of risk. The measure that efficiently constructs the stress-testing scenarios is the expected shortfall (ES). ES describes the expected loss once the VAR measure is exceeded and can potentially stand for an alternative historically based stress-testing scenario for all sources of risk (market, credit and operational). An explanation on the use of ES was given in this chapter. Clustering analysis was also proposed to define the size of the tail as well as for the time dependency. Both are very critical issues in the analysis of extreme values. The proposed approaches are based on how the observed values are distributed in common clusters. Examples were illustrated to show visually the applicability of these approaches to the aspects of extreme-value theory.

In the quantification of market risk there are several alternative models that can be used. Some of them produce higher VAR values making doing business safer. Also, the Basel Committee rewards these models with a multiplication factor that depends on the failures these models exhibited to predict actual portfolio changes. Apparently, VAR models that consistently produce higher values are assigned an equal or lower multiplication factor. In order for the efficient models to be truly rewarded, the lower multiplication factor assigned to them should eliminate the effect the higher VAR estimation would have in the calculation of capital requirements. However, this is not the case in the calculation of capital requirements under the Basel II regulatory framework. All these properties of the Basel II accord were examined in Chapter 5.

The Basel Committee proposes two approaches for measuring the capital requirements for credit risk: the *standardised approach* (SA) and the *internal ratings-based approach* (IRB). In the SA, risk weights are specified for certain types of claim. Under the IRB, banks use their internal estimations to assess credit risk. The estimates are translated into potential future loss, defining the basis of minimum capital requirements. In order to encourage a larger number of banks to move to the IRB approach, the Basel II Accord provides for two alternative methodologies: the simpler *foundation IRB approach* and the *advanced IRB approach*, the latter being based on a broader use of banks' own internal assessments of risk components. These issues were analysed in the second section of Chapter 5.

In terms of operational risk management, the Basel II accord has made much effort to deal with the measurement and management of this important risk, which were not considered at all in the Basel I framework. One of the foremost benefits for the new Basel II accord in terms of operational risk management is the fact that regulatory capital has been allocated for it as a separate discipline. Furthermore, it has given a definition of operational risk that can be adopted in credit institutions. The Basel II accord permits regulators to allow "sophisticated" banks to use their own internal systems to establish risk levels rather than those assigned by private credit-rating agencies. Notwithstanding its many benefits, there are numerous criticisms that are made of Basel II in the operational risk framework.

Chapter 5 later discussed concerns over the complexity of the requirements and the continuing ambiguity surrounding operational risk practices. There have also been concerns about how difficult the requirements will be to implement and how challenging it will be for supervisors to monitor compliance. Some of the issues – such as operational risk transfer, assessment of operational risks, data availability, difficulties in operational risk modelling due to data availability, the differentiation between expected and unexpected losses, and the distinction between the beta values set for the business lines – were highlighted in this section.

Chapter 6, which consisted of three sections, presented several aspects of the integration between all sources of risk: market, credit and operational. Several paradigms were presented in order to illustrate the interrelation among these sources of risk. Integrated risk identification is based on both qualitative and quantitative risk appraisal. The qualitative aspect maps all key activities that relate to financial products and can also indicate risks, whereas the quantitative aspect identifies integrated key-risk indicators (IKRIs) and their parameters to define measurement functions. The identification analysis of the integrated risks is then used as the basis for designing the model. Based on the correlation analysis that identifies the significance values of the above information, the models are defined. The correlation analysis was used in the first section of Chapter 6 as a foundation to illustrate the integrated three-dimensional correlation model in terms of the financial products and their integrated risks. Mapping and monitoring integrated risks gives an overview of risk hazards. Risk managers must be able to understand how one type of risk can affect other risks and how parameters of risk indicators are intertwined. These were also discussed in this section.

Later in Chapter 6, it was shown how the integrated risk can also be based on the distribution of market, credit and operational losses. By the use of the methodology called *integrated risk loss mountain surface* (IRiLMoS), the identification of such an integrated model was defined and illustrated in this section. The surface defined by this method illustrates the actual exposure for the different types of risk. The mapping of losses is mainly based on the distribution of past losses for a set time period. However, for monitoring the losses, their distribution needs to be dynamically updated.

Chapter 6 then presented several paradigms to illustrate the interrelation among the different sources of risk. The concepts of aggregating and integrating the economic and regulatory capital were also exemplified. The risk management community are keen on the idea of aggregating the regulatory capital and/or integrating economic capital, although the latter remains in its early stages. The chapter then illustrated a method for integrating the regulatory capital. The Basel Committee neither permits such treatment nor explicitly prohibits such methodology. Albeit supervisory authorities are not, currently, familiar with such treatment, in future years they will search for methodologies in order to improve the fair regulatory quantification of risks. The methodologies presented in this book move towards this direction.

Finally, the Appendix presents the theoretical background necessary for the quantification of market risks. The material introduces the use of the essential financial derivative products, for an understanding of their properties and their valuation. Moreover, financial derivative products, for the derivation of implied risk parameters, are presented, irrespective of their use as portfolio components. Furthermore, the fact that data, for some financial products, are not always available was taken into consideration. In order to overcome the lack of data, especially for products for which data are not readily available (such as options and futures), benchmarking is used. Finally, when the benchmarking of product prices does not yield reliable results, it is of high importance for the risk manager to use interpolation techniques. Techniques employed involve *linear*, *exponential* and *polynomial interpolation*. Interpolation techniques depend on the types of financial data and product. All these techniques are examined in the Appendix.

There are some important challenges for risk integration and risk aggregation that need to be considered when one is designing an integrated risk management system. Some of these issues include ensuring accountability and responsibility while also taking advantage of local knowledge and expertise. There might be possible conflicts between economic/risk reporting and accounting/regulatory standards. Furthermore, there is a need to ensure that a proper treatment of legal entity issues. There is also the matter of how to use economic capital to make improved decisions. It is to be emphasised that, while integrated risk management concepts are currently still in the developmental phase, they have a substantially promising future. These concepts and their related products will be in a continuous state of development, specifically because the main area of application for such concepts is the dynamic business environment, characterised by increasingly rapid changes.

Appendix

CAPITAL ASSET PRICING THEORY

When dealing with risk factors, the reader should bear in mind that normal distribution is the underlying distribution. However, in Chapter 4, different measures were involved for the estimation of location and dispersion parameters.

According to Capital Asset Pricing Model (CAPM) theory, the mean, the variance and the standard deviation of asset returns are defined as follows:

$$\mu_x = E(x) = \sum_{i=1}^{n} p_i x_i \qquad (1)$$

$$\sigma_x^2 = E[(x_i - E(x)^2)] = \sum_{i=1}^{n} p_i (x_i - E(x))^2 \qquad (2)$$

and,

$$\sigma_x = \sqrt{\sum_{i=1}^{n} p_i (x_i - E(x))^2} \qquad (3)$$

where x_i's are the S_i's asset returns estimated by the arithmetic returns measure:

$$x_i = \frac{S_{i+1} - S_i}{S_i} \qquad (4)$$

or by the logarithmic returns measure:

$$x_i = \ln\left(\frac{S_{i+1}}{S_i}\right) \tag{5}$$

where $i = 1 \ldots n - 1$, corresponding to the number of the available observations for the asset, p_i is the probability of the random event x_i and n is the total number of prices concerning the asset value. Whenever each event has the same probability of occurrence, the above typology is transformed into a representation, according to which the probability p_i is omitted and the measure is divided by the number of observations or the number of observations minus one, such as:

$$\sigma_x = \sqrt{\frac{\sum_{i=1}^{n}(x_i - E(x))^2}{n-1}} \tag{6}$$

It should be mentioned here that in literature, the sum of the squared differences around the mean value is divided by either n or $n - 1$ as shown above. This happens because the first case refers to the estimation of the population's standard deviation while the second case refers to the estimation of the standard deviation of the sample. The book focuses on the estimation of the standard deviation of the sample returns. Thus, whenever the standard deviation of returns is denoted, the standard deviation of sample returns is implied.

The difference between the aforementioned measures of returns is that the later implies a continuously compounded evolution of returns over time. This means that, according to the logarithmic measure, returns do not exhibit gaps between two points in time, that is, the changes are not as sharp as in the case of the arithmetic measure of returns. This means logarithmic returns exhibit a continuous distribution.

In order for the parameters to be applied on a portfolio-wide basis, it is important to introduce a metric of common movements between two sequences of asset returns. Although in recent years new measures have been proposed (such as copulas), the classical metrics are the covariance and the correlation. The first metric depends on the general level of the sequences under examination, while the second measure ranges between -1 and 1, irrespective of the level of returns. The mathematical representation of the covariance and correlation are as follows:

$$\sigma_{xy} = \frac{\sum_{i=1}^{n} (x_i - \mu_x)(y_i - \mu_y)}{n-1} \tag{7}$$

$$\rho_{xy} = \frac{\sigma_{xy}}{\sigma_x \sigma_y} \tag{8}$$

where σ_{xy} is the covariance metric for x and y time series, μ_x and μ_y are the mean values for x and y time series, respectively, σ_x and σ_y are the standard deviation values for x and y time series, respectively, and ρ_{xy} is the correlation metric.

Modern bank portfolios consist of more than one risky asset, making the need for the estimation of a portfolio-wide measure of mean, variance and standard deviation more apparent. In order for these parameters to be estimated more easily, it is useful to impose the basic properties applied to the estimation of mean and variance. The main properties are as follows:

$$\mu_{(x+c)} = \mu_x + c \tag{9}$$

$$\mu_{(xc)} = c\mu_x \tag{10}$$

$$\sigma^2_{(x+c)} = \sigma^2_x \tag{11}$$

$$\sigma^2_{(xc)} = c^2 \sigma^2_x \tag{12}$$

where c is a constant term.

A portfolio of two risky assets, x and y, both normally distributed, with w_x and w_y percentage participation of asset x and asset y in the portfolio, respectively, has a mean return that equals:

$$\mu_p = \mu_{(w_x x + w_y x)} = \mu_{(w_x x)} + \mu_{(w_x y)} = w_x \mu_x + w_y \mu_y \tag{13}$$

and a variance value that equals:

$$\sigma^2_p = \sigma_{(w_x x + w_y x)} = w_x^2 \sigma_x^2 + w_y^2 \sigma_y^2 + 2w_x w_y \rho_{xy} \sigma_x \sigma_y \tag{14}$$

The extension of the above methodology to more than two assets provides the following representation:

$$\mu_p = \sum_{j=1}^{m} w_j \mu_j \tag{15}$$

$$\sigma_p^2 = \sum_{j=1}^{m} \sum_{k=1}^{l} w_j w_k \rho_{jk} \sigma_j \sigma_k \tag{16}$$

where ρ_{jk} becomes unity when $j = k$. This happens because the common movement of an asset return time series with itself is perfect. The same representation in the form of matrixes is extensively presented in Chapter 1, where the value-at-risk (VAR) methodologies are described analytically.

The methodology of the estimation of mean, variance and standard deviation measurements generally refers to products that show evidence of linear behaviour. The linear behaviour is mainly observable in spot financial markets. Spot financial products are non-derivative financial products, traded and settled at most within three business days. Their linear behaviour lies in the fact that any percentage change in the traded value of a portfolio, consisting of one asset, would have an equal effect on the value of the portfolio. However, this is not always the case. When derivative financial products are involved, the percentage change in the value of the underlying asset does not have an equal effect on the value of the derivative product. The properties of complex financial instruments will be presented in the following section.

COMPLEX FINANCIAL INSTRUMENTS
Portfolio products
Futures
Forward products have been traded, unofficially, throughout all eras of human history. Once a trader has agreed to deliver or receive a product on a future date, at a specified price, with a counterparty trader, the transaction is said to be a *forward contract*. In other words, a forward contract is a bet on the price that will prevail on a future date if the forward contract is traded on a standalone basis. The naked positions in forward contracts are distinguished between short and long positions. The short position

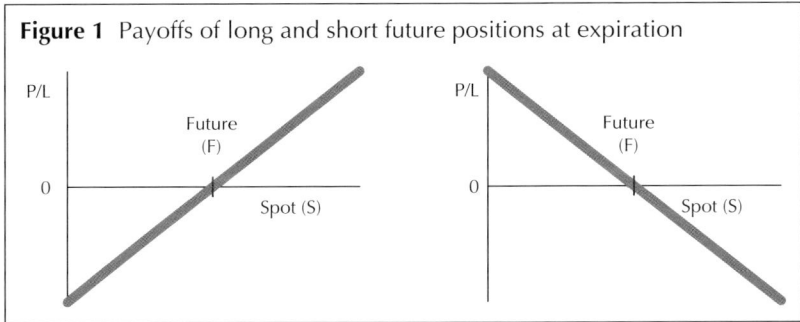

Figure 1 Payoffs of long and short future positions at expiration

grants the holder the obligation to sell the underlying spot asset to the counterparty at a specified price on a given future date. On the other hand, the long position imposes on the holder the obligation to buy the underlying spot asset from the counterparty at a specified price on a given future date. Traders will profit or lose an amount according to the behaviour of the future spot price of the underlying asset. The payoffs of these positions are shown in Figure 1.

However, when forward contracts are traded on an organised exchange under its regulations, at specified volumes for certain products, they are named *futures* (for more details on differences between forwards and futures see Sutcliffe, 1997).

The present value of a forward or future contract is given by:

$$S_v = Fe^{-rT} \tag{17}$$

where S_v is the fair present value of the forward contract F, r is the relative discount rate and T is the time in years up to the expiration date of the forward contract.

Otherwise approached, the forward or future fair value, based on the spot price of the underlying asset is given by:

$$F_v = S_0 e^{rT} \tag{18}$$

Irrespective of the way it is done, however the fair value of a future contract is arrived at, market participants determine its value by buying or selling contracts according to their expectations about the future spot prices. Thus, the expectations of market participants generate an unbiased predictor of the future spot price of the relevant underlying asset. Even though the prediction is unbiased, given that the market is efficient, all market participants have access to the same information set and nobody can exploit confidential information. In any case, the price of the future contract tends to equal the price of the future spot price as the expiration date of the future contract gets closer.

Instead, if a trader retains a position that coincides with the underlying asset of the forward contract, the forward contract has the ability to hedge the initial position. For example, a farmer wants to sell his milk production at the end of a three-month period, but he is afraid of the future spot price of milk and wishes to protect himself from the price variation. So he agrees to sell a forward contract, that is, an agreement to sell the milk at a certain price. Thus, whatever is the future spot price of the milk, the selling price of milk is guaranteed by the price of the forward contract. These transactions also exist in the financial markets as long as traders have special needs for buying or selling products on a future date. The differences between forward contract and future contracts are functional rather than significant (see Sutcliffe, 1997).

Options
Options are derivative products that give the holder (or buyer) the right, but not the obligation, to transact (buy or sell, according to the contract) with the buyer (or holder), an underlying asset at a specified price (the strike price). This transaction can be made at any time until, or on, the expiration date, depending on the type of the option (American or European option, respectively). On the other hand, the seller has the obligation to deliver the underlying asset, upon a request from the holder, or settle in cash any profit or loss from the transaction, under the terms specified in the contract.

In order to be more specific, the options are separated according to two main categories.

❑ *Put options* give the buyer the right, but not the obligation, to sell an underlying asset at a specified price (the strike price) at any time until, or on, the expiration date depending on the type of option (American or European option, respectively). This type of option has positive value when the price of the underlying asset

Figure 2 Payoffs of call and put options at expiration

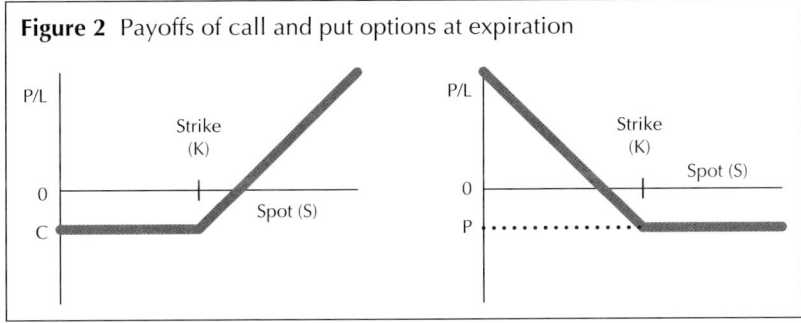

falls below the level of the strike price. This happens because the holder (buyer) has the opportunity to sell the underlying asset at a price greater than the market price of the underlying asset, making a profit.

❑ *Call options* give the buyer the right, but not the obligation, to buy an underlying asset at a specified price (the strike price) at any time until, or on, the expiration date depending on the type of option (American or European option, respectively). This type of option has positive value when the price of the underlying asset increases above the level of the strike price. This happens because the holder (buyer) has the opportunity to buy the underlying asset at a price lower than the market price of the underlying asset, making a profit.

The payoffs of the options are illustrated in Figure 2.

Although this type of derivative product was, originally, invented to protect investors who hold the underlying asset from unfavourable price movements, in recent years, credit institutions retain options as naked positions in their portfolios.

Every option contract has a value. The value is initiated from either the market participants (*traded options*) or the appropriate option-pricing model (*over-the-counter options*). Whichever is the marketplace for the trading of options, the pricing model is necessary in order to determine the fair value of the option. As mentioned above, the holder has the right to buy or sell the underlying option in a strike price K at a future date T years from the present date. The strike price of K in the future equals a strike price of Ke^{-rT} today. Since the price of an option always depends on the price S of the underlying asset, traded in the spot market, the following relationships will always be fulfilled:

$$C \geq S_0 - Ke^{-rT} \tag{19}$$

$$P \geq Ke^{-rT} - S_0 \tag{20}$$

where, C and P are call and put option prices, respectively, r is the risk-free rate and S_0 is the spot price of the underlying asset, given there are no dividends paid on the underlying asset if this is a stock or stock index.

The aforementioned relationships designate that the value of an option is affected by the strike price, the price of the underlying asset and to some degree by the interest rate and the time until the expiration of the contract. If the time to expiration equals zero, that is the pricing of the option takes place at the expiration date, then the values of call and put options become:

$$C = \max\{0, S - K\} \tag{21}$$

$$P = \max\{0, K - S\} \tag{22}$$

Nevertheless, the sign of "equal or greater than", in Equations 19 and 20 shows that option values may also be affected by other factors. A profound factor that may influence option values is the estimated volatility of the underlying asset. Thus, the greater the volatility the higher the option's fair value. Alternatively, the higher the volatility of the underlying asset, the higher the possibility for the option to became profitable for the holder.

It is obvious that market participants, who are the seller and the buyer of the option, determine the market value of exchange-traded options. However, their expectations about the price in which they would place the bid or the ask quote are affected by several factors, as shown above. Black and Scholes (the BS model – see Hull, 2003) developed a concrete framework for the valuation of a European call and put options on a non-paying dividend stock at time zero as follows:

$$C = S_0 \, N(d_1) - Ke^{-rT} \, N(d_2) \tag{23}$$

$$P = Ke^{-rT} \, N(-d_2) - S_0 \, N(-d_1) \tag{24}$$

where,

$$d_1 = \frac{\ln(S_0/K) + (r + \sigma^2/2)T}{\sigma\sqrt{T}} \qquad (25)$$

$$d_2 = \frac{\ln(S_0/K) + (r - \sigma^2/2)T}{\sigma\sqrt{T}} = d_1 - \sigma\sqrt{T} \qquad (26)$$

$N(\bullet)$ is the cumulative normal distribution and σ is the volatility of the underlying asset. However, since there is no unique error-free model for the estimation of the latter, risk managers rely heavily on the so-called *implied volatility*. Implied volatility is the volatility derived by inverting the option-pricing model, described in Equations 23 and 24, given that all other variables, including option prices taken from the marketplace, are certain.

Accordingly, based on the BS model, options are priced for a number of underlying assets (see Hull, 2003). Analysis presented in the book focuses on European options, which are options exercisable only at their maturity, but they can be priced and traded at any time before expiration.

Swaps
By the word "swap" financial engineers, risk managers and derivatives traders mean the exchange of a certain set of cashflows with another set of cashflows, in order to hedge the risk undertaken by an original position. Swaps are directed to hedge all types of risk, namely, foreign exchange, commodity, equity and interest rate risk. However, the most widespread type of swap, and mostly used by credit institutions, is the interest rate swap.

Interest rates in the modern financial environment are an additional market risk factor. Banks are exposed to interest-rate-related positions. When banks possess a long position in an interest-rate-related financial product they are subject to the risk of interest rate increases. On the contrary, when banks are exposed on a short interest rate position they are subject to the risk of interest rate decreases. Thus, banks, in general, are exposed to an interest rate risk in cases in which they are exposed to positions linked to fixed long-term interest rates. These positions retain an extra portion of risk in the sense that banks have no room for manoeuvring except for promptly selling the position. Banks retaining positions exposed to longer interest rate positions have the higher interest rate risk.

A plain vanilla interest rate swap (PVS) involves the exchange of cashflows generated by different types of interest rates, namely, fixed and floating interest rates. The most common case is the receipt of a floating rate (usually Libor) and the simultaneous payment of a fixed swap rate. In other words, a PVS, at time t_0, is a commitment to exchange interest payments related to a notional amount N at pre-specified settlement dates $\{t_1, t_2, t_3, \ldots, t_n\}$. The buyer of a swap makes fixed payments and receives floating-rate payments. The floating rate (usually Libor) is determined at set dates $\{t_0, t_1, t_2, \ldots, t_{n-1}\}$. Suppose that the periods between settlement and set dates are in years, cashflows generated by fixed-swap-rate and floating-rate payments are shown in Figures 3 and 4 respectively.

The fixed swap rate is the interest rate equivalent if the corresponding floating-rate note with the same maturity. Swap interest

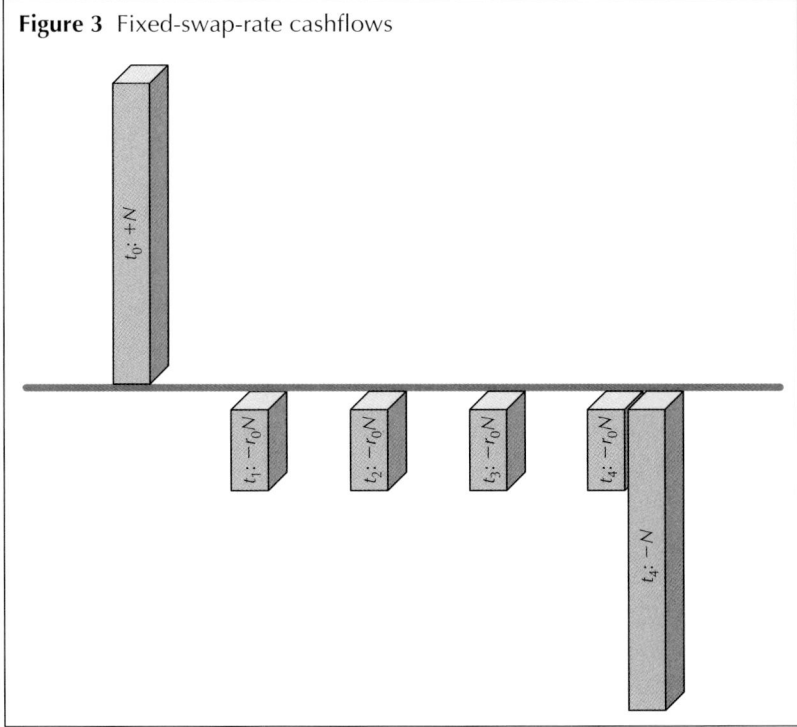

Figure 3 Fixed-swap-rate cashflows

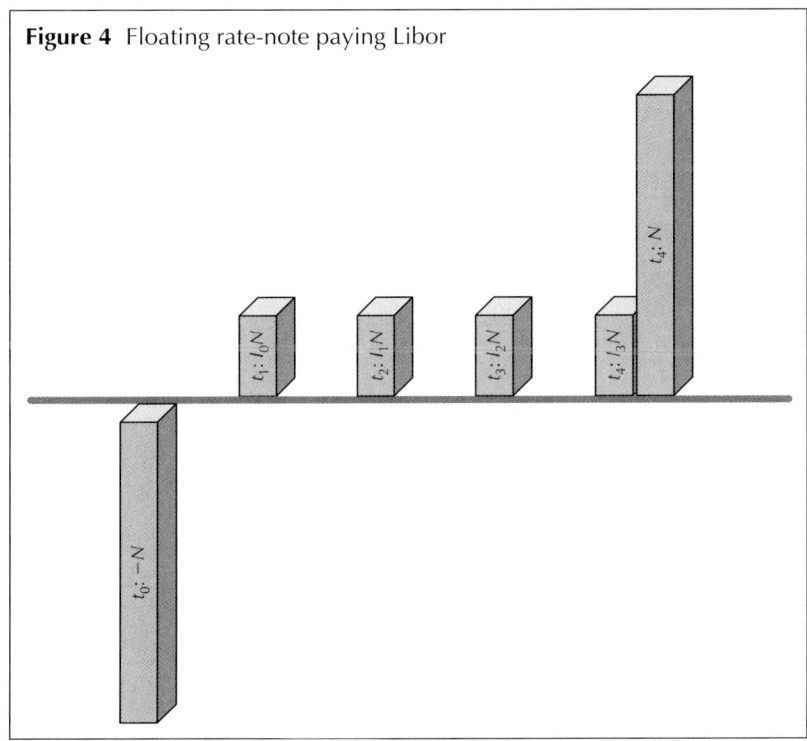

Figure 4 Floating rate-note paying Libor

rates are interest rates that are stable and unchanged throughout the maturity of the swap. Thus, r_0 interest rate is expected to be paid at every distinct settlement date. In order to estimate the present value of the fixed-interest-rate cashflows shown in Figure 3, the following formula should be applied:

$$PV(fix) = \frac{r_0 N}{(1+l_0)} + \frac{r_0 N}{(1+l_0)(1+l_1)} + \frac{r_0 N}{(1+l_0)(1+l_1)(1+l_2)}$$
$$+ \frac{r_0 N + N}{(1+l_0)(1+l_1)(1+l_2)(1+l_3)} \tag{27}$$

On the other hand, floating-rate notes do not assume certain interest payments. The level of interest payments exclusively relies on the level of the base interest rate (Libor in the case examined). The Libor rate l_i ($i = 0, ..., n - 1$) is set at date i and paid at the settlement date $i + 1$. However, the only l_i known with certainty is l_0 that is the Libor rate set at time t_0 and paid at time t_1. The present value of the floating-interest-rate cashflows, shown in Figure 4, is given by the following relationship:

$$PV(fl) = \frac{l_0 N}{(1+l_0)} + \frac{l_1 N}{(1+l_0)(1+l_1)} + \frac{l_2 N}{(1+l_0)(1+l_1)(1+l_2)}$$
$$+ \frac{l_3 N + N}{(1+l_0)(1+l_1)(1+l_2)(1+l_3)} \tag{28}$$

By examining the cashflows of the present-value formula referring to floating-rate notes, it is easy to prove that their present value equals N at every set or settlement date. Assume that:

❑ valuation of the floating-rate note takes place at the issuance of the instrument; and
❑ forward interest rates are unbiased predictors of the future spot interest rates.

Going backwards, the value of the last cashflow $l_3 N + N$ or $(1 + l_3)N$ at t_3 is given by discounting it from $(1 + l_3)$. In other words, its value at t_3 is N. Furthermore, the original cashflow expected at t_3 is $l_2 N$ and the discounted cashflow, as described above, is N. The aggregate cashflow is $l_2 N + N$ or $(1 + l_2)N$. Similarly, the value of cashflows (actual or implied) at t_2 is N. Repeating this methodology, the value of the floating-rate note at t_0 is N. Variation in relation to par value of the note may be observed only between two consecutive set (or settlement) dates.

Thus, by definition, the present value of the above formula at every set date is N. Except for l_0, all other l_i's set at a future time i and paid at $i + 1$ can be approximated by the relative forward interest rate implied by forward-rate agreements described below. The valuation of a swap interest rate implies that, given that all other factors are known, $PV(fix)$ and $PV(fl)$ are equal. By equating the second parts of Equations 27 and 28 and solving for r_0, the swap interest rate is derived. However, the swap interest rate is traded in the marketplace and its market value may deviate from the value derived above. In such cases there are arbitrage opportunities for market participants.

Products for implying risk parameters

Forward-rate agreements

Like all other forward contracts, forward-rate agreements (FRAs) are contractual agreements for future payment or receipt of interest rate cashflows. These products are valued in the same way other forward contracts are. A typical FRA is an agreement between two counterparties according to which the buyer pays a specified interest rate to the seller, while the seller pays an unknown interest rate that will be specified at the expiration of the contract. The long position is retained by the buyer while the short position is retained by the seller. A typical FRA at expiration usually involves the following payoffs for the buyer of the contract such as:

$$FRA_m(0, m, q) = \frac{[L_m(q) - F(0, m, q)]\left(\dfrac{q}{365}\right)}{1 + L_m(q)\left(\dfrac{q}{365}\right)} \tag{29}$$

The settlement of an FRA is made at the expiration of the contract. However, interest rate payments should be paid q days thereafter. In order for the settlement to be made at m day, the interest rate cashflows for both $L_m(q)$ and $F(0, m, q)$ must be discounted by using the floating interest rate that prevails at day m for time deposits with duration q. The price of a plain vanilla FRA for a notional amount of €1 on day d is given (see Chance, 2005) by:

$$FRA_d(0, m, q) = \frac{1}{1 + L_d(m - d)\left(\dfrac{m - d}{365}\right)}$$
$$- \frac{1 + F(0, m, q)\left(\dfrac{q}{365}\right)}{1 + L_d(m - d + q)\left(\dfrac{m - d + q}{365}\right)} \tag{30}$$

where,

$FRA_d(0, m, q)$ is the value of an FRA at time d arranged at time 0 for a contract that expires in m days and for an interest rate valid for $q - m$ days after day m,

$L_d(m - d)$ is the floating rate (usually Libor or Euribor) that prevails at day d for a time deposit with duration $m - d$,

$F(0, m, q)$ is the fixed rate the buyer is obliged to pay, arranged at time 0 for a contract that expires in m days and for an interest rate valid for $q - m$ days after day m.

The first element of the second part of Equation 30 represents the present value of the notional amount discounted using the time deposit floating rate that prevails at day d for the next $m - d$ days ahead. The second element of the second part of Equation 30 represents the upfront payment including the notional amount and the fixed-interest-rate payment at day d. The fair value of an FRA is given by combining the above-mentioned elements.

However, the marketplace price of an FRA and the fair value of the contract may differ from the traded price. In that respect, the forward interest rate for q days after m days from the present time may be given by solving for $F(0, m, q)$. Forward interest rates are very useful in order to value other derivative products such as swaps.

Credit default swap
All the above financial products were designed in order to hedge against price changes that take place due to market turbulences. On the other hand, a major component of the banking portfolio is the set of loans granted to various obligors. Those loans, mainly, possess credit risk that is described in Chapter 2. Although the credit risk of a loan portfolio will not be analysed extensively here, it is necessary to describe credit default swaps (CDSs) in order to become familiar with the product before using it for the quantification of credit risk. CDSs are used in order to hedge a certain portfolio of loans against the appearance of a prespecified credit event or a prespecified set of credit events. These products allow credit risk to be managed in roughly the same way as market risks, that is, by purchasing a financial product traded in the marketplace.

The scope of this book is not to depict all available set of CDS products. The only CDS that will be described is the plain vanilla CDS, because this contains all available information about implied parameters needed to estimate credit risk. Thus, a plain vanilla CDS (see Hull and White, 2000) is a contract that provides insurance against the default risk (credit event) by a particular company (reference entity). The bank that buys the insurance retains the right to sell a particular bond (reference obligation) issued by the reference entity for its par value, also considered as swap's notional principal, when a credit event occurs. The aforementioned bond consists of part of the credit portfolio of the bank that buys the protection.

The total payments per year, as a percentage of the notional principal of the CDS, for a newly issued CDS with €1 notional principal, are given by the following formula:

$$s = \frac{\int_0^T [1 - \hat{R} - A(t)\hat{R}] q(t) v(t)\, dt}{\int_0^T q(t) [u(t) + e(t)]\, dt + \pi u(T)} \quad (31)$$

where T is the life of credit default swap; $q(t)$ is the risk-neutral density of probability of default; $\hat{R}$ is the risk-neutral expected recovery rate on the reference obligation; $u(t)$ is the present value of payments at the rate of €1 per year on payment dates between time zero and t; $e(t)$ is the present value of an accrual payment at time t equal to $t - t^*$ where t^* is the payment date immediately preceding time t; $v(t)$ is the present value of €1 received at time t; w is the total payments per year made by the CDS buyer; s is the value of w that causes the credit default swap to have zero value; π is the risk-neutral probability that the credit event will not occur during the life of the swap; $A(t)$ is the accrued interest on the reference obligation at the time t as a percentage of the face value.

The above-mentioned valuation of a plain vanilla CDS provides the fair value of such products. However, the prices of CDSs are also disseminated in the marketplace and may differ from what was expected by the fair-value calculation. Information about CDS market prices can be used to derive implied probabilities of default when recovery rates are known or recovery rates when probabilities of default are known.

Mark-to-market

Time series data for different types of product should be constructed in a reliable and consistent manner in order to be used for the estimation of VAR measures presented in Chapter 1. In the case of derivative products the construction of time series is a very difficult and time-consuming task. The first characteristic that should be taken into account is the underlying asset, that is, each element of options or futures time series should refer to the same underlying asset. Furthermore, another obstacle that has to be overcome is that options and futures have limited life. Thus, it is necessary to use, invent or construct time series that correspond to the remaining life of an option or future the day they are examined for the determination of VAR.

In order for a given position to be analysed, the collection of options or futures time series should fulfil the following prerequisites for each observation:

❑ the same type of option (call or put or, so the called, "European" or "American");
❑ the same underlying asset; and
❑ the same time to expiration with the existing portfolio position.

Even though the first and second prerequisites should hold in any case, there may be no data available in order for the third prerequisite to be fulfilled. In this case, the data should be generated through an interpolation technique described in the following section.

For example, if the risk manager would like to construct time series corresponding to call options with 41 days remaining to expiration and the available values €5.37 and €5.92 correspond to 34 and 64 days to expiration, respectively, the value produced would be somewhere in between, depending on the interpolation method used. However, there is no unique interpolation technique appropriate to apply on all derivative financial products. The reason lies in the fact that options possess different "degrees of non-linearity" in relation to futures. Thus, it is logical to use different interpolation models in order to determine the interpolated value of the derivative product.

Mark-to-model

Whenever the data for some financial derivative products are not available, it is essential to produce those data by assuming that a product valuation model holds universally for a specific class of financial product. In order for those data to be produced, the valuation models presented above are exploited. For the application of the technique under discussion, it is essential that all inputs be available at all times. If a specific variable is absent, a benchmarking or an interpolation technique should be applied in order to derive this variable. However, the absence of an input introduces an extra assumption or, alternatively, a second source of potential error. Bearing in mind all the above, the model with the lowest number of required inputs is preferable against all other models.

BOOTSTRAPPING
Bonds held by credit institutions are characterised, mainly, by:

❑ price;
❑ maturities;
❑ frequency of coupon payments;
❑ level of coupon payments; and
❑ current level of interest rates used for discounting.

In order to calculate the fair price of a specific bond all the above factors are essential, apart from the traded price of the bond. However, modern risk management does not see the bond as a unique product but it has to value it by discounting each one of the future expected cashflows, separately. Still, each cashflow is realised at different future points at which different interest rates are expected to prevail.

The current level of interest rates is implied from existing market prices by inverting the bond valuation formula and solving for interest rates. This procedure produces a unique interest rate corresponding to all cashflows realised at different maturities. The inconsistency of this technique lies in the fact that, given that the frequency and the level of coupon payments are different, bonds with the same maturity produce different interest rates for discounting. In order for the effect of those factors to be eliminated, bootstrapping techniques are involved.

Bootstrapping assumes that interest rates of shorter maturities act as a basis for the estimation of interest rates for longer maturities. According to this approximation, the yield to maturity of a bond that pays no coupon, and has the shortest remaining life, is used in order for the initial discounting factor to be estimated. The yield, usually, is selected from one-year zero-coupon bond or from one-year Libor. Consequently, the initial discounting factor is estimated as follows:

$$B(t, t_1) = \frac{1}{1 + y_1} \qquad (32)$$

where $B(t, t_1)$ is the initial zero coupon discount factor and y_1 is the one-year zero coupon yield.

While the initial discount factor is used for discounting the first cashflow that will appear in one year, the same par yield is used to estimate the appropriate yield for discounting the corresponding cashflows. The zero-coupon interest rate for the second year's cashflow is estimated by using the initial zero coupon yield as follows:

$$r(t, t_2) = \left[1 - \left(y_2 \frac{1}{1 + y_1} + y_2 \frac{1}{(1 + y_1)(1 + y_2)} \right) \right]^{-\frac{1}{2}} - 1 \qquad (33)$$

The discount factor for the second year's cashflow is given by the following formula:

$$B(t, t_2) = \frac{1}{\left[1 + r(t, t_2) \right]^2} \qquad (34)$$

where $B(t, t_2)$ is the zero coupon discount factor for the second year and y_2 is the two-years' par yield.

The generalisation of the above methodology (see Deacon and Derry, 1994) for n periods is given by:

$$
B(t, t_n) = \frac{1}{\left\{ 1 + \left[1 - y_n \sum_{j=1}^{n} \prod_{i=j}^{n} \frac{1}{(1 + y_i)} \right]^{-\frac{1}{n}} - 1 \right\}^n}
$$

$$
= 1 - y_n \sum_{j=1}^{n} \prod_{i=j}^{n} \frac{1}{(1 + y_i)} \qquad (35)
$$

Linear interpolation

The simplest approximation of the estimation of the aforementioned data is the *linear interpolation*. According to this approximation, the data points that are located in between the actual data are assumed to be on a straight line. Thus, the estimation of a zero coupon rate r^* corresponding to time distance τ, located between zero coupon rates r_{n+1} and r_n corresponding to time distances τ_{n+1} and τ_n and, given that τ belongs to $[\tau_n, \tau_{n+1}]$, is achieved by the following formula:

$$r^* = r_n + \frac{r_{n+1} - r_n}{\tau_{n+1} - \tau_n}(\tau - \tau_n) \tag{36}$$

The advantage of the linear interpolation is its simplicity and the fact that, in many cases, it can produce good approximations of reality. On the other hand, if the yield curve is seen as a whole, the method produces sharp changes between time points under consideration, even if the actual corresponding part of the yield curve may not be. This drawback is efficiently overcome by using the polynomial interpolation instead of linear. Polynomial interpolation assumes that a yield curve exhibits smoother alterations in its shape. It is analytically described below.

Exponential interpolation

Exponential interpolation constitutes another natural candidate for producing missing data. The exponential approximation is used whenever the shape of the yield curve is considered of a similar shape. The exponential interpolation is expressed as follows:

$$r^* = r_n e^{-(\ln(r_{n+1}/r_n)/(\tau_{n+1}-\tau_n))*\tau_n} + e^{(\ln(r_{n+1})/(\tau_{n+1}-\tau_n))*\tau} \tag{37}$$

However, this rarely happens with interest rates. In contrast, it happens with discount factors. Thus, the technique is suitable for interpolating between discount factors corresponding to different maturities. In this case, interest rates in Equation 37 r_n and r_{n+1} should be supplanted by the respective discount factors and the result would be in terms of discount factor.

Cubic spline interpolation

One of the most widely used techniques in financial engineering is cubic spline interpolation (see Holton, 2003). It is the most appropriate technique for modelling yield curves, zero curves and forward curves. The term *structures of interest rates* consists of interest rates that correspond to discrete points in future time. The risk manager has to construct term structures that not only enclose interest rates corresponding to the above-mentioned points but also contain interest rates that match the maturity of some portfolio assets. These maturities of portfolio elements are, almost always, located between the prespecified interest rates. In order for the intermediate interest rate r, which corresponds to maturity τ, to be found according to cubic spline interpolation, a number of polynomials $f_k(\tau)$ on different intervals $[\tau_k, \tau_{k+1}]$ should be fitted, such as:

$$f(\tau) = f_k(\tau), \quad \tau_k \leq \tau < \tau_{k+1} \tag{38}$$

In order for the polynomial interpolation to hold, the following conditions must be fulfilled. Each polynomial should pass through the end point of its respective part of the term structure such that:

$$f_k(\tau_k) = r_k \quad \text{and} \quad f_k(\tau_{k+1}) = r_{k+1} \tag{39}$$

First derivatives of successive polynomials should match at all points of the term structure that link together subsequent parts of the curve such that:

$$f_k(\tau_{k+1})' = f_{k+1}(\tau_{k+1})' \tag{40}$$

Second derivatives should fulfil the same condition as follows:

$$f_k(\tau_{k+1})'' = f_{k+1}(\tau_{k+1})'' \tag{41}$$

Second derivatives should be eliminated at the end points of the term structure such that:

$$f_1(\tau_1)'' = 0 \quad \text{and} \quad f_k(\tau_{k+1})'' = 0 \tag{42}$$

Suppose that the term structure of interest rates consists of 10 points or 9 intervals, the polynomials that should be estimated, according to cubic spline interpolation, are 9. The equations to be used should take the following form:

$$f(\tau) : \begin{cases} r_1 = \delta_1 \tau^3 + \gamma_1 \tau^2 + \beta_1 \tau + \alpha_1 \\ r_2 = \delta_2 \tau^3 + \gamma_2 \tau^2 + \beta_2 \tau + \alpha_2 \\ \qquad \cdots\cdots\cdots \\ r_9 = \delta_9 \tau^3 + \gamma_9 \tau^2 + \beta_9 \tau + \alpha_9 \end{cases} \tag{43}$$

Table 1 Term structure of euro zero-coupon rates as at 20 December, 2005

Remaining maturities	Euro zero-coupon rates (%)
1 year	2.8511
2 years	3.0085
3 years	3.1042
4 years	3.1710
5 years	3.2347
6 years	3.2929
7 years	3.3530
8 years	3.4056
9 years	3.4678
10 years	3.5242

According to the aforementioned conditions and assuming that τ belongs to the respective time interval of the term structure, the following numbers of equations should be estimated:

❑ 18 equations corresponding to the first condition;
❑ 8 equations corresponding to the second condition;
❑ 8 equations corresponding to the third condition; and
❑ 2 equations corresponding to the fourth condition.

Thus, a system consisting of 36 equations should be calculated. In any case, the size of the system equals the quantity of polynomials for the estimation multiplied by 4.

Although the cubic spline interpolation is the most appropriate technique for approximating term structures of interest rates, it may produce wrong results if some data are more concentrated in relation to some other.

Interpolation case studies
Suppose that the term structure consists of the following rates and their respective maturities as shown in Table 1.

If the maturity of a cashflow that needs to be interpolated corresponds to 500 days, it should be interpolated between one-year and two-year maturities. Two out of the three interpolation techniques, depicted above, produce the following results:

❑ linear interpolation produces a zero-coupon interest rate equal to 2.9093%; and
❑ exponential interpolation produces a zero-coupon interest rate equal to 2.9083%

Finally, the polynomial interpolation is far more complicated in relation to the other two interpolation techniques. From the conditions described above, it is inferred that a polynomial should be estimated for the interval between two points in time. Cubic spline methodology is not applicable for only one time interval. Moreover, it is not efficient for fewer than five simultaneously estimated polynomials. However, in the present case study it is intuitively applied for two time intervals. For this reason the following number of equations should be estimated:

❑ 4 equations corresponding to the first condition;
❑ 1 equation corresponding to the second condition;
❑ 1 equation corresponding to the third condition; and
❑ 2 equations corresponding to the fourth condition.

This is a system comprising of eight equations with eight unknowns, expressed as follows:

$$
\begin{pmatrix}
1 & 1 & 1 & 1 & 0 & 0 & 0 & 0 \\
8 & 4 & 2 & 1 & 0 & 0 & 0 & 0 \\
0 & 0 & 0 & 0 & 8 & 4 & 2 & 1 \\
0 & 0 & 0 & 0 & 27 & 9 & 3 & 1 \\
12 & 4 & 1 & 0 & -12 & -4 & -1 & 0 \\
12 & 2 & 0 & 0 & -12 & -2 & 0 & 0 \\
6 & 2 & 0 & 0 & 0 & 0 & 0 & 0 \\
0 & 0 & 0 & 0 & 18 & 2 & 0 & 0
\end{pmatrix}
\begin{pmatrix}
\delta_1 \\ \gamma_1 \\ \beta_1 \\ \alpha_1 \\ \delta_2 \\ \gamma_2 \\ \beta_2 \\ \alpha_2
\end{pmatrix}
=
\begin{pmatrix}
2.8511 \\ 3.0085 \\ 3.0085 \\ 3.1042 \\ 0 \\ 0 \\ 0 \\ 0
\end{pmatrix}
$$

After solving the system of equations the following results are derived:

$$
\begin{pmatrix}
\delta_1 \\ \gamma_1 \\ \beta_1 \\ \alpha_1 \\ \delta_2 \\ \gamma_2 \\ \beta_2 \\ \alpha_2
\end{pmatrix}
=
\begin{pmatrix}
-0.0154 \\ 0.0463 \\ 0.1266 \\ 2.6937 \\ 0.0154 \\ -0.1388 \\ 0.4968 \\ 2.4469
\end{pmatrix}
$$

which correspond to the following polynomials:

$$r_1 = -0.0154\tau^3 + 0.0463\tau^2 + 0.1266\tau + 2.6937$$

$$r_2 = 0.0154\tau^3 + -0.1388\tau^2 + 0.4968\tau + 2.4469$$

The zero-coupon interest rate that has to be estimated corresponds to 500 days' maturity, that is $500/365 = 1.37$ years. The interest rate level should be estimated by using the first of two polynomials. Finally, 500 days' zero-coupon interest rates given by cubic spline interpolation technique is 2.9142%, which is different from the respective interest rates derived by using linear or exponential interpolation.

REFERENCES

Chance, D. M., 2005, *Valuing Forward Contracts, The Professional Risk Manager Handbook* (London: PRMIA).

Deacon, M. and A. Derry, 1994, "Estimating the Term Structure of Interest Rates", Working Paper, No 24, Bank of England, July.

Holton, G. A., 2003, *Value at Risk: Theory and Practice* (London: Academic Press).

Hull, J. and A. White, 2000, "Valuing Credit Default Swaps I: No Counterparty Default Risk", Working Paper, April.

Hull, J. C., 2003, *Options Futures and Other Derivatives*, 5th international edn (NJ: Prentice Hall).

Sutcliffe, C. M. S., 1997, *Stock Index Futures: Theories and International Evidence*, 2nd edn (London: International Thomson Business Press).

Glossary of Abbreviations

AMA	advanced measurement approach
AR	autoregressive model
ASA	alternative standardised approach
BIA	basic indicator approach
BM	block maxima approach
CAPM	capital asset pricing model
CDS	credit default swaps
ClORiP	clustering operational risk profile
CREC	credit risk economic capital
CRRC	credit risk regulatory capital
EAD	exposure at default
EI	exposure indicator
EL	expected loss
ES	expected shortfall
EVT	extreme-value theory
EWMA	exponential weighted moving average
FHS	filtered historical simulation
FRA	forward rate agreements
FX	foreign exchange
GBM	geometric Brownian motion
HS	historical simulation approach
IKRI	integrated key-risk indicator
IMA	internal measurement approach
IRB	internal ratings-based approach
IRiLMoS	integrated risk loss mountain surface

IRiMoS	integrated risk mountain surface
KRI	key-risk indicator
LDA	loss distribution approach
LGD	loss given default
LGE	loss given such an event
MAE	mean absolute error
MC	Monte Carlo simulation approach
ME	mean error
MREC	market risk economic capital
MRRC	market risk regulatory capital
OREC	operational risk economic capital
ORRC	operational risk regulatory capital
OTC	over-the-counter
P&L	profit and loss
PD	probability of default
PE	probability of loss event
POT	peaks-over-threshold
PVBP	price value of a basis point
PVS	plain vanilla (interest rate) swaps
RMSE	root mean square error
SA	standardised approach
VAR	value-at-risk
VC	variance-covariance approach

Index